Teachings of the
Santería
Gods

"No hay forma más mágica para sentirse cerca de los orichas que a través de patakies. Es ahí donde uno se transporta a la imaginación. La manera tan espiritual que tiene Ócha'ni Lele para elevar mi imaginación a través de su escritura es un toque especial. ¡Maferefun orichas! Lo que se ve no se pregunta. Este es un libro especial para aquellos que llevamos lo nuestro de corazón y sin maldad. ¡Ócha'ni Lele, te felicito, querido mío"!

"There is no more magical way to feel close to the orishas than through the patakís. It is there that one is transported to one's imagination. Ócha'ni Lele has a very spiritual manner in elevating my imagination through his writing, which reveals a special touch. *¡Maferefun orichas!* What is seen is not questioned! This is a special book for those of us who go forth from the heart, without malice. Ócha'ni Lele, my dear, I congratulate you!"

IVY QUEEN, VOCALIST, MUSICIAN,
AND QUEEN OF REGGAETON

Teachings of the Santería Gods

THE SPIRIT OF THE ODU

Ócha'ni Lele

Destiny Books
Rochester, Vermont • Toronto, Canada

Destiny Books
One Park Street
Rochester, Vermont 05767
www.DestinyBooks.com

Destiny Books is a division of Inner Traditions International

Library of Congress Cataloging-in-Publication Data
Lele, Ócha'ni, 1966–
  Teachings of the Santería gods : the spirit of the Odu / Ócha'ni Lele.
    p. cm.
  Includes index.
  ISBN 978-1-59477-332-7 (pbk.)
  1. Cowries—Miscellanea. 2. Divination—Cuba. 3. Mythology, Cuban. 4.
Santeria. I. Title.
  BF1779.C64L42 2010
  299.6'7413—dc22

                                                          2010012682

Printed and bound in the United States

10 9 8 7 6 5

Text design by Virginia L. Scott Bowman and layout by Priscilla Baker
This book was typeset in Garamond Premier Pro with Greymantle and Thornton
used as display typefaces

To send correspondence to the author of this book, mail a first-class letter to the
author c/o Inner Traditions • Bear & Company, One Park Street, Rochester, VT
05767, and we will forward the communication.

For my godparents, Banacek Matos and Angel Jimenez: They gave me ocha; and with that, they gave me the world. For that, and other reasons, I love them both more than I can ever say.

Contents

Preface

Ten years ago, I published my first book about the Lucumí faith, *The Secrets of Afro-Cuban Divination: How to Cast the Diloggún, the Oracle of the Orishas*. Regarding my initial vision for that work, I wrote the following passage in its introduction:

"I hoped to include a very important element of divination: the *patakís* [sacred stories] told by the *odu* [divination patterns]. These are the legends of our faith, comparable to the parables of the Christian Bible and the mythologies of other pagan faiths. Some tell about the lives of the *orishas* [spirits] on earth; some tell of the lives of our spirits in heaven. Many tell about the beginning of humans, earth, and Cosmos, and also the lives of ancient humans who lived and died following the way of the orishas. Finally, there are stories about each odu itself, for even the odu were once alive on earth as mortals, walking among men and women as they would. It is from these myths that many of our customs are born. It is through a diviner's study and interpretation of patakís that the meanings of odu expand and evolve. But since there can be anywhere from two to twelve patakís in any single pattern, adding even one pataki to each chapter would have made this book unmanageable. Several companion volumes are in the works to explore these exciting avenues of cowrie-shell divination."*

After *Secrets,* I wrote two more books: *Obí, Oracle of Cuban Santería*† and *The Diloggún: the Orishas, Proverbs, Sacrifices, and Prohibitions*

---

*Ócha'ni Lele, *The Secrets of Afro-Cuban Divination: How to Cast the Diloggún, the Oracle of the Orishas* (Rochester, Vt.: Destiny Books, 2000), 7.
†Ócha'ni Lele, *Obí, Oracle of Cuban Santería* (Rochester, Vt.: Destiny Books, 2001).

of Cuban Santería.* In the text of those volumes, I was able to write about a few of the ancient stories; and in *Obí,* I had the chance to play storyteller and actually write my own versions of a few patakís. But I wanted to do something more expansive, and in 2002, after submitting the manuscript for *The Diloggún,* I began drafting an extensive collection of short stories based on the Yoruba and Lucumí myths. Beginning with the root odu of Okana, continuing through its composites, and moving chronologically through each family of odu, I drafted, wrote, and rewrote more than a thousand stories in eight years. It was a lot of work—more writing than I've done in my entire life.

Finally, ten years after the publication of *The Secrets of Afro-Cuban Divination,* a volume devoted to the patakís of the *diloggún* is complete. It has been a long journey toward the accomplishment of this goal.

As I wrote, I faced an uncomfortable task—turning the oral fragments into stories worthy of publication. Those who study diloggún understand the difficulties involved. Written records of these myths in handwritten notebooks are often little more than fragmented notes of even more fragmented stories. They lack substance and form. Truly, the only way to learn about the myths of this religion is to hear them from one's godparents, who are, hopefully, elders in the religion. Barring that, initiates who work in the *igbodu* of *ocha* (the sacred room of the religion), might, if they are very quiet and very respectful, hear the elders talk about the old stories among themselves. It is there, when faced with a seasoned priest or priestess, that one learns the true wisdom found in the patakís.

Still, an oral recitation of a patakí differs from a written work; and what works orally doesn't always translate into a good short story. When I began my own versions of these tales back in 2002, I had no idea of the amount of work involved. But now that the first volume of patakís is ready for publication, I am very happy with what I've done. The countless lonely hours spent writing and rewriting were worth all the effort.

---

*Ócha'ni Lele, *The Diloggún: The Orishas, Proverbs, Sacrifices, and Prohibitions of Cuban Santería* (Rochester, Vt.: Destiny Books, 2003).

As I present this volume, I must admit that while this work might seem exhaustive to those with little knowledge of the diloggún, in truth, it in no way, shape, or form exhausts the bulk of what the diloggún is. For every patakí that I present, as many as one hundred or more remain unexplored. If I write four stories in one chapter, there can be hundreds of others not mentioned. Books are finite entities with limited space, and the diloggún is an infinite receptacle of wisdom that evolved over centuries.

What this book is, however, is expansive. Following the road I began a decade ago when I first put pen to paper, I have catalogued as many patakís as possible in the confines of a single work. This book is but a small part of my own calabash of wisdom, and my calabash is but a fragment of what exists in the world. I have opened the lid on my calabash so that others with knowledge and wisdom can add mine to theirs. And I pray that in time, more people will come together to write and share their own knowledge of the diloggún with others. For as the odu Unle Odí (8-7) teaches us: Olódumare spreads all knowledge and wisdom throughout the world; and if we are to evolve and grow, we must bring that wisdom back together, and share.

May we continue to grow and evolve!

Acknowledgments

There are many people I need to thank for their help and support over my writing career. I'll get the professional acknowledgments out of the way first:

Susannah Noel, the editor for my first book, *The Secrets of Afro-Cuban Divination*. I learned so much by working with her on my first major project. Susannah, three books later, the comments and suggestions you made as you edited my first volume are still fresh in my mind, and I remember each and every one you made as I wrote this volume.

Doris Troy, the editor for my second book, *Obí, Oracle of Cuban Santería*. She did a wonderful job with that project, and she, too, made suggestions for my work that I still follow today. While editing the patakís for that volume, Doris wrote to me that I was an incredible story-teller, and it was her encouragement that made me believe . . . I could tell a story. This book is nothing but stories, and I thank her from the deepest, most secret places of my heart!

Nancy Ringer, the editor who ripped and shredded the volume that became *The Diloggún*. Well, perhaps ripped and shredded is too harsh a phrase, but she did help me acquire the critical eye needed for the books I write now. I was flabbergasted by the amount of rewrites I had to do on that volume, but in hindsight, I have to say this: Nancy, you are wonderful! I hope all the authors with whom you work appreciate your eye for detail.

Patty Capetola, the editor who helped shape this volume, *Teachings of the Santería Gods*. Patty, I appreciate your eye for detail; and I want you to know that the wonderful comments you made about my writing have encouraged me to work on yet another book of patakís! Thank you!

Laura Schlivek, my project editor throughout all my work with Inner Traditions. There are many reasons I need to thank you, but perhaps the most important reason is that you were able to encourage me and motivate me when I felt I wasn't good enough to complete a book. You're a goddess, and I love you for it.

Jon Graham, my acquisitions manager at Inner Traditions. I'm sure there are a thousand manuscripts that come across your desk more worthy of publication than mine, but somehow, you work your magic and come up with yet another contract. Olófin blessed me the day he sent my work to your desk. You're a god, and I love you for it.

Inner Traditions: I offer my eternal gratitude to you. Every publisher wants books that will reap huge sales, and often, books that need to be published because their content is important are overlooked because there are other books that will draw in huge sales and reap vast financial rewards. You didn't have to publish any of my books. You could have spent your financial resources on other books that would have given you greater returns in a broader market. I understand that, and thank you, from my heart, for putting my work out there.

And, as always, I am grateful for the day Marjorie Stevens pulled me out of high school English to tell me, "Stuart, this is fantastic stuff. Have you ever thought of being a writer?" And I thank Olófin for the day that my college English professor, Ann Refoe, kicked me out of English class (yes, truly, she kicked me out!) and told me, "You don't belong here. Just write whatever you want, and turn it in at the end of the semester for your grade." Of course, I amazed her when I walked in the last day of class with a book contract. If she hadn't thrown me out of class, none of this would have begun.

And for the record . . . I got a perfect 4.0!

And now, for the personal acknowledgments:

My godparents, Banacek "Checo Yemayá" Matos and Angel "Coquí Oshún" Jimenez: Because of you both, there are few men in this world who are as blessed as I. Every day, people write to me about the night-mares they lived in their quest for ocha; and they tell me about the trau-mas they go through on a daily, weekly, monthly, and yearly basis with their own godparents. Too many santeros wander the world, lost and incomplete, because once ocha is given, they are abandoned, turned out into the world to fend for themselves spiritually and otherwise. Each year that passes, I feel closer to you both; I hope we stay like this forever.

My god sister, Jamie Vargas: You might be my baby sister in ocha, but it was your Oshún who lifted me, and I'm thankful for that. And know this: You are young in ocha, but you are wise beyond your years, and I'm so glad it's you who cares for my New York godchildren when I'm 1,500 miles away, in Florida. But know that I trust you with more than my godchildren; I trust you with my life. I hope Oshún keeps you on this earth forever.

Ivelisse Pesante, a.k.a. Ivy Queen. When I met you, I was about to give up: I was tired, exhausted, lonely, and sad; and our nightly conver-sations about love, life, and the religion inspired me to try one more time. You are a muse, and I'm thankful you took so much of your per-sonal time to inspire me.

I need to thank all of the "serious" godchildren in my life at this time: Ashara Yvonne Watkins, Katelan V. Foisy, Amanda R. Kaczmarek, Robert Young, Rebecca Payn, Vivienne D'Avalon, and Sandy Short. Every time I put my pen to paper, or my fingers to my keyboard, you are the ones who inspire me to continue this work. After I'm gone, each of you will still be around, and each of you will have your own godchil-dren. In my absence, my books will be here to instruct you, and my pri-vate notes will be in your hands to guide you. Seriously, I think about things like this—what will become of you when I'm gone. For no other reason, that's why I keep writing, and putting absolutely everything I know, and everything I learn, on paper. The printed word, published and otherwise, will live after my death; and my spiritual descendants will have a part of me with them as they grow spiritually. This is but a small part of my legacy to each of you—and it is for this reason, and no other, that I stay up all night writing.

The world should thank you for inspiring me.

And finally, I would like to thank Irma Miranda Baez (Olobatalá): Irma, you spent hours translating obscure Cuban texts and manuscripts that flowed across my desk on a monthly basis. Many times, you thanked me for allowing you access to those rare texts. With the world as my witness, I want to thank you for helping me. Truly, Obatalá blessed me when he put you in my path, and I love you for all that you have done. May you live a thousand years.

An Introduction to the Diloggún

The diloggún is one of the most complex yet beautiful systems of divination practiced by orisha worshippers throughout the world. It is a living, oral body of wisdom born with the first stirrings of the universe; it took on flesh when the sixteen principle odu (patterns of cowrie shells that can fall in the diloggún) became mortal, living beings, each in one of the sixteen ancient kingdoms of the Yoruba Empire. It spread as priests and priestesses shared their knowledge of its patakís (sacred stories) and proverbs with one another; it acquired spiritual and religious depth as the orishas themselves instructed humans by its wisdom; and it grew, as each generation that lived added the stories of their own lives, loves, conquests, and failures. With this oracle, a diviner accesses the knowledge and *ashé* (spiritual power) of all creation.

In spite of the complexity and beauty of this divination system, books studying it are all but nonexistent. Scholars turn to the Yoruba oracle known as Ifá when analyzing Yoruba thought and religion; and the diloggún remains in shadows, mentioned but not examined. A prominent American scholar who studied both Ifá and diloggún as it exists in Nigeria and the New World, Dr. William Bascom, Ph.D., once wrote of the Ifá oracle, "Ifá is the most respected, in many ways the most interesting, system of divination of five to ten million Yoruba in Nigeria and millions more of their African neighbors and their descendants in the New World."*

*William Bascom, *Ifá Divination* (Bloomington: Indiana University Press, 1991), preface.

1

Years later, in his study of the sixteen-cowrie-shell oracle (the diloggún) as it existed in the mind of his only research subject, Sàlàkó, he wrote, "'Sixteen cowries' *(èrìndínlógún, owó mérìndínlógún)* is a form of divination employed by the Yoruba of Nigeria and by their descendants in the New World. *It is simpler than Ifá divination and it is held in less esteem in Nigeria,* but in the Americas, it is more important than Ifá because it is more widely known and more frequently employed. *This may be due to its relative simplicity . . ."* [italics mine].*
Later, in the introduction to his book *Sixteen Cowries,* Bascom continues, "Compared to Ifá divination with its manipulation of sixteen palm nuts or even the casting of the divining chain, *sixteen cowry divination is simple"* [italics mine].† In spite of Bascom's thesis, there is nothing simple about this system. Orisha worshippers devote massive amounts of time to the diloggún's study before casting their first hand of shells; it is common to apprentice with an elder for years before adherents have competency in the system. Because of Bascom's writings, scholars accept his simplistic view of the diloggún as truth, yet there is nothing simple about this oracle. Sixteen-cowrie-divination is richly nuanced as is the Yoruba practice of Ifá—unfortunately, it is less well known.

This mind-set remains with modern American scholars; each academic researcher begins their work with Bascom, and Bascom, as a leading *academic* authority on Yoruba divination, plants this seed of cultural calumny in the minds of his readers. His thoughts on the importance of the diloggún, at least to Yoruba descendants and Lucumí adherents in the New World, have become accepted by those who should have investigated its cultural importance more deeply. It has left a huge hole in the study of Yoruba thought and religion.

Nevertheless, one can forgive Bascom and his students: They were outside observers, unable to see the bigger picture because they were neither part of Yoruba culture nor part of Yoruba religion. Those who

---

*William Bascom, *Sixteen Cowries: Yoruba Divination from Africa to the New World* (Bloomington: Indiana University Press, 1993), 3.
†Bascom, *Sixteen Cowries,* 5.

live and die by the orishas know the importance of the diloggún and its oral corpus to our lives.

Perhaps the only overgeneralization in Bascom's works regarding diloggún that I agree with is this: "Divination with sixteen cowries is related in mythology, perhaps historically, and certainly morphologically, to Ifá divination."* If Dr. William Bascom had spent more time studying the very things he theorized about, in time he might have grasped a greater picture of the whole.†

As Lucumí priests and *aborishas* (initiated worshippers), we cannot depend on writings such as Bascom's to understand our own oracle; we cannot bury ourselves in the study of any academic tome written, because those who study divination from a culturally sterile point of view are unable to grasp the spiritual significance of our practices. We must turn to our own odu, and the stories they tell, to unravel the spiritual history and the significance of the diloggún to our faith. For these stories are legends comparable to those found in the ancient myths of Greece and Rome; they are as culturally significant as those in the Torah, Talmud, or Christian bible; they are rich with jewels of wisdom like the I Ching, and they are as vast as the Vedas of the Hindu faith. There are stories about the creation of the world, the birth of Olódumare (God), and the resulting Irunmole (the first orishas) who awakened in Heaven; there are myths describing the lives of the holy odu themselves as they walked on Earth in mortal form. There are histories about ancient priests, and kings, and commoners—people who lived and died following the ways of the orishas. Finally, there are stories about the orishas themselves—the loves, losses, conquests, and defeats making them the powerful beings they are today. There are mantras and songs, hymns and chants, ritual customs and secular teachings: one finds all this, and more, in the patakís of the odu.

As an oracle, the diloggún employs sixteen cowrie shells to access an odu. In its natural state, a cowrie shell has on one side a smooth,

---

*Bascom, *Ifá Divination*, preface.
†The stories presented in chapter 12 of this volume explore the relationship between the oracles of diloggún and Ifá.

rounded back and on the other side an elongated, serrated opening resembling a mouth; unaltered, a cowrie shell cannot be used for divination. Each shell is prepared, or opened, to create the cowries used in divination. With a knife or file, a priest removes the rounded back of the cowrie, popping off the rounded hump to make a flat back. He files down the new surface so it has no ragged edges. Almost every orisha in the Lucumí faith has eighteen of these shells in its possession except the orisha Elegguá; he has twenty-one cowrie shells. Because orisha priests believe Elegguá was a witness to creation, diviners use his diloggún for divination. Elegguá saw the world begin; Elegguá knows everything in it, and Elegguá knows what will happen. His knowledge is flawless.*

To read or cast the diloggún, the diviner selects sixteen shells at random from the set of consecrated cowries. He keeps the remaining shells to the side, with the natural "mouth" facing down. Diviners refer to the cowries left to the side as witnesses, and while present for divination, they remain unused. The mechanically opened side of the shell has a value of zero; the natural mouth has a value of one. When a diviner casts the sixteen shells on the mat, he obtains a numerical value from zero to sixteen by adding the values of the shells. The number corresponds to a particular odu in the divination system, and the orisha uses this odu to speak to the priest.

To employ this oracle effectively, one must know all sixteen names and their numerical equivalents. They are:

> 1 mouth = Okana
> 2 mouths = Eji Oko
> 3 mouths = Ogundá
> 4 mouths = Irosun
> 5 mouths = Oché
> 6 mouths = Obara

---

*Keep in mind, however, that almost all the orishas posses a set of cowries, and with these they do speak; the diloggún of orishas beyond Elegguá, however, is accessed by the *oriaté*. They are the priests with the skill and knowledge to put any orisha on the mat to speak.

7 mouths = Odí

8 mouths = Unle

9 mouths = Osá

10 mouths = Ofún

11 mouths = Owani

12 mouths = Ejila Shebora

13 mouths = Metanlá

14 mouths = Merinlá

15 mouths = Marunlá

16 mouths = Merindilogún

It is important to note that a diviner's level of skill and training dictates how deeply he is allowed to read with the diloggún. In the Lucumí faith, there is a special division of priests known as oriatés. These are the masters of Lucumí ceremony and lore. To be an oriaté, one must study with an oriaté; and only after years (sometimes decades) of training does one's teacher vouch for his level of skill. During this time, the apprentice's teacher gives a number of lavish, expensive ceremonies and rare orishas not available to the general priesthood. A large part of the apprentice's training centers on diloggún and odu; and with this rank of skill and knowledge, the diviner has the right to read all sixteen patterns of the diloggún, Okana (one mouth) through Merindilogún (sixteen mouths).

Those diviners without the skill of an oriaté read freely from the combinations falling between Okana (one mouth) and Ejila Shebora (twelve mouths). The final four patterns (Metanlá, Merinlá, Marunlá, and Merindilogún) reference spiritual currents so intense that their appearance on the mat is rare.* If one falls, the novice diviner performs a simple ceremony to close the oracle; and the client is sent to a more experienced oriaté.†

---

*In my seven years as an active diviner, these patterns have never fallen on my mat. After reading hundreds of transcribed *itás* (divinations given to initiates by oriatés), I have seen only five combinations of these odu.

†For more information on these special rituals, see my previous work *The Secrets of Afro-Cuban Divination: How to Cast the Diloggún, the Oracle of the Orishas.* Pages 315–17 detail this ritual closure.

By comparing the oral corpus of the sixteen parent odu to a library, one can envision each odu as a book in that library; and just as books are divided into chapters, each of the sixteen parent odu, as a separate book, has smaller divisions. We know these chapters of each book as the *omo odu* (children of odu). Each omo odu is a part of a spiritual family linked by the parent giving it birth, just as each chapter of a book is part of the book's greater whole.

By casting the diloggún, a diviner accesses one of these "chapters" on behalf of his client. Initially, the diviner does not know which section of the book to read. First, he awakens, gently, the orisha whose diloggún he uses with an invocation paying homage to Olódumare, the earth, the ancestors, and the orishas. After this series of prayers, the diviner makes two initial castings, recording the numbers of each. With these numbers, the orisha identifies the omo odu applying to the client. The first casting names the parent odu and the second creates the omo odu, narrowing the reading down to one of 256 possible combinations. For example, if the first casting of the diloggún results in a pattern of nine open mouths on the mat, the parent odu is Osá. Casting the cowries a second time, if the diviner counts three mouths, the odu Ogundá has fallen. The resulting omo odu is Osá Ogundá (nine mouths followed by three mouths), and the diviner searches his memory for the meanings of that particular composite letter.*

Each of these omo odu forms a spiritual organism, a complete entity that foretells various blessings (known collectively as *iré*) or misfortunes (known collectively as *osogbo*). After casting a composite letter, the diviner uses the eight *ibó* (auxiliary divination tools such as certain black stones, seeds, or pottery shards) to extract from it the qualities of iré and osogbo. Depending on the question asked, the diviner uses the ibó in a number of pairings; together, the diviner and client manipulate the cowries and ibó in tandem to determine the orientations of the odu.

---

*For more information on this process, see my previous work *The Diloggún: the Orishas, Proverbs, Sacrifices, and Prohibitions of Cuban Santería*. Chapter 1 gives complete directions for manipulating the diloggún safely and completely from its opening to its closure.

From these are the predictions of any one letter drawn, and the *ebós* (offerings) needed to placate volatile essences are determined. One creates harmony, and evolution unfolds.

Ebó is a central concept to this religion; and many of the stories found in the diloggún's odu speak of animals, humans, and orishas making ebó to avoid misfortune. To the Lucumí, everything in this world has its price—that price is known as sacrifice, or ebó. In a world of instant gratification the concept of sacrifice might seem strange, but in truth, every moment that one lives, sacrifices are made for the betterment of both one's self and one's community. Each day that one goes to work to pay bills, it is a sacrifice of free time to obtain money. Every time someone puts money in a savings account instead of buying a new pair of shoes, it is a sacrifice to ensure a stable future. Parents sacrifice personal needs to save for a child's college education, while communities might sacrifice the expansion of recreational facilities for better schools. At all levels in life, resources are limited and no one person or group can have it all.

Ebó, at its core, is sacrifice; and Lucumí adherents practice this in many forms. Some of the odu mandate behavior modification—simply, to achieve desired results, something in a person's life must be changed or removed, literally sacrificed, to avoid misfortune and evolve. Still, many of these ebós are material: a diviner might advise his client to offer fruits, grains, cooked foods, candles, prayers, herbs, or cloth to various orishas. The client does these things to obtain the spirit's favors; and if the diviner's knowledge of both odu and ebó are great, miracles ensue. The patakís, the sacred stories found in the oral corpus of the diloggún, are the foundation from which these ebós are drawn. Simply—someone with a problem similar to ours did this once and it worked; so, if the client does the same thing, it should work as well. Each odu contains stories rich with examples illustrating the benefits of making ebó versus the risks of not making ebó; and somewhere between these two extremes is a twilight area where one suffers and fate curses or blesses at its whim.

One of my favorite stories in this volume illustrating the simplicity of ebó is "Oshún's Ebó" in chapter 11. Oshún's character is familiar to students of Yoruba folklore; she is a goddess given great reverence in the Lucumí faith. Simply, she is the orisha of love, abundance, eroticism, fertility, and sweetness—all things making life worthwhile. "Things were not always like this," the story tells us, for once Oshún was impoverished. The patakís tells us this outright—it does not investigate why she became poor—and it tells us that she went to see a diviner and make ebó. At the mat, she told him, "In spite of what I do not have, all I have left is my faith." That faith was tested—the diviner told her to use all of her remaining wealth (and from the story, one knows her wealth was not much), buying all the red palm oil and honey she could. Then, he told her to make ebó with that, pouring it all into the river.

To most, such an act would seem a wasteful thing: If one has little, the modern mindset would imply that it is foolish to spend limited resources on an ebó as extravagant (comparatively speaking) as this. Yet Oshún had faith and did as the diviner instructed. As she slept outdoors, the elements of her ebó transformed, and Oshún awoke a rich woman.

The moral of the story: The simplest ebós bring the greatest results. Yet we learn more about the nature of ebó through this patakís. Sometimes, what the orishas demand of us might seem huge. We need something but we have next to nothing, and divination tells us to sacrifice what little we have to gain something more. Part of any ebó is faith—and Oshún told the diviner she had plenty of that; yet she had to act on that faith, sacrifice every little bit of what she had to evolve away from her poverty. In addition, this story teaches us something about Oshún; she was not always rich materially, but she was wealthy in spirit.

To the Lucumí, the risks of not making prescribed ebós are real, but the risk lies with the client, never the diviner. There is a proverb: "Those who fail to make ebó turn the diviner into a soothsayer." "The Story of the Cat and the Rat" found in chapter 1 illustrates both this proverb and the risks of unmade ebós well. It reads as a child's fable, not unlike something from the Brothers Grimm, and it is narrated by the odu Okana herself. Surrounded by her grandchildren, one of the little girls becomes overwrought that their household cat kills a mouse, and in a moment of exasperation, she asks, "Why do cats do that? Why do they kill mice?" Against her better judgment (for small children, this story might be frightening as are many children's tales), Okana gathers them together and settles in for a bedtime rendition of a story best described as macabre.

For the cat and the rat were once friends, and when the world went bad and food was scarce, the cat went to the diviners to have divination and make ebó. The wise man who read for the cat that day assured her, "For our world to be in balance, there must be both good and bad in our lives. Don't worry, cat; soon the rains will come, the forest will green-up, and there will be prey. You, however, have more pressing concerns." The cat opened that day in Okana an odu that brings all the bad into life before allowing all the good to come; but the odu had specific warnings of treason, and it warned the cat to make ebó.

Of course, overwhelmed by many of the odu's warnings, the cat forgot to make ebó. By the end of the story, one learns that refusal by omission is just as perilous as refusal by stubbornness.

All the cat's children died.

Without revealing the delightfully dark twists and turns of the story, as Okana closes the patakís, she tells her granddaughter, "And that . . . is why cats kill mice." A simple omission of ebó brings misfortune into the world, and the fabric of everything wrinkles permanently. More importantly, Okana's closing remarks are difficult points to ponder—does osogbo come in spite of itself, or does osogbo come by one's refusal to make ebó? If one refuses to make ebó, truly, who is responsible for the evil wrought, the stubborn client or the transgressor? All these are difficult points to ponder.

Finally, there are times that one exists in a twilight between iré and osogbo—one is safe, but danger abounds; and the orishas watch to see if one will be obedient, making ebó, or disobedient, resigning oneself to whatever life brings. Chapter 3 contains one of my favorite stories illustrating this twilight concept: "King Olushola Makes Ebó." Olushola was a monarch with two envious brothers—Abiodun and Adejola. While Olushola made his biannual trip to see his diviner, Mofá, the two younger brothers plotted to overthrow his rule by assassination. At first, Olushola refused to make ebó, his refusal coming in the midst of treason. His brothers' greed, an assassin's mistake, and a guard's ill luck allow the king momentary reprieve,* and a timely ebó assures his future safety.

Beyond such heavy morals and illustrations of ebó and faith, the patakís of the diloggún are meant to be entertaining. Years ago, when an elder priestess of Yemayá found out I was writing volumes of patakís, instilling new life into them, she wrote to me, "You should continue with your work, and publish as many volumes as you want. For in the old days before the Internet, radio, or even television, and during the time we had no written books, only oral memories, these were the novellas of the day." She continued to emphasize their instructional and moralistic natures, but insisted that these fragments were part of something larger, and added, "Each storyteller had his own version of the patakís, ways of telling them that made them distinctly his own. It is time that they were put down on paper, and you should do just that."

I took her advice to heart then, and I still do. For when studying the orisha faiths of Nigeria and the New World, it is time for us, as orisha worshippers, to turn to the study of the odu through the diloggún exclusively. With the cowrie shells comprising its mechanical system, we have our own way to access the 256 sacred patterns of creation, the letters by which Olódumare created the universe; we have our own methods of saving and cataloguing the body of lore encapsulating the lives of the ancient humans, the orishas, and the existence of Olódumare himself. Throughout this book remember: Although the odu contain all the facets of our faith and lives, they are not stagnant, unchanging, mere collections of sacred stories and scripts conceived centuries ago. Each is alive in the universe; each exists in our hearts. They are organisms of energy, creatures of symbiosis awaiting connection with our own human energies as they open on the mat.

This system of wisdom and divination is the heart of orisha worship.

---

*Chapter 3 records the stories of Ogundá, and the number *three* represents this odu. Please note the three tragedies befalling the king before making ebó. Observant readers will note simple nuances such as this in every patakís presented in this book.

1

Okana

One Mouth on the Mat

*The head feels only two things—the rage of the heart,
and its desire to love.*

Okana is a perilous odu, fraught with danger—it is a sign of fervor, passion instilled by both love and hate. The patakís found in its oral corpus deal with the theme of passion in myriad ways. Although there are dozens of myths detailing the interactions between both mortals (animals and humans) and immortals (spirits and orishas), to illustrate the redemptive power of passion in relation to this odu, I chose to focus on the woman's life for whom this section of the diloggún is named, Okana.

Lucumí diviners and storytellers know her as a woman born of two spirits named Sedikoron and Ajantaku. Orphaned at a young age, her godmothers Osá Oché and Metanlá Ayui brought her up in the world; and when grown, she set out to fend for herself. Her parents left her wealth and her godparents taught her witchcraft; and Okana had an obscene abundance of both. Still, it was not enough. Her village shunned her as a witch, and her loneliness consumed her until she turned her talents to self-gratification. The turning point in her life was her obsessive love directed at the orisha Shangó; and he thwarted her powerful spells by consulting his diviners and making ebó.

11

Loneliness, lust, and malcontent, central themes of this odu, are self-destructive; and Okana embodied all the bad this letter has to give.

Yet those same things—loneliness, lust, and malcontent—can be powerful motivators for evolution. In spite of herself, when Okana was at her darkest hour, the healing energies of this sign directed her life, and without magic or even a plan, when Okana put herself into the hands of God, she evolved. It was neither deliberate nor calculated; it just happened. As the final story in this chapter illustrates, she ended her life a wealthy, happy widow surrounded by dozens of children and grandchildren.

One might have power, one might have wealth, one might have needs and desires binding better judgment; however, Okana guarantees that everything born of base human desires will fail. It is only when letting go of the things that push us to use our talents for self-gratification, focusing on the greater good, that we move with the tide that is both life and evolution. Still, in the face of Okana both are necessary for human evolution, and the greater the tribulations, the greater the ecstasy brought by this odu. "If there is nothing bad," my godfather once told me, "there can never be anything good." Okana lives and offers both good and bad in exquisite abundance.

Okana Brews a Love Potion

It was late, and Okana was alone, gazing at herself in a full-length mirror. She admired the fullness of her face, her creamy black skin and high cheekbones, and the full pout of her lips. She blew herself a flirty kiss and turned to the side, throwing her shoulders back so her breasts plumped up to their full size. She ran her hands over her own tiny waist and shook her head gently, so the hundreds of carefully woven braids cascading just below its hourglass curve shimmied and shook against her buttocks. Okana was gorgeous, and she knew it.

She turned away from the mirror, looking over her shoulder to see her backside before walking away; and she paced through her home, a mansion by anyone's standards. Her parents had done well during their brief life together, and had died while Okana was still young, but they had provided well for her, and she wanted for nothing.

Nothing, that is, except love.

For while Okana was a pretty woman, and a rich woman, she was a lonely woman; she had no man with whom to pass her days. Desperately, she craved love.

Okana sighed deeply as she paced; it was a troubled breath that lifted and dropped her ample breasts in sorrow. "If only I wasn't alone," she thought. A gentle breeze wafted through an open window and caressed her skin gently, as if to soothe her.

She barely noticed. There was no soothing her troubled mind.

Okana walked into her kitchen and looked around at shelf upon shelf of herbs, a virtual apothecary of remedies to cure all ailments, physical or spiritual. She was well-stocked with both the baneful and the beneficial, for Okana was a witch. Her mother had been a witch, as had her mother before her, and as everyone in her village knew, "A witch always gives birth to a witch."

That is why she was lonely; that is why she could not find a man. No one wanted to love a witch.

That moment, she decided to use her witchcraft to find love.

As midnight came and the moon set over the horizon, Okana was alone in her kitchen, experimenting with her herbs. She peeled, pounded, mashed, and mixed every ashé she had that dealt with love and matters of the heart. Little else mattered to her beyond her work; for just as those in love cannot see clearly, those who crave love can see little beyond their desires. Strange scents and fumes wafted through her home and were carried into the world with the night-winds that blew.

The air was alive with magic.

Finally, after hours of work, Okana created a philter that was love liquescent: it embodied all the sweetness of love, the desires of love, and the dangers of love. Its scent was intoxicating; one drop and her skin glistened with a preternatural glow, a sheen that hinted of sexual ecstasy and exotic delights. "Surely," she thought to herself, "no man can resist me now!"

At her opened window, she lit a coal in a brazier, and put a single drop of her oil on the red-hot ember. Fumes like fog rolled into the night. "Bring me love," she whispered as they rolled into the darkness.

Her spell was potent. It did not take long.

The next night, she found herself in the arms of a strong, black man whose loins burned her own like fire. The magic of her potion ensnared them both, and she abandoned herself to the waves of pleasure that erupted in her body. So intense was the spell that neither man nor woman knew where one body began, or the next ended; and they were joined so deeply that they did not care. Spent, both collapsed into the other's arms, and still ensnared by her spell, Okana thought, "I know what love is!"

The scent of magic died as they slept, and when she awoke the next morning, she felt empty. He awoke with a strange, feverish glow in his eyes; he dressed silently, kissing her on her forehead, and promised to return that night.

Okana didn't care. Nor did she want to care. She only wanted to try her potion again on another man.

Early evening found Okana wandering through the streets of town, alone. She was freshly bathed and dressed in a robe showing more skin than it hid; and as she had been the night before, she was liberally oiled with her own magic philter. Like a lioness in heat she walked, seductively, through the streets, laughing as women grabbed their children and hid in shadows from the witch. She heard their whispers, but didn't care.

Then, she saw him—a man younger and stronger than last night's love. His skin was rich and supple, stretched tight over muscles toned from hard labor. He walked with the grace of a leopard. Reaching into her bag, she pulled out the vial of potion and anointed herself freshly, giving in to the dosed vapors that rose from her skin. Boldly, she introduced herself, and watched as her magic ensnared the young man with desire.

That night, she knew ecstasy greater than the first. And while they slept, as it had the night before, the spell evaporated with the first morning light.

Okana awoke, once more feeling empty inside. She looked down at the strange lover as he slept beside her; he didn't seem as handsome anymore. There was a strange rattle in his chest as he snored, and his skin was covered in slick sweat. The sheets around him were damp. He was feverish.

With the young man still sleeping in her bed, Okana walked outside, wrapped only in a white sheet, to breathe in the morning air. It invigorated her, and chased the sleep from her head.

Then she saw him, her first lover, sleeping by the door. He awoke and rubbed his eyes. "I knocked last night. You did not hear?"

Okana took in a sharp breath. She thought of the young man still sleeping in her bed, and not knowing what the first man might have heard as he camped outside her home, she said, "No, I didn't hear. I woke up too early yesterday, and was exhausted come night. I slept fitfully. I might have made noise in my own sleep. But I did not hear you."

He stood close to her, taking her shoulders into his hands, and kissed her lightly on the cheek. His own lips were hot and feverish. "I will come back tonight for you," he said, almost a threat. This close, she could see the delirium in his eyes, and felt his breath hot on her face as he whispered, "I think I love you."

He left her standing, alone and shaking. "He is crazed," she whispered to the wind before going back inside to the arms of her newest lover. They spent all day in bed.

That evening, Okana returned to town, leaving her newest lover at home, sleeping. He was exhausted from a night and a day of love, and even her roughest shakes could not wake him. She did not care; she might need him when she returned home.

She sat in a little chair outside her favorite merchant's shop drinking a glass of palm wine, as she thought about the spell she wove. "This was my most powerful magic!" Okana congratulated herself with a little hug. She inhaled deeply; the scent of love rose off her skin like steam. Before leaving home, she rubbed the oil all over, finding its smell as intoxicating as the most powerful drink, and wanting to see if she could find a love even stronger than the first two. "I will simply go to the next man's house," she thought, "And when I am done with him, I will return to the other in my bed."

After many drinks, Okana's mind was clouded; she forgot about the man she had at home and simply searched for someone new. And then, she saw *him*. Walking toward her was an eye-filling man. His skin was deep, rich, dark ebony with a subtle sheen; it seemed to glow preternaturally. He walked forcefully, like a lion, each step purposeful, with his own loins swaying seductively from his hips. His arms were huge, powerful; they seemed strong enough to hold the sun, and his chest was chiseled like a marble statue's. So huge were the muscles in his thighs that his legs bowed out slightly. Okana felt fever burning in her secret place, like a fire.

Driven by her desires, Okana stood in front of him in the street, blocking his body with her own; and with a boldness that surprised even her, she kissed him before he could protest. Powerful magic was made in that moment; he was ensnared, the lion by the trap, and he kissed her back. People in the streets shuddered and gasped in surprise. Some watched, whispering "witch," while others tried to hide their eyes, but couldn't; and there in the street, Okana and her prey groped and rubbed and squeezed as the sun set over the town.

Okana knew nothing except desire, and wanted that man in her bed. Desperately. She forgot there was someone already wrapped up in her sheets.

Like a lioness in heat, she led him to her lair; and he followed, not questioning. Okana was confused when she saw the first man standing outside her door, trembling and covered in sweat. "I don't know what is wrong with me!" he called out, his voice louder than it needed to be. He was shaking as if chilled; and even in the evening twilight, she could see that sores covered his face and arms.

"Pox!" she gasped. She looked at her own arms, worried that the contagion might erupt on her own delicate skin.

"You did this to me," he cried. "You are a witch!"

His words stung; anger consumed her, melting her fear. "I did this?" she cried. "You are the one covered in sores. My skin is clean!"

Strong hands grasped her shoulders from behind. "We must go. We should not be so close," a deep voice warned. In her drunken haze, Okana had forgotten that her newest love-conquest stood behind her.

Slowly, they backed away from the man as the front door to her home opened, and lover number two came stumbling out. He was naked, almost delirious, and covered with the same sores as the first man, though not as deeply. "What have you done to me?" he moaned.

It was then that the third man realized, "These men, you have slept with them?"

She turned quickly and wailed, "No!"

It was there that Okana's witchcraft was broken, and he backed away from her in disgust. The other two mindlessly wandered into the streets and walked their separate ways.

That very night, word was spread through town that not only was Okana a powerful witch, but also she was a promiscuous woman who spread disease with her touch. And while her own charms and potions kept the pox at bay so she never got sick, her reputation spread, and nothing she tried would quell it.

From that moment on, not a man in town would lay with her. For many years, Okana remained a lonely, loveless creature.

Okana's Seduction of Shangó

It was late afternoon; the sun still hung high in the sky, and even in the oppressive heat, the marketplace was packed with people. Okana was one of many, another face lost in the crowd; there were no taunts of "witch," and no one seemed to remember that it was she who spread the pox through town. Here, lost among the many colored trinkets and covetous faces, she was merely a woman, and an exhausted one at that. The heat was draining.

A great cry rose through the streets; it started as a distant murmur and spread, creating a cacophonous roar. The crowds parted, and Okana stood and stared. From the distance she could make out a man's body floating above the crowd. In the light of day, his blackness was impressive; his skin sparkled and shimmered like hematite in the afternoon sun. He bobbed slowly, gently, and his body rippled and rocked with each rising and falling. As he came closer and the crowds parted, she saw that he was not floating; he was seated on a white horse, attended by many muscled, armed men on foot. Heat rose in her face; she thought it was the oppressive heat of the dry season, but as she felt that familiar tingle in her loins, she realized it was the heat of desire.

"Who is that man?" she asked to no one.

"That is the new king, Oranmiyan's grandson, Shangó," said an unfamiliar face.

Okana was in love.

Shangó rode past her; she stood, unmoving, while the crowd continued to part, and Shangó noticed her, briefly. Their eyes locked; and for a moment, Shangó's seemed clouded with desire. He nodded his head toward her, and smiled. Then, as quickly as he noticed her, he turned away. The crowds closed around her again, and she watched as his supple form bobbed away gently until she could see him no more. The crowds quieted down to their normal roar, and everyone continued about their business.

Okana turned to the woman who had answered her. "That is the new king? What was he doing here?"

The woman smiled. "He wants his subjects to know who he is. So every day at the same time, he travels the same road with his guards so we can see his face." Her eyes grew moist, filled with longing. "Isn't he the most handsome man?"

"Indeed, he is," agreed Okana. And to herself, she murmured, "I will be his queen!"

Shangó was back in his palace, surrounded by his guards and his priests. "I don't know what happened to me," he said. "I felt fine, and then I saw her. The most beautiful woman I've ever seen. I've known many beautiful women in my life, but there was something about her. I almost jumped off my horse; I wanted to take her in my arms and run away with her. But as soon as I turned my head and gathered my thoughts, the desire was gone, and I only wanted to run away. It is not normal for me to want to run from a woman!"

The diviner cast his shells on the mat: One mouth opened. "That woman was a witch," whispered the diviner. "The eyes of a witch were on you today, and she desired you. You will see her again, because she is plotting to ensnare you. But don't worry, as with all the misfortunes in life, there is ebó."

Okana was home that night, mixing and mashing herbs; skillfully, she combined them into a philter whose scent would overpower the senses of any man she desired. When her work was done, her home was filled with the exotic scents of magic and love, and she fell into a fitful sleep.

The next day, at the same place, and the same time, Okana stood and awaited Shangó's approach. "My magic is strong," she told herself. "This time, he will notice me. I will speak. And he will be mine!"

When she saw the king's approach, Okana doused herself with the potion, and she stood in the middle of the street. Shangó stopped his horse in front of her.

The desire he felt the previous day rose in his loins; and for a moment, his eyes were locked to hers. Yet Shangó made ebó before riding that day, and the force of ebó was stronger than the magic surrounding Okana. He took a deep breath, and as quickly as it tried to overpower him, the magic was broken. Still, he smiled as if entranced by her charms. "Good day, beautiful woman," he said in a low, baritone voice. Okana smiled seductively as Shangó asked her, "What is your name?"

"I am Okana," she said, throwing her shoulders back so her ample breasts and deep cleavage were in full view of the king. Shangó's eyes, however, were not on her breasts; his thoughts were on the name of the odu that fell from his diviner's hands: *Okana.*

"Let me tell you a secret, Okana," Shangó said quietly, bending down from his horse so his face was close to hers. "I am a descendant of Odúduwa; the heavenly, royal blood of my ancestor runs in my veins. The wiles of a witch cannot touch one with the sacred blood of the orishas in his body."

Shangó rode away, and Okana, in grief, collapsed to the earth, crying in despair. Once again, her obsessive love went unreturned.

Okana's Curses

Wealth weakened her drive, loneliness hardened her heart, and taunts of, "Witch!" from the townspeople warped her mind. "If I can't be happy," she seethed to the darkness that filled her soul, "no one can be happy."

Okana turned her witchcraft to evil things; she brought osogbo to the town in which she lived. She conjured storms. She set fires. She ruined farms and dried up milk-cows. She created poverty. Mothers mourned and fathers feared as their children suffered.

Yet Okana was confused when these tragedies touched her own life. When the storms unleashed their wrath over the town, the roof of her own home was destroyed. When fires burned, she coughed from the smoke. When crops withered, she had nothing to eat, and when milk-cows dried up, she had nothing to drink. Poverty recessed the village economy, and the luxuries she loved were hard to obtain in spite of her wealth.

This only made her angrier and her curses more severe.

One by one, the townspeople sought out Mofá to make ebó. One by one, they cured Okana's curses. She sought to destroy, but in the end, made everyone stronger. For through Mofá's skilled hands, each osogbo was soothed, and iré brought back to the land.

So confused and angry was she that her rage grew until her humanity was all but destroyed. Everyone was afraid of the evil witch.

Okana's Final Loss

There comes a time when enough is enough, and the townspeople were tired of the constant afflictions suffered by Okana's witchcraft. An angry mob gathered in the center of town. It was night, and fires were lit.

"I lost my children to the pox," wailed a woman. "It was Okana who brought this on us!"

"The rains haven't touched my land in weeks," said an old farmer whose skin was leathered and wrinkled by the sun. "My crops are all dead!"

"I am bankrupt." said another man. "Okana cursed my business."

Women were angry over their losses in love; men were angry because their women abandoned them. A cacophony of complaints disturbed the night.

"Ebó is never enough," said an elderly man over the roar. "You can make all the ebós you want, but if the problem isn't removed, you will have to make ebó all over again."

Right there, the townspeople decided to drive Okana from town.

With torches lit, they stormed her home; the angry mob broke her windows and doors with stones and set fire to all she had. Okana was in her workroom practicing her witchcraft when the assault began; and when it ended, she was fleeing for her life. Osogbo followed her that night, and all the curses cast came back to her to roost.

She was weak, ill, homeless, and powerless.

And since osogbo fled the town with her, everyone there became prosperous and healthy again. They cheered the destruction of the witch and all she owned.

Okana Makes Ebó

When one has everything, one must lose everything to change, to evolve: So it was with Okana. Afflicted by the osogbo she once commanded with her witchcraft, she sought out the diviner, Mofá, to make ebó and change her life. With all the money from her pockets in her hands, she sat on the mat, and prayed for help as the old man opened the diloggún.

The once-powerful witch was reduced to asking for help. With the loss of all her possessions, she no longer had the tools of her craft at her disposal. She was powerless. With the weight of osogbo bearing down on her head, she was hopeless.

Her own sign fell, Okana. "In the streets at times is where one encounters happiness," said the wise man as he prepared to make ebó.

There were eight plates on the mat that day, each with different items: a coconut and two candles; black-eyed peas and toasted corn; okra and cornmeal; strips of cloth in red, blue, white, and yellow; pumpkin; charcoal; a mask; and one rock. One by one, Mofá prayed over each plate and cleansed her.

Okana left the diviner's home, still powerless and helpless, but she knew: "There is gain, and there is loss." She took her ebó to a crossroad in a neighboring village, for Mofá had told her, "You can no longer live in the village of your birth. You must go away to a place no one knows you if you are to find happiness again."

She sat on the street corner, and for the first time in her life, she cried. Okana cried for her dead parents. She cried for her losses in love. She cried for the evil she had wrought on her own people, and she cried because she knew not what else to do.

Okana was a lost creature, indeed; but ebó has a way of renewing all things.

Okana's Lesson in Love

It was over for Okana: She had no home, no money, and no magic. With nothing left, she lay in the street, her clothes tattered and her face ashen. Beside her was a mud puddle, and she looked at her reflection in its dirty waters. She thought herself to look older than her years. "So this is what I have come to?" Lightly, she ran her fingers over the water's surface and watched the ripples disturb and distort her reflection. When the puddle settled again, she saw another face reflected behind her own. She gasped, flipped over, and looked up.

Over her towered a late-middle-aged man with salted hair; his face was deeply creased, but his eyes bright and youthful. He wore robes of fine linen and held in his hands a purse stuffed with coins. Cautiously, he held his hand out to her.

"It is not seemly that a woman with your talents should be lying in the streets," he said, offering to help her up. She took his hand. It was strong.

"And where else am I to lay? I have no home anymore." A single tear slid down her face, streaking the dirt and ash on her skin. She let the stranger bear the burden of her weight as he pulled her to her feet, but once she stood, she stood on her own, and backed away cautiously.

"I came looking for you, Okana." Her eyes narrowed when he said her name; he knew who she was. The townspeople had burned down her house and taken away her land—there was nothing left to take except her own life.

"Leave me alone. Haven't I suffered enough?" She shook with anger and fear. "You people have ruined me. You have punished me for my witchcraft. You burned my house and stole my land. You banished me from the town of my birth. My wealth was stolen. You have taken away everything I had. I have nothing left except my life, and you will not take that!"

People in the streets stopped and stared. Someone whispered, "She's a witch?"

The stranger grabbed her firmly by her arm; he was middle-aged, but he was as strong as a youth, and he pulled her away from the slowly growing crowd. "My name is Salakó," he said quickly. "Let us go somewhere else and talk."

Together they ran through the streets, leaving behind the dumbfounded townspeople who could only wonder what the man would want with a ruined witch; when the crowd was far behind, they began to walk, and eventually came to a modest home on the outskirts of the village. "This is my home," he said, opening the front door, "and the home of my father."

It wasn't as nice as her home had been, but the house was clean and well-maintained. He led her to the back, and pushed on a door, then stopped. "Why am I here?" Okana asked.

Salakó put his hands by his side and looked at her. "You are right. I need to explain things to you." He took a deep breath and sighed. "My father is in this room. He is an old man, and he is dying. He also has the pox, and no one will come to nurse him as he lays helpless. I've heard that you once fought off the pox; it is a disease that you have power over. I want you to help him."

Salakó held the bag of coins out and gently put it into Okana's hands. "I can pay you well for your skills."

She pushed past him, but gently, and opened the door. The room reeked of sickness and death. In the center of a bed that was much too large for the body it held lay a withered old man, breathing heavily and covered with sores. Cautiously, Okana walked to his side. The sheets were soiled.

"He is too sick. There is nothing I can do to heal him."

"But can you care for him? Can you care for him without getting sick yourself?"

"I can. There are things I will need from town, herbs and salves and supplies." She recited a list to him, careful to leave nothing out. "If you bring me these things, I can make him comfortable and pain-free, and I will stay with him until he passes."

For many days and nights, Okana labored over the old man; she tended his sores and dressed his wounds. She turned him, and cleaned him when he soiled himself, and she made sweet-smelling potions that put him in a twilight place pain could not reach. Whenever he awoke, she offered him cool water to drink and food to eat if he would open his mouth, and then administered the medicines that would return him to that safe place free from worries.

Salakó watched as Okana cared for his father as if he were her own; he watched the wicked woman transform in the face of the old man's impending death. She had a kindness to her, and tenderness in her touch. When, finally, the old man passed and Salakó mourned, she took care of him as well, comforting him and offering him light potions that eased him through the darkness of a loved-one's death.

Through it all, Salakó fell in love with Okana.

Early one morning, he walked into the kitchen where she was cooking breakfast, and as he wiped the sleep from his eyes, Okana said, "It is time for me to go."

"Go? Where will you go?"

"I don't know. But my work here is done." Her back was to Salakó, and with her hand, she wiped away the tears that gathered in her eyes. "I need to go."

Okana was surprised and let out a stifled scream when Salakó grabbed her fearfully from behind. He turned her on her heels and took her face in his own aged hands. "Do not leave, Okana. I love you. I need you to stay."

Her body tingled and her face froze, and she stammered, "You . . . you love me? But I used no witchcraft. I used no charms." Her voice trailed off.

"Love isn't about magic or potions or charms. Love just . . . is. It happens. It happens on its own, and all by itself. And I am hopelessly in love with you, Okana."

The two of them were married that day, and lived happily as husband and wife. Together, they worked and built wealth equal to what Okana had known in her youth. They bore children together. Finally, when the day came that Salakó passed away from old age, Okana herself was still a middle-aged woman with many years ahead of her. She had children, and she had grandchildren, and she knew love.

She had everything she had ever wanted.

The Story of the Cat and the Rat

It was late. Okana sat by the hearth, warming herself; her grandchildren lay on the leopard-skin rugs, exchanging playful taunts and blows. She watched and smiled. Okana was an old woman: She had been a mother, and then a grandmother, and she was even a great-grandmother with more progeny than she could count. If old age was golden and children were wealth, she was a rich woman.

One of her granddaughters screamed and pointed into a dark corner. "Grandma," she cried out, "look at the cat!"

Okana rose with effort. "I am blessed in my old age," she thought to herself, "but youth still has its advantages."

She walked stiffly, as old women do, to the corner, and shooed the cat away. It ran, leaving behind a dead mouse. She picked it up by the tail, holding it at arm's length. "It's just a mouse," she told the child.

"Why do cats do that? Why do they kill mice?" she wailed. The other children stopped playing and gathered around their grandmother. They wanted to hear her answer.

Without a word, and with the children at her heels, she opened her front door and threw the dead mouse into the night. "That's just what cats do," she said.

"But why?" whined the little girl.

"Sit down, child," she said. "Sit down, everyone. I'll tell you the story of why cats kill mice."

Sixteen eager children sat on the rugs in two semicircles between Okana and the fireplace; she sat, facing the fire. Its warmth lit up and softened her face. One by one, she looked each of her grandchildren in the eyes, waiting for them to settle down. They settled quickly; grandma's stories were always a treat.

When they were settled, she began, "This isn't a story for the faint of heart. Maybe I shouldn't tell it?" She smiled that mischievous smile that makes little children act crazy.

"No!" they wailed in unison.

"This isn't a story for frightened little children. Maybe I shouldn't tell it?" She looked to her side and down at the youngest girl, grinning a wickedly playful grin.

"No!" they wailed again. "We're big!" they chanted in unison.

"I'm not frightened," the youngest girl said.

Okana took in a deep breath, as if weighing her answer carefully. "Well, all right; you are all big boys and girls. I don't think you'll be too frightened. This is the story of why cats kill mice."

Eager eyes were on Okana as she told the story.

Once, there were two close friends: the cat and the rat. They lived together in the time when the world was new, and things weren't always as plentiful as they are now. Together, however, the two of them survived very well. For the cat was a stealthy hunter; she would spend her days slinking through the forests in that special way cats slink, and when her prey was in sight, she would pounce in that lightning fast, silent leap only cats can do. Nothing got away from her claws.

The rat was an excellent cook, and he knew the herbs and roots of the forest. When the cat brought home her catch each day, the rat would throw it in his pot with whatever things he foraged from the earth, and they would feast on a huge, delicious meal. It was because she was an excellent hunter, and he an excellent cook, that the two of them became and remained fast friends.

There came a drought one year, and all the tiny prey of the forest ran away in search of water. The roots and herbs dried up. And even though no creature was more skilled at the hunt than the cat, and even though no animal could forage and cook the roots and leaves of the forest better than the rat, food was scarce. They were starving.

And the cat was a mother as well; she had three small kittens.

So the cat did what anyone in hard times does—she went to see the diviners. She sat on the mat that day with a wise old man who told her, "For our world to be in balance, there must be both good and bad in our lives. Don't worry, cat; soon the rains will come, the forest will green-up, and there will be prey. You, however, have more pressing concerns."

"And what might those be?" asked the cat.

"You have a relative in a far away place that you love dearly, but have not seen in quite some time. He is ill, and needs your help. Go there, and when you return, your life here will be better. I promise."

"That is my cousin the leopard!" the cat cried. "I have not seen him in years. But I cannot travel that far now. I have children."

"You must go," said the diviner. "The orishas are saying this is how you will bring balance back to your life."

"Then go I must," she said. "I can leave my children with my friend the rat. But will they be safe without me? He is not very strong. I do not think he could protect them if someone attacked them."

"Your children will be fine . . . if you make ebó." And there on the mat the diviner prescribed all sorts of ebós and adimús (types of offerings) the cat was to make to ensure her cousin's health, her blessings, and the safety of her children.

That afternoon the cat had every intention of making ebó, but she was distracted when she saw some prey in the distance. Two young quail were pecking at the earth, and quietly, she stalked them. When she was close enough, she pounced on them and caught one in each paw. The poor birds never saw her coming. "My luck is returning already!" she cried, holding up her kill. Biting down on both with her sharp teeth, she carried them in her mouth as she ran through the forest, back home to her kittens and the rat, and she forgot about making ebó.

The cat told the rat about her visit with the diviner, and while he was cooking the quail in his huge stew pot, she asked, "The distance is far, and I cannot travel with three children in tow. Will you watch them for me, and keep them safe?"

"For you, my best friend, I will do anything."

The cat trusted the rat with her own life, and she felt he would take good care of her kittens. That night, she set out to visit her cousin. She never made ebó.

Okana paused and looked at each child. Sixteen sets of eyes were staring back at her; the children hung on her every word.

"Grandma," the same little girl whined. "They were friends! That doesn't tell us why the cat kills mice!"

Okana sighed and smiled. "I'm getting to that part, child. Will you let me finish my story?"

One of the boys poked the girl in the ribs, "Be quiet and let grandma tell the story." The two children smiled at each other and got quiet.

Okana continued:

The cat never made ebó. Food was still scarce. Rats are not known for being patient creatures, and between the hunger, and the three hungry, whining kittens, he grew impatient. And he grew hungrier. For many days the cat was gone, and when the last bit of quail stew was eaten, and when there were no more roots and leaves to cook, the rat began to look at the cat's kittens as if they were . . . food.

In unison, the children gasped.

"Cats aren't food. They're pets!" argued one boy.

"That's nasty!" said another.

"You can't eat cats," said the youngest girl, scrunching up her face in disgust.

"Animals live by their own rules, children," said Okana. "They don't think as people do. To an animal, anything weaker is food."

> One by one, the rat separated the three kittens, and with the others out of eyesight, he sliced them with his small claws and bit them with his tiny teeth. Neither his claws nor his teeth were very big, but the kittens were small and unable to fight back. When all three were dead, he skinned them and put them into his big stew pot, and cooked them up into a meal. Anything he could not eat—the skin and bones—he simply threw outside the house.
>
> Rats are sloppy like that!

Okana paused in her story again, and looked at the children, one by one. She saw the wide eyes and horrified expressions on her grandchildren's faces. "I told you this story wasn't for the faint of heart," she said. "Shall I continue?"

"Yes," they agreed in unison, holding each other tightly in fear of what might come next.

> While the rat was eating her children, the cat was on her way home. She had nursed her cousin, the leopard, back to health, and he rewarded her greatly with dozens of cowries. For you see, back in those days, cowries were money, and the leopard was a wealthy animal. With her newfound wealth, the cat could buy the necessities she could not hunt, and she could provide well for her three kittens and her friend the rat.
>
> Imagine her horror when she came home and found the skin and bones of her three children scattered outside her home. And imagine her anger when she found the rat bloated and stuffed with meat, the meat of her children.

It was there that the cat flew into a rage, and with her razor-sharp claws, sliced and diced the rat into a thousand pieces, but not before torturing him slowly for the great evil he had done.

That is why cats "play" with rats and mice before they kill them. And that is why, even today, cats hunt and kill every rodent they can find. Each one slain is done out of vengeance for the three kittens the rat ate while his friend, the cat, was away.

"And that," Okana said as she sat back in her chair, "is why cats kill mice."

"He deserved it," said the little girl, sitting up and crossing her arms with that defiant bounce little girls do when they know they are right. "He ate his best friend's children."

"Yes, he did," agreed Okana. "But don't forget—the cat never made ebó. So at the end of it all, whose fault was it, really? Is the rat to be faulted for being hungry, or was it the cat's fault because she did not do what the diviner said? Now, it's late children. That was your bedtime story. Off to sleep with all of you."

Each hugged and kissed their grandmother before scurrying to their beds. The little girl hung back and kissed Okana last, and when she did, she said, "I love you, grandma, and I'll never forget to make ebó!"

"Then your life will be blessed, child. Sleep well."

2

Eji Oko

Two Mouths on the Mat

Enjoy the moment for it is all you have, and that,
too, will soon be gone.

Eji Oko is a deep, mysterious pattern; it seethes with darkness, change, separation, and imagination. The pattern has no parent in the dilogún; born of Olódumare's unfolding, it emerged after the odu Unle* and stands in opposition to that sign in the west. Eji Oko is the balance to Unle. Unle is light. Eji Oko is darkness. Unle stands at the east, and is the harbinger of creation, life, light, and awakening, while this letter bars the west, turning all back into primal darkness. Eji Oko begins the cycle of death, decay, and destruction, yet feeds the cycle of life, growth, and creation through its work.

Its spiritual implications are nothing short of awesome. Eji Oko teaches us that transitions are inevitable: there is the transition from womb to birth, the transition from childhood to adulthood, youth to old age, and this world to the next. Central to all these transitions is death. Our life in the womb dies so we may be born; our childhood dies so we may reach old age. We die so we may move from this world to the next. Death in some form is at the core of any and every change—something must die before something new can take its place.

---

*Unle was the first odu born in Heaven after God's awakening.

31

Of all the patakís in the oral corpus of Eji Oko, I found those about Ikú, the Lucumí personification of death, to be the most vital. For after Eji Oko created both the sunset and the night, the night created Ikú; she was born of the darkness permeating the earth. After her birth, before that first night was over Ikú discovered her ashé, and soon she discovered Ejioko (the mortal form of the heavenly odu). Not knowing that he was her grandfather, spiritually speaking, Ikú fell in love with him, and they married. She being death, and he the father of the darkness from which she sprang, theirs was a barren marriage and Ejioko sought solace in the arms of another woman—an act that destroyed his marriage and set the stage for future heartbreak and sorrow.

While these stories form the foundation of Eji Oko's divinatory meanings, no exploration of the odu would be complete without at least a mention of Ochosi. A secondary theme of Eji Oko is that of blind justice, and as the dispenser of justice, Ochosi's presence is integral to this odu. According to the Lucumí cosmos, Ochosi was the orisha responsible for sacrificing to Olófin, the spiritual father of the orishas; however, it was a role fulfilled in secret. It was a symbiotic relationship—Ochosi fed Olófin, and Olófin renewed his ashé on a daily basis. One day, Ochosi's wife became curious about his hunting habits; and when her curiosity got the best of her, well, the story speaks for itself.

Change, separation, death, and justice—these are all central themes in the odu known as Eji Oko; and when the sign falls on the diviner's mat, all these things will come into focus in varying degrees in the client's life. With skill and a thoughtful recitation of the patakís, the diviner can and will help the client make wise choices in life, but the responsibility to choose wisely and act ethically remains a burden that the client himself must bear. Evolution is no simple task.

The Birth of Ikú

Evening shadows lengthened as the sun set on the first day; they stretched over the earth beneath a rich, black velvet cloth that unrolled from the eastern sky. Soon everything was dark, and animals, heavy-eyed and fatigued, lay down to rest; they slept, lost in dreams.

When the last creeping thing closed its eyes, something else on the earth awakened. As shadows deepened, something umbrous and sinister slipped through them; it congealed slowly, rising and taking form: Ikú.

At first she was nothing more than a shadow, a whisper in the night air, insignificant and intangible, but the darkness continued to gather to itself, becoming solid. It created a body. She looked down at herself and felt her new form with eager hands. Ikú was pleased. It was soft but firm; her flesh was smooth and seductive. Wide hips swayed sensually as she relished in her existence; chills coursed through her body as she felt the full breasts meant for suckling children, and tempting men. The color of her skin was darker than the night; she held her hands up to the starlit skies, and saw that her own blackness was deeper than the velvet of space. Though she reeked of danger, she was every woman's dream, and every man's desire.

She closed her eyes, breathing in deeply, and called more of the darkness to herself; it became solid, whipping and folding over her form until she was wrapped in whole cloth made from the cold night air.

Ikú studied the night; though she could not see far, she knew there was something vast hidden in it. She wanted something that was out there, although she didn't know what that something was, and while she thought about that, her belly rumbled. She craved . . . she didn't know. So for countless hours Ikú just stood there, and waited to see what would come after the darkness.

Sunrise came; and as Ikú watched the mottled light erupt in a cacophony of colors on the horizon, she knew *birth*. "This is how all things begin," she thought to herself. "Like the sunrise. It all begins with birth. Everything comes from darkness, as did I, and erupts fresh and new in the world. But how do all things *end*?"

Ikú walked through the world, losing herself in its beauty; and after she walked for some time, over a hill she spied a herd of animals grazing, feeding off the fresh, young grasses. She felt again the emptiness in her stomach, the rumbling that insisted she do something; and there, she realized what she must do. "I must eat." As the animals themselves were doing, Ikú bent down to graze on the earth; the sweet grasses filled her, but they did not sate her. While she pondered this, she saw other animals in the trees, biting at the colorful fruits in their branches.

"This is what I must eat," she thought, "to feel full." So Ikú walked up to the trees, annoyed when all the animals fled her presence; she reached up into a tree and grabbed some of the brightly colored fruits that hung there. As she bit into them, she was pleased; sweet juices flooded her mouth, and once again, the fruits she ate filled her stomach. But it did not sate her. Again, she stood there and pondered that mystery.

Ikú could take the emptiness she felt in her stomach no more; anger flared up inside her, and she went on a rampage, eating and gorging herself on every grass, vine, and fruit she could find. The more food she ate, the hungrier she became, and as her hunger grew, so did her anger. It flared about her like an icy wind, and soon, she noticed that everything she touched turned black and withered; it died right there with her touch. Anger left her; sadness came. "This is how all things end," she realized. "They end with me, in death."

From deep in the forest she heard a primal, hungry growl, and a painful scream that ended too soon; she forgot what she was thinking and ran toward it. She saw a leopard and another fallen animal that she could not recognize, so torn beyond recognition it was; and she watched, amazed, as the leopard's blood-soaked lips and teeth tore again and again into the animal's flesh. Hungry growls turned to purrs of satisfaction, and Ikú thought to herself, "That is what I must eat, to feel full." Ikú felt the cessation of life deep within her being, and knew, "This is what I am. I am the bringer of death." Without a sound, she descended upon the leopard; with her hungry touch, it fell dead, and she gorged herself on its flesh, fat, and blood. For the first time her hunger was gone; but still, she wanted more.

Ikú went on a rampage over the earth, gorging herself on its animals until she could hold no more. But nothing sated her hunger, which angered her more; and one by one, she set out to eat every animal that lived, crept, or crawled on the earth, never noticing that for each animal she ate, yet another sprang up somewhere to take its place. All Ikú knew was that the world was her personal buffet; her greed continued to grow, and she continued to eat. But while she gorged herself, Ikú never really felt full.

So intent had Ikú become on filling herself that she missed the creation of humans; for centuries their race grew, never knowing disease or death. In the beginning, humans grazed only on the grasses, grains, and fruits given freely by the earth. Ikú felt the death of each of these, but paid it no mind; it was no different from the death brought to these things by the animals upon which she herself fed. But in time humans learned, as had Death, that the animals were good for food as well. As the first band of hunters killed their first prey, Ikú felt that death, although she had not brought it. She followed the scent of blood and saw these new, two-legged animals feeding on another with four, and wondered who had such power equal to her own.

For years Ikú watched them evolve, and in time the first of their kind grew weak and died of old age. Death felt this passing, as she had that of the first blade of grass and the first animal formed on Earth, and as she tasted the death of the first human she realized that for the first time, she was full. Her hunger finally abated. The meat was sweet, fulfilling, but in time the hunger returned and Ikú set out to eat her next human.

She fed freely, and great cries were heard all over Earth and in Heaven. People who never knew death faced it every day, and Ikú, in greed, slaughtered humans in the prime of their lives. She found that the younger humans were the sweetest, their meat the softest and tastiest, and the life of a child was rapturous. Out of powerlessness, humans resigned themselves to a fate of continual death, and watched as Ikú picked them off one by one.

It was during this time that Ejioko incarnated among mortals. At first Ejioko saw the wisdom in death, for not even humans could be allowed to propagate and live forever. They would destroy the earth in a matter of centuries. Yet Ikú was intoxicated by the scent of human flesh and if allowed, would one day wipe out the world. The orishas, as well, were concerned, for all the hard work they put into the world was being swallowed up by this one being. Ejioko divined, and came up with a solution. He marked an ebó of one goat, sacrificed to Eshu (a manifestation of Elegguá), its meat cooked with a thousand small pebbles, and a rooster for Elegguá, to be sacrificed the following day.

That day, they gathered and sacrificed, and as night fell over the earth, they sat around a fire and cooked the meat with the pebbles. They feasted silently, eating around the stones. The air was thick with their fear as they watched the darkness for any sign of Ikú. Sleep, however, overcame them, and as they sat ringing the fire, one by one they slumbered. Finally, the last human closed his eyes; and Ejioko tied Elegguá's rooster close to the fire so it would not escape and would stay warm during the cold night. Then he settled in and waited for the enemy to arrive.

In spite of wanting to stay awake, he, too, fell into a deep sleep.

In the last hours before sunrise, Ikú came; quietly, like a leopard stalking its prey, she crept into the camp, cloaked by darkness. The fire was but a collection of embers, yet it was still hot, and she knelt beside it to warm herself. She took in a deep breath, enjoying the scent of so many sleeping humans crammed into one space.

But something smelled different.

Ikú followed the strange scents; sniffing at the air in short, rapid bursts, she came to Ejioko's side. He looked human, delicious in his slumber, but there was something different about his odor. Carefully, she touched his face, almost a loving caress, and then she knew. "It's the soul of an immortal trapped in human flesh!" She licked her lips hungrily. "This one will sate my hunger for a long, long time."

Then Ikú traced the other scent back to the fire. Sitting off to the side was a large pot of stewed goat's meat, still warm and steaming. She looked around at the sleeping humans and saw that each had a gourd of the meat sitting at their side. "So this is what humans eat," she thought. "They love the goat's flesh as I do."

Knowing that Ejioko would fill her so she could eat no more, she decided to feast on the stew first. She took her first bite, and as she bit down, something hard in the meat shattered her teeth. She cried out in pain.

"What are these animals?" she gasped, spitting out a mouthful of tooth fragments and stones into her hands. "They can eat rocks? They are getting stronger! What has this immortal taught them?" It was then that the rooster tied to Elegguá's shrine awoke and felt Ikú's presence, and it crowed in fear. Everyone around the campfire awoke, grabbing for their weapons and letting out their own fearful cries. Ikú ran away from the humans that day, afraid of the race that had evolved to eat stones with their own teeth. So afraid was she that she never again lifted her own hands against those who could eat such hard food.

Since the time that Ejioko taught humans how to fight death by making ebó, Ikú has been afraid to feast freely on humans. To eat, she can do so only by the graces of the orishas, who say who, when, and where their children on Earth may be taken. And those that live by the orishas' will do not suffer untimely death; they see to it that those who make ebó live the full lives granted by Olódumare.

The Marriage of Ikú and Ejioko

Ejioko was alone in the forest. It was night, and he warmed himself by the fire he built. Over the pit roasted the meat from his day's kill; its juices snapped and sizzled as tongues of flame licked at it. Pleading for food, his stomach rumbled, and in response, Ejioko poked at the meat. It was still rare. "Soon," he thought, eyeing it hungrily.

Later, when his belly was full, Ejioko spread his animal skins on the cool earth and curled up beside the fire. Sleep came quickly.

It was then that Ikú slipped from the shadows and stood silently over Ejioko's sleeping body. For a moment he stirred, and it seemed he would awaken. Ikú put her index finger over pursed lips, and whispered, "Shhh . . ." Ejioko fell back into a deep, dreamless sleep. This was but one of Ikú's powers, for sleep is but a form of light death, the soul slipping into the world between Heaven and Earth.

"What a beautiful man," she thought to herself, eyeing the thick chest, thin waist, and muscled legs. His arms were toned, defined, and venous from handling the bow and arrow every day. She trembled with desire. "And we are both hunters, he and I," she thought. For Ejioko spent all his days in the thick jungles tracking game, and she was a huntress whose jungle was all of creation. There was only one animal Ejioko could not hunt: humans. They were her prey exclusively.

"And what a clever man he is," she whispered into the night. For hunt him she had, but Ejioko had the wisdom to make ebó, and thwarted her each time. "Still," she thought, "If I cannot eat him . . . I can have him another way." A lustful fire burned in her loins. "One way or another, I will have him inside me." She smiled a wicked smile and retreated into the shadows.

Ikú thought she was clever each day that she followed Ejioko, but he, ever the hunter, knew he was being hunted. Time and time again he tried to focus his preternatural senses on the thing at his heels, and each time, it melted into the forest so quickly he lost track of it. "It's not an animal," he thought, breathing deeply and trying to take in its scent. "It's not a human, either," he realized, when the air was filled with everything but the smell of humans.

In that moment, Ejioko knew fear.

Slowly, quietly, he lifted an arrow from his quiver and loaded his crossbow. He lifted it to the sky and cried out, "Let this arrow pierce the heart of the evil that follows me!" His muscles tensed and then relaxed as the arrow sailed into the sky.

He ran as fast as he could, following the arrow as it arced and came sailing back down; and at the projectile's end, he saw a dark form, waiting. He watched in awe as its hand came in front of its own chest and caught the arrow, just mere inches before it would have sliced through. It was then that he realized he was being followed by Ikú, the one who had tried to kill him. And by daylight, he found her most beautiful.

"No one has ever come so close to killing me," she said as Ejioko walked toward her.

"And no one has ever been able to track me so well," he answered.

"We are very much alike. We are hunters, you and I."

"Yes," agreed Ejioko. "We are." Desire flooded him, and he embraced her. They were wed that night.

Ikú and Ejioko spent many years together, in bliss, in love and making love. But as centuries passed, it became painfully obvious to both of them that they would never have children. For Ikú was the mother of death, not life, and her womb was like that of a dead thing. In spite of their love, this was the one thing that, in time, caused Ejioko to seek out the embrace of other women.

Ikú never knew he was cheating on her: Ikú never knew of the children he fathered with his mistresses.

After many years and many affairs, Ejioko found himself in the arms of Nanumé. Of all the women he had known, none made love better than she. When he was with her, the world was timeless, and each night, he spent more and more time away from Ikú, and more and more time in Nanumé's arms.

One morning, things went too far: Ejioko awoke, confused; and was shocked when he discovered it was morning. Sunlight slipped through cracks in the bedroom curtain. "Have I been here all night?" he thought.

He looked at Nanumé, and sighed. Her body was youthful, supple, with ample breasts that rose and fell with each breath. He pulled the sheets down just a bit, exposing the narrow curve of her waist. Below that . . . "I could spend the night in worse places," Ejioko thought to himself.

Nanumé stirred and woke under Ejioko's lustful eyes; as she moved, a ray of sunlight caught her black skin. In the light, it dazzled like polished onyx. "You're still here," she whispered, her voice tangled in sleep and dreams.

"I couldn't leave if I tried." Ejioko kissed her neck in the soft spot between the collarbones and nibbled at her throat for just a moment. His tongue tasted something rough and sour. He drew back, surprised, and saw a hard, crusty pustule where before he had seen only silky smoothness. "What is this?"

Nanumé brushed her fingertips lightly against her throat, and when she touched the tiny pustule, she drew in a deep breath. "Something must have bit me, a bug." She sat up, pulling the sheets to her chin. She inhaled deeply, arching her back and shrugging her shoulders. "I love you so much," she whispered, leaning over to kiss him. Ejioko forgot about the small pustule rising like a grain on Nanumé's skin; Nanumé, however, was worried. "Not again," she thought. "How many more times must I suffer the family curse?"

Ikú was furious with Ejioko when he came home that morning. "I was lost in the forest," he said. "It was dark, and I was confused."

"Don't lie to me," she wailed like a banshee. "No one in the world knows the forest better than you. You do not get lost."

Ejioko hung his head in shame. "Forgive me," he said. "But I was. I was lost, and all I could think about was getting home to you." His face was sincere, for truly, he was lost—lost in the arms of Nanumé, lost in her embrace. Ikú believed him when she saw the sincerity on his face. Forcefully, he took her into her arms and kissed her. Desire rose in her loins, and for the moment, Ikú forgave him. She forgave him all day and all night.

So intense was their lovemaking that Ejioko forgot all about Nanumé. It was as if he knew Ikú for the first time.

It took only a few days before the sores broke out on Ejioko's skin. Soon, Ikú's skin erupted. "Smallpox!" Ikú cried. "We have smallpox." Ejioko healed quickly, with only a few scars hidden in places that most would never see; perhaps it was because Nanumé's love was like a healing ashé, and spared him the full scourge. He never knew.

Ikú's skin became ugly and deformed, and Ejioko never forgave Nanumé for infecting him, and in turn, his wife. He never, ever went back to see her.

Nor could he bear to look at the deformed face of Ikú; disease marred her beauty and turned her into an evil-appearing creature.

Nanumé could not forget about Ejioko. She was with child—his child. As sores erupted over her body, her belly grew, and her agony was great. So disfigured was she that she did not go out into the world to look for Ejioko; she hid in darkness, and waited for the contagion to pass.

He never came. He never knew that she was pregnant with his child.

Nobody came to help Nanumé with the baby's birth: Not Ejioko, not the doctors, not the midwives, not even the other orishas. For nine months, her flesh ripened with life and ripped with foul, pus-filled pustules that filled the room with an acrid odor. Her beauty was still there, but marred by disease; her womb, full, was stretched and painful as her belly tore around the sores with the added pressure. A contraction came, sharp and earnest; she cried out as wetness poured from between her legs. She screamed, and only an echo answered her. There, exhausted, lying on the floor, with consciousness fleeing her like a shadow, she gave one final cry, and heard another faint one, not unlike her own. Her child was born in her misery.

Eventually, the sores on Nanumé's body healed, and as was her ashé, when the sickness passed, she was again young and beautiful. The child born that painful night grew quickly into a toddler, and to ease the loneliness in her heart, the longing for Ejioko, she spent all her days in the fields playing with her. She was walking; and until now had shown none of the family's curse, the scourge of smallpox. Nanumé smiled. *Maybe,* she thought, *it all ends with her?*

Unknown to Nanumé, Ikú was stalking her. For since Ejioko had brought home the rotting disease, she had been an outcast, forced to wander at night and stay in shadows. Unlike Nanumé, smallpox was not her ashé, and her form remained blighted. Rumors spread in the world, and eventually she knew that Ejioko slept with Nanumé; she left him, and set out to exact revenge on the woman who dishonored and disfigured her.

Ikú found her in the forest; Ikú watched as she played with the child, her husband's child, and she realized, "This is her source of happiness now that my husband has left her."

Ikú drew herself up to her full height; she blocked out the sun, and a great shadow fell over the girl. Nanumé looked up at the sky; horror melted her beautiful face as she saw Ikú, menacing, so strong that not even the sun dared shine on her. Nanumé rose from beneath her tree and ran toward her daughter to protect her; by instinct, she knew that Ikú was about to exact revenge on both her and Ejioko for their adultery. But before she could reach her, her daughter's step faltered; her body went limp, and the breath left her as she crumpled on the earth, dead. Nanumé collapsed over her lifeless body and wept. For years, she wept over the corpse of her child. The pain seemed eternal.

After that, Ikú banished herself from the light of day, and crept in shadows, a horrible figure that brought fear and despair to those who saw her. In anger, her three sisters rose up, and swore to destroy Ejioko and all his children on Earth: Arayé, Ano, and Aro. Their sole purpose became vengeance, and they sought to destroy any good that Ejioko brought to the world.

But before they could do that, they had to destroy his iré.

Ejioko Loses His Friend Iré

In spite of everything, Ejioko led a charmed life.

Because of his skills as an archer and a tracker, there was little he lacked. He never knew hunger, because he never failed to find and kill his prey. He never knew poverty, because he felled the healthiest, mightiest animals, and sold their flawless pelts for huge sums of money. He never knew loneliness, because he was one of the most handsome men on Earth. Women threw themselves at him.

Ejioko was blessed; he was blessed because Iré was his best friend and followed him wherever he went.

Still, the three sisters Arayé, Ano, and Aro never forgot that it was his adultery that brought disease to Ikú, disfiguring her, and they sought out ways to separate him from Iré. After much plotting and planning, they decided to do it through his dreams.

At night, while Ejioko was sleeping, they entered his mind and made him dream of a bright, new future. In it, Ejioko was no longer a hunter; he was a warrior. It was through war and conquest that he amassed many followers and became ruler of his own kingdom. Night after night, they brought these dreams to him, and before long Ejioko believed them to be prophetic.

Still, Ejioko knew that not all dreams were true, and he sought out the diviner Mofá to make sure and make ebó.

The old man sat him on the mat and cast his cowries: two mouths fell. He continued to cast the cowries, and a deep frown lined his face. "These dreams, they are not what they seem," he said. "You have some very powerful spirits angry with you, and they are using these dreams to take you away from your destiny. You are not meant to be a warrior, nor are you meant to be a king. You already know your ashé, and your purpose in life. Feed your head and forget these dreams, lest you lose the blessings you have."

"But my dreams promise a greater future, Mofá," he argued. "It is the future of my dreams that I desire. Mark ebó so my dreams can come true."

He shook his head sadly. "I can't. Your dreams do not speak of your destiny. They bring your downfall. Clear your head immediately so the dreams leave you, and you can continue walking your path with your friend Iré."

Ejioko knew it was no use to argue with the diviner, so he thanked him and promised he would return quickly to make ebó.

Instead, he went to sleep and dreamed.

Put aside your bow and arrow, the voice in his dream insisted. *Pick up the sword instead. A great war is coming to the land, and if you fight in this war, you will be a hero!*

Ejioko saw himself leading a great army into battle, and they cheered as their enemies were killed, one by one. Of all who fought, no one fought more valiantly than he, and they cheered him. He was brought home and given a hero's welcome, and before long, the town's king died. They crowned him king in his place.

As he slept, the three osogbo-sisters laughed and giggled joyously.

Ejioko awoke from the dream. "Surely, this is the will of the orishas," he thought to himself. That night, Ejioko put away his bow and arrow and picked up a sword. He set out on the road the three osogbo sisters revealed to him in his dream, searching for the army he was to lead.

As he left, he left behind Iré, who was still sleeping.

The next morning, Iré awoke to find himself alone. He waited. "Surely," he thought, "Ejioko will remember he has left me behind, and he will return." Then, he saw the bow and arrow sitting on the floor, discarded, and he saw that the sword Ejioko kept as a curiosity was gone. Iré knew that he succumbed to the dreams sent to him by the three osogbos. And he set out to find the diviner Mofá.

For days, Ejioko walked in the forest along the path that was shown to him in his dream. He was starving. Ejioko made no provisions for food before he set out on his journey. So used to just finding and killing his prey was he that he didn't think about taking food. But now, when he tracked his game, he was unable to kill it. Before he could get to it with his sword, it fled deep into the forest, and once again he would have to track something new. The hunger overwhelmed him, and he began to doubt his dreams and believe in the words of Mofá. Weakened by his hunger, Ejioko collapsed on the forest's floor and cried.

Mofá again sat on the mat, this time with Iré himself, and marked ebó. "Do this quickly," he said. "And then set out on the forest road to find your friend Ejioko. Take the bow and arrow with you. He will need it."

Before night came, Iré returned to Mofá with two roosters: one for Eshu, and one for Elegguá. Mofá performed the sacrifice. Quickly, Iré ran through the forest, looking for his friend Ejioko; with him, he carried the odu's bow and arrow and the meat of the two roosters. He found his friend sleeping, dreaming the dreams sent by the three osogbos, and weakened from hunger. Tenderly, Iré woke his friend, put his bow and arrow in his hands, and said, "This, Ejioko, is the true source of your blessings. Never abandon your own iré or ashé again."

Thankfully, Ejioko took the bow and arrow, and in silence, ate the meat Iré brought. By morning, his strength returned.

Never again did Ejioko listen to advice from his dreams; instead, he sought out the diviners on all important matters.

Ochosi Feeds Olófin

It was early morning; the sun was barely above the horizon, and a thin, cool mist rose from the forest floor. Its dampness made the earth soft, muffling Ochosi's slow, careful steps. His body was poised but his muscles relaxed; and in his left hand, he carried a simple bow. With eyes narrowed and ears focused, he concentrated on the woods, and tried to feel life around him. A twig snapped somewhere ahead, and another; he knew there was an animal walking, almost as soundlessly and carefully as he. Ochosi barely breathed as he tried to focus on it.

It was a buck, wandering and nibbling mindlessly on wild grasses and leaves; it was oblivious to Ochosi's presence. In one quick, fluid motion, he lifted his bow with his left arm, and with his right hand snapped an arrow in place. It took only a single heartbeat for him to tense the line and send the arrow slicing thin air. The buck never saw Ochosi; nor did it feel the arrow. It pierced his heart so cleanly that he fell down, dead, before his body could feel its mortal sting.

The wet thud on the forest floor alarmed the birds in the trees, and a massive flock flew away in fear. It was thunderous for a moment, then dead calm. The orisha stood over his kill, and for the first time, he let himself breathe deeply and sigh. In the morning silence, it almost echoed.

Ochosi hoisted the carcass on his back, the legs dangling over his shoulders and brushing his chest. The buck's head bounced limply on his left shoulder as he walked. He went deep into the forest; so far did he go that it was noon when, finally, he laid the body at the feet of an ancient Iroko tree. Pointing his arrow to the sky, he began to sing the sacrificial songs sung since humans first had a voice, and a blinding white shaft of light from Heaven engulfed the tree.

Olófin stood in that light and watched as Ochosi slit the deer's neck, letting the blood flow into the earth. He removed the head and offered it to him. In acceptance, Olófin touched the head; a great current of ashé traveled from his hands to Ochosi's.

"Once again, our pact is fulfilled," said Olófin. "You feed all of

Heaven, and Heaven gives you the ashé that makes you the great hunter you are. You will be blessed forever among the orishas."

Ochosi saluted Olófin, and he tapped him on the shoulders, bidding him rise. Then, the shaft of light faded, and the forest returned to normal. Ochosi was left with a headless, bloodless carcass. He gutted it, removing its vital organs, and left these at the foot of the tree as well. What was left, he carried back home.

This was Ochosi's mission every day: to hunt, feed Olófin, to give ashé back to the earth, and to feed his family. In return, Olófin refreshed his ashé every day, making him the most skilled hunter on Earth or in Heaven; but, Olófin gave Ochosi his ashé for hunting with one string attached. No one was to know that he sacrificed to Olófin every day. It was to be a secret thing, done at the feet of Olófin's favorite tree.

This part of the pact would have been simple had it not been for Ochosi's wife. She was curious and wanted to know everywhere he went and everything he did. Night after night, when he came home with his kill, she wondered why every animal was missing its head, and she wondered why every animal was drained of blood.

When she could wonder no more, she demanded answers from her husband. "I never get an answer from you, and I want to know now," she whined, her voice shrill and caustic. "Why are all these animals cut as if in sacrifice?"

Ochosi was quartering meat when he looked up at her and said, "Woman, what are you talking about?"

"The animals you bring home are always drained of blood. And they are always missing their heads. And the vital organs are already removed. The legs, the heart, the liver, everything is gone. Why?"

"There are some things that a wife should not know about her husband," said Ochosi, continuing his work.

Back inside the house, the woman's curiosity consumed her. "My husband is a good hunter, yes, but how can he kill so much game alone? And what happens to the heads, or the entrails, or the blood? And why won't he tell me? I am his wife!" She had to know the answers; and she plotted.

The next morning, as always, Ochosi woke before the sun rose; silently, he dressed. In darkness, he stood over his marriage bed and kissed his wife lightly on her forehead. True—she was a source of aggravation for him, but he was fond of her. Sometimes, he thought he loved her.

Still shrouded by the night, Ochosi went into the dark forest as he had for years, alone; he was its master, and it was his source of life. He closed his eyes for a moment, breathing in the musky, damp air, and reached out into the woods with his mind. This was part of the ashé Olófin gave him—to meld with the life of the forest, to feel its heartbeat, to know what lay within it without using his eyes. It was all darkness as he felt the forest's strength closing around him; a part of him was there, in his body, breathing deeply, while a part of him went forth among the thickets and the trees and the rivers and the streams, in search of his prey. He felt the deer in the forest, sleeping soundly on mossy banks; they were quiet in their thicket, curled together for warmth, their chests rising and falling in unison as they slept.

A stag lifted its head, sniffing at the air. Warily, it narrowed its eyes and lifted its snout, as if trying to focus on an unseen enemy. This happened each time Ochosi used his inner vision to find his prey; one of the animals would feel him, sense him, and try to find him. It was part of his ashé, to not only track his prey, but call them to their death. The buck rose to its feet, first the front legs, and then the back, and walked cautiously in Ochosi's direction. Little did it know that its own curiosity was leading it to Ochosi, and its death. At first, the orisha focused on it with his mind; there was no way he could track it physically, for the animal was too far away. Focused so sharply on the stag, Ochosi did not notice the occasional snap of a twig behind him; he didn't hear the light breathing that was mere yards away from his back.

Ochosi was being followed, and he had no clue.

When finally Ochosi and his prey were within eyesight of each other, before the animal could run, Ochosi sent a single, swift arrow to make its kill. The stranger who followed marveled at the orisha's skill; and so focused was he on his prey, he still felt not the stranger's presence.

Ochosi gathered up the carcass and continued to walk; the stranger followed him to the sacred Iroko and watched him lay the buck reverently at its feet. Once done, he prostrated himself before the mighty tree, singing the ancient, sacrificial songs.

At first the lights came down from Heaven gently; small, bright sparks falling like rain, and these were followed by larger orbs that pulsed and shimmered as if alive. The Iroko glowed; the stranger could not tell if it was its own light, or light borrowed from the sparks and orbs reflecting off its surface. Then there was a flood of white-hot brilliance; it was so intense that the stranger's eyes burned. "What ashé is this?" Ochosi's stalker whispered.

A final flood of white light came, and as the glow dimmed tolerably, the stranger saw a figure inside: Olófin. "He makes sacrifice to Olófin himself!" In fear, knowing this was somewhere no one should be, the stranger backed into the forest slowly, but still watching as Ochosi slit the deer's neck, and the blood flowed into the earth at Olófin's feet. Finally, when there was enough distance and the trees hid the view, the stranger turned and ran.

Ochosi was down on one knee, holding the head up in offering to Olófin. Instead of taking it, he glared at the orisha and demanded, "Who did you bring with you to my sacred place?"

The anger in Olófin's voice frightened Ochosi; he was confused and dared not look up. "No one, Father," he said. "I am all alone!"

"No, we are not alone. There is another. You were followed without your knowledge."

Ochosi was angry. He stood up and spun around wildly, looking for the trespasser. He saw no one. Olófin stood, watching him, as if to see what he might do. Ochosi's anger flared. No one in the world was able to hide from him, but Olófin insisted there was another in the forest. "With your permission, Father, I will punish the one who has defiled your temple."

Olófin said not a word; he merely shook his head once and narrowed his eyes, as if giving permission.

Staring up at the heavens, Ochosi loaded his bow with an arrow, and pulled its cord taut. Mustering all his ashé behind his words, he incanted, "Arrow of justice, strike him who has defiled this sacred place. Pierce his heart and take his life!"

Like a silver flash, the arrow sliced into the heavens; and so quickly did it move, forced onward by Ochosi's wrath, that neither he nor Olófin could trace its arc. It simply disappeared into the distance.

Then they heard the scream.

It was a frustrated, pained cry that was part defiance and part disbelief; it echoed through the forest as the arrow struck its mark. It ended as suddenly as it came. Ochosi ran toward it, tracking it from its sound. He stopped running when he saw the limp body with the arrow deep in its back, and his jaw dropped when he realized: "It's a woman." Slowly, he walked to it, and froze. "It can't be." He fell to his knees. "It can't be!" Gently, he turned the body over, and cried when he saw his wife's face, eyes wide in terror, and mouth frozen in a painful grimace. In his anger and vengeance, he had killed his own wife.

3

Ogundá

Three Mouths on the Mat

There is no day so distant, nor so far away,
that it never comes.

Everyone loves to watch drama unfold in others' lives; everyone fears drama unfolding in their own lives. Perhaps it is for this reason that we love and fear the odu Ogundá. As an aborisha, I loved listening to my godfather speak of this odu and the patakís found in its corpus; yet as both a santero and a diviner, when this letter opens for a client during divination, I get a cold tingle running down my spine. That tingle is excitement, because I have the chance to speak on some of our most dramatic patakís, and it is fear, because I know the client might suffer, and suffer greatly, before the energy of this sign passes.

"Fatal eventuality" is a phrase by which I describe Ogundá. Bad things happen to good people, and often without reason. Fortunately, the patakís of this odu give clues as to what is coming and how it comes; and it assures us that with timely ebó, we can always lessen, and sometimes avoid, the random destruction of our world. "How the Crocodile Became Powerful" is such a story. For once the crocodile was a weak creature, tormented and tortured for no reason other than his delicate nature, but through the energy of Ogundá and the power of ebó, he became the most powerful creature in the river. More importantly, the prey became predator, and everyone who ever treated him poorly suffered—death being their punishment. "King Olushola Makes Ebó" is another story of fatal eventuality; and again, with divination and ebó, his enemies destroy themselves, and in the midst of unavoidable tragedy, Olushola evolves safely.

Just as bad things happen to good people, so do bad things happen to bad people, and with even more fatal consequences. "Why the Rooster Was First Sacrificed" is an example of this. It is no secret that the Lucumí faith practices animal sacrifice, nor is it a secret that humans eat meat to survive. This story is one of many found throughout the corpus of the diloggún that describes not only why animals are sacrificed and eaten, but also how they came to be victims of slaughter to satisfy both mortal and immortal appetites. The rooster was a naive creature who overestimated his importance to the world; and when that naïveté granted him true status in the world, the power went to his head, and he betrayed the very orisha that gave him purpose. In the corpus of Ogundá, betrayal is always met with a bad ending—and the story speaks well of this theme.

There are hundreds of patakís in Ogundá repeating these themes, and throughout the composite odu (a pairing that combines a parent odu with a second odu), there are dozens more. I chose these three for the simple reason that they are my favorites. With the amount of drama and suspense they hold, I am sure they will become your favorites as well. More importantly, they reinforce a central theme of this sign: there is no day so distant, nor so far away, that it never comes. That day is the price we pay for our moral and ethical transgressions.

Why the Rooster Was First Sacrificed

It was early morning, but still night, and the rooster stood on the forest floor, calling his friends to witness his power. "It is time," he called out into the darkness, and one by one, the birds awakened and fluttered down to the forest floor. It was dangerous to be on the ground;

predators hid in bushes and waited to ambush the unwary. Yet the mystery of the rooster's supposed powers was too much a temptation, and for a time, they forgot about the dangers that might be lurking in shadows. Soft coos and crows filled the forest, and the rooster held a single wing to his beak. "Shush," he ordered, but softly. "It is time for me to call the sun!"

Gently, the rooster sang.

It was a soft clucking at first, like that of any other rooster or hen, but soon he gathered air in his lungs, and changed his song. It was unlike any sound any bird ever made; it was shrill and sharp, filled with a cacophonous, ragged vibrato that filled the forest. It hurt to listen, but listen the birds did, and they watched the eastern sky, waiting for the sun to rise.

Elegguá awoke to the sound of the rooster's crooning. It wasn't loud inside the palace walls, but so sensitive were his ears that the slightest noise disturbed his sleep. Begrudgingly, he got up from his soft bed and walked down the long, cold stone floor to Olófin's chambers. His head still swimming with sleep and dreams, he knocked lightly, and when there was no answer, he knocked louder. There was only the sound of his knuckles rapping on wood, and then silence.

"Every century, Olófin is harder to wake," he sighed.

Elegguá knocked more forcefully, and when there was still no answer, he banged with all his might. The doors opened, and Olófin stood before him, smiling and cheerful, well-rested from his night's slumber.

"As always, thank you, Elegguá," he said.

Elegguá smiled faintly, and walked back to his own room, overwhelmed by Olófin's cheerfulness. "I got out of bed for that," Elegguá said to himself. "I'm so glad tomorrow is Ogún's turn to wake him. The world would not stop if Olófin himself just slept in for one day."

Behind his doors, Olófin heard every word Elegguá said; he was old, but his ears were sharp, and he heard every sound on Earth when he wanted. He shook his own head sadly. "Oh, but it would. It would hurt the world if I slept too long." Quickly, he banished the thought and set about making the sun rise.

He was surprised when he heard the rooster crow in the distance.

While Elegguá was waking Olófin, the rooster was crowing, each stanza of his song growing in strength and volume. A small bird turned to another and said, "He is a fraud. The sun does not rise."

"It does," said the other bird. "Some days are harder than others, for the sun is a deep sleeper. That is why the rooster's voice is so important to the world. Just watch."

Hundreds of birds sighed as one when the first rays of sunlight peeked over the horizon; and their voices joined that of the rooster's joyously with the dawning of a new day. In a world so harsh and dangerous, small miracles such as these were a reason to wake up each day. When light suffused the world, they took flight, leaving the rooster alone on the forest floor. He ruffled his feathers proudly, and picked at the earth with his beak. "Of all the birds in the world," he thought, "only I can call the sun. I am an amazing creature, indeed!"

The next morning it was the same; all the birds in the forest gathered around the rooster, and the rooster, softly at first, began to call the sun with his songs. Elegguá was sleeping in his bed when he heard the rooster crow. Wearily, he sat up and looked at Ogún. He lay peacefully in his bed.

"Ogún!" Elegguá called out, "Ogún!"

He stirred. "What?"

"It is your turn to wake Olófin."

Ogún sat up; Elegguá lay back down and closed his eyes, pulling a pillow over his head to block out the rooster's call. When Ogún saw that Elegguá was sleeping, he, too, went back to sleep. "Just a bit longer," he thought to himself before giving in to dreams.

"What is wrong?" cried the birds when the sun did not rise. The rooster's voice was worn; it cracked and crumbled under the stress of strenuous singing.

"I don't know," said the rooster, fearful. The darkness was deepening; the sun did not rise. "Maybe the sun sleeps too deeply this morning. We must move closer to its home, closer to the east."

All the birds took flight, and the rooster ran as fast as he could, toward the east, screeching as loudly as he could. Thousands of wings beat at the air, and there was fear in the forest when the animals heard hundreds of birds fleeing to the east. The rooster was tired and breathless, but his voice was strong and shrill, breaking into something horrible as he ran toward the sun's home.

Olófin awoke to the sounds of their panicked, massive migration; and even though he knew it was late, he rushed outside to see what was happening. He marveled at the sight; a dark, living cloud of birds flapping through the darker skies, and the rooster, running and screeching beneath them. "Stop!" he called out and the birds landed. "What is happening?"

"The rooster failed to call up the sun this morning, and the world lives in darkness!" they cried.

Olófin smiled, and looked at the rooster. "Sing for me," he said.

Olófin stretched his arm out to the eastern sky while the rooster crowed; and slowly, the sun rose from its resting place.

"We have to speak, you and I," he told the rooster. The birds were amazed when God himself carried the bird into the palace.

It was well after noon when Elegguá pulled himself out of bed; and his heart fell when he saw Ogún sleeping still. "Ogún!" he cried out. "Ogún! Did you wake Olófin?"

"No," he said, wiping sleep from his eyes. "It is your turn."

"No, it is yours!" Elegguá screamed, running out of their room. Ogún followed behind him, and they burst through Olófin's doors. He was already awake, the rooster sitting at his feet.

For the first time in centuries, Olófin was frowning. "Now," he said to the bird, and the rooster let out a cry that shook the palace walls. "This is the creature that woke me up this morning," he said. "Sunrise was late, and all the birds of the forest were in a panic. The world does stop if I sleep in, Elegguá."

Both orishas' mouths dropped open, and Elegguá felt shame.

"From now on, it is the rooster who will serve me. It is the rooster who will wake me. For this morning, I overslept, and the world woke to darkness and fear. Of all the animals in the forest, his voice is the loudest, and he alone woke me this morning. He alone will wake me, and I will awaken the world."

"And I," thought the rooster, "will always be the most important bird in the forest."

As punishment for their failure, Elegguá and Ogún were banished from Olófin's home. They left sadly; but in their hearts, they were plotting their revenge on the rooster.

Olófin sat in his chambers with the rooster and taught him one of life's great mysteries. "It was never you who woke the sun," Olófin told him. "It was your voice who woke Elegguá and Ogún, and one of them came to awaken me. After I was awake, I called the sun up over the horizon."

The rooster thought about that for a moment. "But my voice was the one first heard. It was my voice that started the process!" he said. In his little head, he was still convinced that he alone had the power to call up the sun.

Olófin agreed. "Yes, by waking up Elegguá and Ogún, you started the process. From now on, you will live inside the palace and wake me yourself!"

The rooster's pride was intact, and he wasted no time going out into the world to announce his newfound importance to all creation.

Elegguá and Ogún were having none of the rooster's boasts; together, they went through the world and shared the truth: it was Olófin who called the sun over the horizon.

The rooster, being arrogant, corrected the two orishas everywhere he went. "It is true that Olófin calls the sun," he said, "but the sun would not rise at all if I did not wake Olófin every morning! I live in God's palace, and it is my duty to call him from his slumber every day."

"He does not live in the palace!" the two orishas announced. It was a lie, but they were angry at the rooster, and they wanted to torment him.

"Prove it," cried the birds.

So every night while Olófin slept, the rooster crept quietly through his walls, opening every door there was. Bit by bit, he learned Olófin's most intimate secrets, and to prove to the animals of the forest that he lived inside the palace walls, he divulged these secrets to them.

Elegguá and Ogún smiled. It was treason, and quickly they took word of this treason back to Olófin himself.

"This cannot be!" cried Olófin when Elegguá and Ogún told him the news. "He is a trusted servant and would not betray me. The two of you are jealous."

"No, father," said Ogún.

"Yes, father," said Elegguá, not wanting to lie. "We are jealous. But what we tell you is true. Your ears hear every word said on Earth. Use them now to listen to how the rooster speaks of you."

Olófin frowned, but in his heart he was afraid that the orisha was being truthful. He held his right hand up to silence them, and closed his eyes; with his ears, he sought out the rooster's voice on Earth. "It is true!" he heard the rooster telling the animals, "I myself have seen the secrets that Olófin keeps hidden in the most guarded places of the palace!" And Olófin listened while the rooster told the animals just what those secrets were.

"Bring him to me now," Olófin said with the hurt of betrayal in his voice.

It was early evening when Elegguá and Ogún returned with the rooster; Elegguá held him tightly, and Ogún eyed him hungrily.

Olófin's back was turned to all three when he spoke. "I am very sad, rooster," he said. "I trusted you. I brought you into the palace and made you my servant. Your only job was to wake me up every morning, and you had a simple, pampered life."

Elegguá let the rooster go; he ruffled and straightened his feathers. "And I serve you loyally and willingly," said the rooster. "I wake you up every morning so you can call the sun up over the horizon. Without me, the world would live in darkness."

"No!" Olófin turned to face the rooster. "Without me, the world would live in darkness. Anyone can wake me. Elegguá and Ogún did it for centuries. But only I can call up the sun. No one else, not even you, has such power."

The rooster's heart sank. "Then I will learn my place from this, and serve you loyally all my days."

"No, you won't," said Olófin. "For you abused my trust. While I slept, you went through my most private rooms and learned my secrets. That in itself was treasonous enough. But then, you took those secrets out into the world, sharing them with all the animals of the forest. Thankfully, Elegguá and Ogún discovered your treason before you could do too much damage."

"And what is the punishment for treason, father?" asked Elegguá.

"It is death." Olófin crossed his arms on his chest.

The rooster tried to escape, but Ogún caught him before he could make it to the door. With a quick flick of his wrist, he twisted off the rooster's head and took the first taste of his blood, and together, he and Elegguá feasted on the rest.

Thus was the rooster first sacrificed, and since that day, it has always been Ogún who takes the first taste of blood, and Elegguá who feasts next. To pay for their ancestor's treasonous ways, he and all his kind soon became the favored sacrifice of all the orishas in Heaven and on Earth as Ogún, and Elegguá, shared their blood with them all.

How the Crocodile Became Powerful

The crocodile was the largest, most graceful creature in the river; his body was a deep, rich, earthy brown covered in soft skin, and he swam smoothly through the deepest water. Yet his beauty brought envy, and all the fish and frogs sharing the river with him were jealous. Every day, they ganged up on him as he ate from the reeds and grasses that grew on the riverbanks, and soon the crocodile feared everything around him.

"Why do you put up with it?" asked Elegguá when he found the crocodile cowering in tall reeds, hiding from the other fish in the river. "You are so big! Why do you let them scare you?"

Quietly, so no one else could hear, he whispered, "Because the frogs make terrible noises; I can never sleep because they wake me. And the fish have teeth, and they bite me when my back is turned. I can't take it anymore!"

"You need to make ebó!" the orisha told the crocodile. "Bring me twenty-one coconuts and twenty-one iron spikes. You'll never be afraid again!"

The crocodile had never heard of ebó before, but for some reason, he trusted the orisha. At night when the other river creatures were sleeping, he slid from his hiding place and gathered the things for which Elegguá asked. By morning, the orisha had his coconuts and nails.

"Open your mouth!" Elegguá said, and one by one, he slipped the iron spikes in the crocodile's gums, giving him sharp teeth. "Turn around," he ordered, and while the crocodile's back was turned, Elegguá split the coconuts and put the shards down his spine and on his sides. They formed a rock-hard armor that nothing could break. "Now you have no reason to be afraid of anything!"

Cautiously, the crocodile slid through the water; and as he swam, the fish bit at him. They broke their teeth on his rough skin. Still, the bites hurt, and the crocodile opened his great mouth and bit down, slicing their bodies in half.

They tasted good, much better than the grasses and reeds he lived on.

Since that day, the crocodile has been the most powerful animal in the river, with skin so hard no one can hurt him, and teeth so sharp he can eat everything.

He was king of the river, and never felt fear again.

King Olushola Makes Ebó

It was midnight, and the moon's darkened crescent barely lit the courtyard. King Olushola slept soundly, but his two brothers, Adejola and

Abiodun, were wide awake. With a small, lit candle to find their way through the palace, they snuck outside into the courtyard, and when they were sure they were alone, they began to speak in hushed whispers.

"Soon," said Adejola, the oldest of the two, "our brother Olushola will make his biannual trip to see the diviner Mofá."

"And when he does," said Abiodun, "he will leave you in charge, as always."

"Only this time, things will be different." Adejola cracked an evil grin; the night's shadows stretched it and made it look sinister. "When he leaves me in charge, I'm not planning on giving the throne back. I've hired an assassin. He will wait outside Mofá's house, and when Olushola leaves, he will kill our older brother."

"And then the throne is ours for good!" Abiodun's words were a bit too enthusiastic. He covered his mouth with one hand and ducked down, as if that would muffle the sound.

"Not so loud." Adejola put a finger to his lips and blew out the candle. For quite some time the two younger brothers crouched, hiding in the darkness. When they were convinced no one heard Abiodun's outburst, he continued. "The throne will be mine for good. You will sit at my side as my advisor."

"Why do you get to be king?" Abiodun hissed. "What if I want to be the king?"

"Abiodun was always the brat," Adejola thought to himself. "When a king dies without an heir, the throne always falls to the next oldest brother. Olushola has no wife. He has no heir. When he dies, by natural law the throne goes to me." Abiodun glared at his older sibling. "Don't worry, brother. I will share my wealth with you, and one day set you up as king of your own kingdom. And if anything ever happens to me, I have no sons. My wife has given me daughters—not sons. The kingdom will go to you, my favorite brother."

Abiodun thanked Adejola; still, he hated the plan. He wanted to be king. *"One day,"* Abiodun thought, *"I will kill you, and be king in your place!"*

ᛩᛪ

The next morning, Olushola was packed and ready for his journey: he had his horse, his sword, and a handful of his most trusted armed guards to see him through the countryside. Adejola and Abiodun were at his side; Adejola's wife, heavy with child and about to give birth, stood at the doorway to the palace. She was too tired to see her brother-in-law off on his travels.

As he packed a few last minute supplies into his saddlebags, he told his brothers, "It is a week's journey to Mofá's house, and a week's journey back. I will stay there at least six days to rest and speak with the king about some personal business. That means I'm leaving you in charge for almost three weeks' time, Adejola."

"As always, brother, I will care for your kingdom as if it were my own."

"It is yours, Adejola," said Olushola with a smile. "I'm not young. I have no wife, and no sons of my own. You are still young. One day I will die, and the kingdom will be yours." The two men embraced.

Olushola turned to his youngest brother and held his hand warmly. "And you, Abiodun, I need you to help your brother. You were always the brightest. If anything important happens while I am gone, I want you to advise him on what to do."

"As you wish, my king," said Abiodun. As always, there was envy in his voice, but Olushola did not notice.

"And take care of that wife," he said to Adejola. "After five daughters, she looks ready to drop another girl any time now!"

"I am blessed, brother!" Adejola said. *Yes, blessed,"* he thought. *"Still, it would be nice to have a son."* He smiled at the king.

Olushola mounted his horse and called to his guards. They left, and his two younger brothers watched and waved until they were out of sight.

Abiodun turned to his older brother. "As king, what is your first order of business?" he asked with an excited grin. Adejola put an arm on his back, and they walked back to the palace.

"It is good to be a king, even if it is only temporary!" Adejola said as he kissed his wife on the cheek.

"Your brother is old," his wife said. "There is hope for you yet!" She smiled an innocent smile. "But I am happy living as wife to the king's brother. I am happy just being with you, my love."

"If nothing else, I have a devoted wife," Adejola thought. He smiled, and it was sincere.

His smile turned to a frown as she grabbed her belly and gasped, doubling slightly as if in pain. Wetness soaked her shoes. "The baby! She's ready!" she said as if amazed.

Adejola lifted her in his arms, "We're having another daughter!"

Abiodun, worried, called for the midwife.

Her sixth labor went quickly; and before the sun set, Adejola was holding his first son. "The heir to my throne!" he said proudly to his wife.

Abiodun was with them. "You aren't king yet," he sneered.

"Yes, husband," his wife said, her exhaustion apparent in her weak voice. "You aren't king yet. Isn't naming your son as heir a bit premature?"

"Can't a father be proud?" Adejola smiled a huge, warm grin at his newborn son.

"This isn't good," thought Abiodun. *"As long as that son lives, I will never get to be king."* Gently, he nudged the midwife. "You know what to do," he whispered to her.

She nodded knowingly.

That night, while everyone in the palace slept, the midwife hovered over the baby's crib. The room was dark save for a sliver of light that came from the waning moon, but it was enough for her to see the newborn's face. He slept peacefully on his back. "I will be rewarded handsomely for this," she whispered. Carefully, she turned the baby on his stomach, wadding up the blanket under his helpless face. He coughed and tried to breathe, but the blanket was too thick; he tried to cry, but those cries were muffled.

"What are you doing?" Unknown to the midwife, the baby's mother was sleeping in a chair at the far end of the room; darkness hid her from the evil woman's eyes. Silently, she awakened when she heard the midwife's whisper and her infant's frail cough. She came to the crib quickly. "Oh, my god!" she said, looking from her baby to the midwife in horror. "What were you doing?" She saw madness in the woman's eyes as she scooped her child into her arms, shaking it gently so it would breathe. "Help!" she screamed as loudly as she could, backing away from the midwife, who stood frozen in shock. "Help me! Oh God, help me!" she screamed again, running to the opposite end of the room.

Doors opened and slammed throughout the palace, and armed men came running. The baby's father, Adejola, and his brother, Abiodun, were at the front. Adejola's wife ran into his arms, sobbing. The infant was breathing normally. "She tried to kill our baby."

Guards surrounded Adejola and his wife protectively. Abiodun bore down on the midwife. "Murderous woman," he roared, his heart racing in his chest. He knew she was caught, and had to move quickly to cover his own tracks. "You tried to kill my nephew!"

She was about to open her mouth, to blame him when Abiodun's fist slammed into her face. She fell to the floor, screaming, blood spraying from her mouth; by reflex, a palace guard grabbed his arm, restraining him. "It was Abiodun!" she screamed through shattered teeth and split lips as he tried to get out of the guard's grasp. He put his hand to the guard's hilt, twisting out of his grip as he slid the sword from its sheath. Everyone in the room shrank back. "Abiodun said he would kill me if I didn't kill Adejola's firstborn son!" Not another word did she say; Abiodun sliced her head in two.

He stood there, panting like an animal. His eyes reddened with anger. "*I was too slow!*" he thought, trying to think of a way to escape the blame. He raised the sword between himself and the guards, buying time while he spoke. "She was crazed, brother!" Adejola's eyes were wide with surprise and rage. "She didn't know what she was saying. I'd never kill my own nephew."

"Kill him," Adejola ordered, partly for his treason and party to shut him up before he said too much. Abiodun was skewered with six swords simultaneously.

෨෧

Six days later, Olushola sat on a mat, on a low stool facing the diviner, Mofá. The old man was disturbed. "You are in danger," he said. "Outside these doors waits treason!"

"Treason?" asked Olushola. "Are you speaking of this empire's king? I have business with him. Surely he is a fair man? He has always been a fair man!"

"No, Olushola." Mofá shook his head, narrowing his eyes. He pointed at the king for emphasis. "The treason comes from those closest to you, your own brothers."

"Nonsense!"

"I am never wrong, Olushola. But if you make ebó, Eshu will take care of the treason for you."

"Mofá, I've known you for a long time. When you were young, you were my father's diviner when he was king. But my brothers love me. Perhaps you have lost your ashé?" He looked at Mofá, but the old man's eyes were unyielding. "I'm going home. I will come back for my business with your king later. And when I see that everything is okay, I will return, and perhaps if you are well-rested and feeling better, you can divine for me again."

Olushola got up off the mat before Mofá could mark ebó and bring the session to closure; grabbing his cloak, he told his guards who were waiting just inside the front door, "We are leaving for home now."

"Let me water your horse first, sir," said one of his guards as they went outside as a group. "There is a trough only a few hundred yards away. It will take me only a moment's time." He hopped on the king's horse while the other guards hopped on their own; the king grabbed the bridle of the guard's horse and stroked its neck.

It was then that an arrow sliced through the air; it was silent and came without warning. It sliced through the guard's chest as he sat on the king's horse; he fell, dead before his body hit the earth with a muffled thump. The air in his lungs came out of him with an audible sigh; arterial blood flooded the dirt around him. There was chaos.

෨෧

Unknown to anyone, the assassin had lain in wait for hours; when the sun rose, he was hiding on the roof of a nearby house. Adejola had given him the address to Mofá's home and told him what the royal horse looked like. When he saw the guard mounting the horse, he assumed it was the king and took aim. When the guard hit the earth, and everyone ran for him, he assumed the king was dead. He ran from that place, thinking his mission was accomplished. "I will be rewarded well!" he congratulated himself.

In horror, those in the streets ran for their lives: men yelled for their weapons, women screamed, and children cried. The king knelt over his guard's lifeless body while the others tried to pry him away, into the safety of Mofá's house. The diviner was still seated. "Will you make ebó now?" he asked.

With a hollow, ashen expression on his face, Olushola agreed. He fed Eshu everything for which he asked.

It took a week's travel, but the assassin made it to the king's palace. Guards escorted him to the throne room, where Adejola sat sorrowfully. *"My own baby brother,"* he thought silently. *"My own baby brother tried to kill my helpless son."* The irony of his words was lost on him as he pondered the treason from his brother's hands. When his guards beat on the great doors, it broke him out of his self-pity, and when he saw his hired assassin, he was thrilled.

"This messenger says he has news for you," one guard said.

"It's about . . . your brother, the king," he said, feigning sorrow.

"Leave us!" Adejola ordered.

"We will wait outside, sir," the guard said.

When the doors were closed and they were assured of privacy, Adejola asked, "How is my brother, the king?"

"Quite dead, I assure you."

"How did he die?"

The assassin feigned a tear as he held his hands to his chest. "A single arrow sliced through his heart, clear out the other side. He was dead before he hit the ground." He looked at the floor for emphasis, and then asked, "Now, about my reward?"

"Yes, about that reward," said Adejola, standing and walking toward the assassin. "You must be rewarded appropriately for killing my older brother, the king." He put his left hand on the assassin's shoulder, and held him close. In his ear, he whispered, "I wouldn't want you telling anyone the story of what happened later." With his free hand, he plunged a dagger into the assassin's stomach. Then, with a flick of his wrist, he pushed him back.

His mouth gaped open and his eyes were wide in surprise as he held both hands over the spot the dagger sliced. There was blood trickling through his fingers. Adejola turned and smiled, looking down at his dagger. Only the tip was bloodied. He heard maniacal laughter behind him.

"You don't think I would come unprepared, do you?" He heard the rustling of cloth and the sound of a sword being unsheathed. In fear, he turned. The assassin was holding a wad of bloody cloth up in the air, waving it like a flag, and in his other hand, he held his sword. "I thought you'd do something wicked. So I padded myself just in case you chose to stick a dagger in me. Now, you can either pay me, or I can kill you."

Adejola let out a primal, angry scream, and rushed the assassin, his dagger held high. Rage and anguish blinded his judgment. The palace guards burst through the door when they heard Adejola's scream, and watched in horror as the assassin plunged his sword through Adejola's chest. Sixteen pairs of arms beat him; they disarmed him and took him down while he screamed, "Adejola had me kill the king! He is the evildoer, not I!"

Adejola heard none of this. He was dead.

Sorrow and mourning filled the kingdom; flags were at half-mast, and villagers wore rags as if mourning the death of a great dignitary. "What has happened here?" Olushola asked his guards as they rode to his palace. None of them knew.

Palace guards met Olushola with great surprise at the gates, and they rejoiced, lifting him off his horse and into their arms. They carried him on their shoulders to the palace, where Adejola's wife was dressed for mourning. A funeral was underway for three men: Abiodun, Adejola, and Olushola; only Olushola's coffin was empty and closed. "You are alive?" Adejola's widow asked, reaching out to touch his face as if he were a ghost. "The assassin said he killed you with an arrow through the heart."

Olushola's eyes were teary at the thought of his slain guard. "The assassin killed the wrong man," he said, sadly.

Adejola's five daughters surrounded their uncle, and the oldest held a baby in her arms. Olushola reached out to touch it. "It's my baby brother, your new nephew. It's a boy," she said, sorrow straining her voice.

"We celebrate one less death today!" announced Olushola to the assembly. "For as you see, I am alive! I made ebó, and I lived through the treason of my brothers!" A great roar of surprise and celebration erupted in the palace courtyard, for King Olushola was alive, and home.

The king questioned the assassin, he questioned the palace guards, and he questioned Adejola's widow. Slowly, the story of treason unraveled. He knew his brothers hired the assassin to kill him. He assumed that Abiodun, worried he would never have the throne, had the midwife attempt to murder the newborn son. And he knew that in anger, and partially to cover his own tracks, Adejola had his younger brother murdered where he stood. The assassin admitted to killing Adejola because he tried to kill him first, and he was put to death himself for his crimes.

In time, Olushola married his younger brother's wife and adopted her children as his own, for they were innocent of any crime, and when Olushola passed away in his old age, peacefully, Adejola's son inherited the kingdom.

His name was Obafemi, which means "the king loves me," for truly Olushola loved the boy as if he were his own. History remembered him as the wisest, most loving king the kingdom ever knew.

Such is the far-reaching power of ebó.

4

Irosun

Four Mouths on the Mat

Nobody knows what lies at the bottom of the sea; but
Olorún and Olokun—they are the ones who know.

Irosun is a mysterious sign: It speaks of the visible, the seen, cautioning the client to open his eyes to what is happening in the environment, yet it also alludes to the invisible realm, those things known only by the soul. Its advice is always simple: "Take care of what lies before you, and let the orishas take care of that within." Born from the pattern known as Owani (eleven mouths), Irosun is younger than Unle, king of all the odu. This letter, however, receives respect equal to its monarch. Symbolically, it alludes to the eyes; it is found in all the body's pairs, those appendages or organs working as twins. While all letters of the diloggún bring enlightenment and evolution, Irosun's nature is to hide more than it reveals, to bring more questions than answers. It is a paradox unto itself, and no one can fully understand its implications. We say that only Olorún and Olokun know what Irosun holds. Nevertheless, a competent diviner can turn Irosun's unknowns into self-discovery and growth if he has studied the letter.

A generalization holding true for most clients opening in Irosun is this: they come with smiles, pleasant faces, and relaxed demeanors; yet the big smiles and bright, hopeful eyes are a mask of this person's hopes, not an accurate reflection of what lies within. Under this mask is darkness; bright eyes hold tears, and smiles hide depression. For some, the surface is no more than a conditioned response to the turmoil seething within. Alone, this person cries. All around are false friends, enemies, gossip, bad tongues, evil thoughts, and treason. Deception hides, waiting for its chance to attack. Irosun himself was such a creature; he was both lonely and surrounded by false friends. Deception filled his life. With Elegguá's intervention, however, he was able to not only find love, but also discover who his true friends were. Two stories chosen for this chapter illustrate this theme well: "How a Man and a Woman Found Love" and "Irosun Discovers His True Friends" show what the odu had to go through to find and fulfill his needs in life. In the body of this chapter, I presented two more stories displaying the inherent osogbo of the sign, the treason and betrayal to which Irosun alludes: "The Story of the Cat and the Leopard" and "The Tail (Tale) of the Little Monkey." Remember—in this odu false friends abound, and friendships are forged for no reason other than someone wants something another person has. Irosun's advice? Never, ever teach all one knows; and never trust anyone implicitly.

Finally, no presentation on Irosun is complete without a discussion of Orishaokó (the orisha who controls the fecundity of the earth) and his place in the corpus of Irosun. For this family of odu gives birth to something very special: funeral rites, and the rite of Itutú (the burial of a priest in our faith). "The Pact between Orishaokó and Olófin" speaks for itself, and speaks well.

In spite of the mysterious, often conflicting themes found in the odu Irosun, a competent diviner can turn all these unknowns into a competent reading if he studies the letter well. It is a powerful sign promising unprecedented growth and evolution if the client listens and applies the morals of the patakís to his life carefully. When this sign came once for me in a reading, my godfather told me, "Open your eyes, and open them wide, for there is much to see. And you, my son, live with blinders on."

"And what if I miss something important?" I asked him.

"Then you will find yourself like the fish in the marketplace—eyes opened, but unable to see."

Such is the depth of danger and intrigue found in this family of signs.

How a Man and a Woman Found Love

It was late evening and the house was dark, but no one slept. The young woman lay in her bed, crying softly into her white sheets as she strained to listen to her parents' conversation in the next room. They thought their daughter was sleeping and felt safe speaking in hushed tones.

"I'm just worried about her," she heard her father say. His voice softened, and the walls muffled his words, but then she heard, "A woman her age should be married by now!"

"I know. I know," her mother agreed. She could almost see her putting both hands on the crown of her head, throwing them up to emphasize her words. That was something her mother always did. "But have you found a suitable husband for her yet? No. All the available men are already wed."

"She's too old as it is. We will never find a man to take her," her father lamented. The rest of their conversation was blotted out as she buried her head in her pillows, crying herself to sleep.

Early the next morning, Irosun sat on the mat facing Elegguá, and the orisha manipulated the cowries on the mat. He smiled at his old friend, Irosun, who fidgeted on the low stool. Elegguá stopped; the cowries were a formality. He always knew the reason his clients came to see him. Irosun smiled back, but the smile was insecure.

"Irosun," Elegguá said, rolling the cowries from his open palm and counting the mouths facing upwards, "I already know why you've come to see me. You're lonely. And you're not getting any younger."

He sighed and attempted another smile, but it was only a sad frown that stretched across his dark face. "I am very lonely," the odu said. "No matter how hard I try, I can't find a wife."

Eleggúa put two ibó in his hands, and cast the shells again to mark ebó. He did this several times in succession. "Oshún will help you," he promised. "But only if you make ebó."

"Anything!" he said, grateful for the help.

"Offer Oshún honey in the river. Take your ebó to the most secluded spot you can find. After you sweeten her, bathe with honey soap, and let her waters bless you. She will set you on a course to find love. Just have faith."

Irosun thanked the orisha and left quickly for the market. As he was leaving, a young woman brushed past him. Their shoulders touched lightly; embarrassed, Irosun said, "I'm sorry. Excuse me for being so clumsy."

She smiled shyly, nodding her head. Eleggúa watched, amused.

He knew she was as lonely as Irosun.

At the river, Irosun walked downstream until he found a lonely, secluded spot to make ebó and bathe. On his knees, he prayed to Oshún as he poured the sweet syrup into the river, touching it with his index finger and tasting it. The honey rippled the river's smooth surface and floated a bit before folding into the water. When the last of it was gone, Irosun stood, stripped, and walked in. Leisurely, he did as Eleggúa said, and bathed.

While he bathed, the river's current strengthened. It was gentle at first, but soon the water pushed at him forcefully, and he was afraid. "Time to get out of the river," he thought to himself.

Irosun took but a single step; his foot slipped on a smooth stone. He yelled as he fell back, but the scream was cut short as the current pulled him under. A forceful kick against the riverbed propelled him back to the surface, but the current carried him farther downstream, where the water was deeper, and no longer could he touch the bottom. No matter how forcefully he swam, Irosun was trapped in the current.

The young woman sat on the riverbank, her legs folded beneath her as she poured honey into the river. It was what Eleggúa told her to do as ebó. When the last of it was gone, she watched the water ripple, breaking her own sad reflection on the surface. She saw her eyes reddened from tears, her cheeks stained with traces of salt; and she sobbed. "Oshún!" she cried, waiting for the echo to fade, "Why am I so alone?"

As if to answer her, she heard a loud splash, and a shout for help as Irosun came flailing down the river. With a gasp, she recognized him as the man she had bumped into at Elegguá's house.

She ran to him, not caring that her skirts were wet, and he swam to her, not caring that he was naked; and when they met in the river, by impulse they embraced, and kissed.

They were wed the next day; such is the power of ebó.

Irosun Discovers His True Friends

The afternoon sun hung high in the sky, filling the world with a heat that was almost stifling. But Irosun and his friend Elegguá felt cool; they lounged beneath a huge tree with thick leaves and branches blocking the sun's rays, and all they felt was a cool eastern breeze that evaporated the sweat from their shiny black skins. There, in the shade of the tree, they chatted.

"I am such a blessed man, Elegguá," bragged Irosun. He smiled at the orisha, who lay back against the trunk with his straw hat pulled over his eyes. Elegguá's chest rose and fell lazily; he wasn't sure if the orisha was awake or napping, but still, he talked. "For not only are you my best friend, but also I have so many good friends. If friends are wealth, then I am a rich man!"

Elegguá lifted his hand and pulled off his straw hat; with the back of his wrist, he wiped beads of sweat off his brow before putting his hat back on his head. "Irosun," Elegguá said, "I am probably your only friend, and your best one at that."

"No," Irosun argued. "Well, yes, you are my best friend. But I have so many other friends it's amazing. All the odu are my friends, and all my neighbors adore me, especially when I divine for them. I am surrounded by friends."

"No, you're not." Elegguá sat up and looked Irosun in the eyes. "You think all those people are your friends, but they aren't. They only use you for your ashé, and what you have to give. If you were a common man with no skills or talents, none of them would give you the time of day."

His words stung Irosun like a wasp; his mouth fell open, and he stood. "How can you say such a thing to me? You're jealous. Say it isn't true. You're jealous because you are not my only friend!"

Elegguá stood to match Irosun's incredulous stare. "I'm sorry if I've hurt your feelings, Irosun, but you know nothing escapes me. The other odu are only friendly to your face; they laugh behind your back. And humans only come to see you when they need something from you. You have no true friends . . . except me. I like you . . . because . . . I like you."

"Since you know so much, prove it. Prove I have no true friends except you."

Elegguá smiled. He thought, "This won't be hard." Instead, he said, "Irosun, no one knows what lies at the heart of a man, but there are ways to make them show their true faces. I can prove to you who your friends are, and who they aren't. I want you to give a party."

Irosun smiled. "A party for all my friends—that will be nice, indeed."

"Yes, but with a twist." Quietly, so not even the tree could hear his words, Elegguá whispered his plans into Irosun's ears. It was devious, but Irosun agreed. After all, he wanted to show Elegguá that he was wrong.

While Irosun sent his servants out and about to make preparations for the party, Elegguá went to each odu and all the humans and announced, "Irosun is having a dinner party, and everyone is invited. There will be food, and music, and dancing all night!" Everyone was amazed; Irosun had never thrown a party before, but Irosun was a generous man, and everyone knew that the dinner would be amazing.

The day of the party came, and people arrived in droves. One by one they crowded into Irosun's house until it was filled, and still, there were more outside waiting to come in. There was music. There was dancing. There were servants carrying trays of finger foods.

But there was not enough for everyone who came.

The guests began to grumble. "Where is the food?" they asked. "Where is the drink?" they cried. "We are hungry. When is dinner?"

"Dinner?" Irosun asked, nervously. He looked to Elegguá, who was standing by his side. "This wasn't meant to be a dinner party. It was meant to be . . . a gathering of friends!"

Grumbles and sighs came up among the assemblage, and angrily, each began to denounce Irosun and their foolishness at coming to his party. Irosun's mouth hung open in shame, and Elegguá consoled him, putting his hand on his shoulder and giving a friendly squeeze. "If these were your friends," Elegguá said, "they would not be so quick to denounce you, and even quicker to leave."

"No," Irosun agreed, "they wouldn't."

"Do you see now that among all your acquaintances and clients, you have only one true friend, and that friend is me?"

Irosun hugged Elegguá tightly. "Yes," he said. "And I'm sorry I ever doubted your wisdom.

Since that day Irosun and Elegguá have been the best of friends, and when others came seeking favors from the odu, he treated them as clients, and no more.

The Story of the Cat and the Leopard

It was dark in the house except for the low-burning candles, and Irosun's two children played quietly on the leopard skin rug. From his chair, Irosun watched them wearily. When he decided they had stayed up late enough, he called to them, "It's time for bed!"

"No!" they wailed in unison.

"Yes," said Irosun, too tired to get up out of his chair. "It's late, too late for little children to be up playing."

As if in agreement the housecat, who had been sleeping on a side table, jumped down onto the leopard-skin rug. She mewed insistently at the children, and began kneading with her claws. She growled softly.

"She loves this rug, daddy!" said the youngest girl, picking the cat up even though it protested with a hiss. Rubbing behind its ears, she turned its protest into purrs of satisfaction.

"To her, it's a trophy," said the father, standing up and taking the cat out of his daughter's hands. He dropped it to the floor, shooing it away. "Now, off to bed."

"A trophy?" she asked. "What's that?"

"A trophy is something you keep, like a souvenir, but it's a reminder of a contest you won."

"The cat won a contest?" asked his older son. "What kind of contest?"

Irosun sat on the rug next to his children. "Perhaps *contest* isn't the best word to use, but to the cat, this leopard skin rug has a history." Irosun looked at his two children, and they looked back at him. There was silence for a moment. "Do you want to know the story behind this rug?"

Two little heads bobbed up and down in agreement. They smiled. Irosun told his story.

Once, there was a leopard that was pathetic among his own kind; he wasn't strong, nor was he fierce. All leopards live by hunting, and no matter how hard this animal tried, everything he hunted escaped his claws. He lived by eating scraps in the forest, food abandoned by other animals. From time to time, he wandered into the city to scour peoples' garbage for food.

He was a very unhappy creature.

One night the leopard was scrounging through our trash cans, just outside this house; and he saw our cat running wildly through the streets. So fast was our cat running that he didn't see the leopard standing in the middle of our trash, and the leopard watched him scale a tree and jump, almost soaring, through an open window.

He was in awe of the tiny animal's strength and agility. "That is such a small creature, a helpless animal, but it seems so self-assured and powerful," thought the leopard. "His legs are smaller than my own, and his claws are tiny, but he runs so fast, and climbs so swiftly. How is he able to do that?" Finally, he decided to make friends with the cat. "I can learn all he knows . . . and then . . . I can eat him!"

"That's terrible!" the small girl wailed, holding the palms of her hands over her mouth in suspenseful fear.

"Don't be a baby," taunted the oldest boy. "You act like a girl."

"I am a girl! I'm not acting."

"Settle down, you two," warned Irosun, "or I won't finish my story."

They hushed quickly, and Irosun continued.

The next night, the leopard hid outside the house, and watched the window the cat jumped into the night before. It was late when it came out; he stood on the ledge, arching his back and flicking his tail as he sniffed the night air, and then, with a graceful jump, he landed on a thick branch, scaling down the tree headfirst.

It was but a simple hop, skip, and jump for the cat. Still, the leopard was amazed. He came out of hiding, and the cat froze in its tracks.

"Don't fear me," said the leopard. "For you and I are as family."

"What do you want?" Every muscle in the cat's body was tense, and its eyes scanned a route for escape. Cats knew well the treason that lived in the heart of a leopard, and our cat did not trust the beast.

"I don't want to hurt you, so you can relax. I want to learn from you."

The cat relaxed a bit. "Learn? You want to learn from me? What could you want to learn from me?"

"You are agile. You are graceful. You scale trees as if they were ladders. I can't run. I can't jump. I can't climb. Teach me how to do these things, and I will be your best student and closest friend."

The cat was no fool. "I know you and I know your kind, leopard," said the cat. "As soon as you know as much as I, you would use that knowledge to catch me. You will eat me as soon as you are able."

"I would never eat a friend!" the leopard promised. "Leopards are many things, but we are all loyal. You and I are kindred spirits. I would learn from you, and use what I learned to protect you, not to hurt you." The great animal put his head to the ground humbly. "I will honor you always as my teacher."

The cat didn't believe a word the leopard said, but if cats are one thing, it's arrogant. Having such a large and powerful beast putting his head on the ground inflated the cat's ego. Against his better judgment, he agreed. "I will teach you all I know," said the cat. And to himself, he thought, "Well . . . maybe not everything. I have to keep some secrets."

Irosun stopped his story for a moment, looking at his children. The cat sat by his feet, looking at him, purring as if in agreement with every word he said. "Wow," said the son. "Our cat was the leopard's teacher."

"Yes, he was," said Irosun.

"He must have been very smart," said the youngest girl.

"Or very stupid," said the son.

"He was neither smart nor stupid. What he was . . . well . . . he was arrogant," said the father. "That's just how cats are."

The two new friends began their lessons the next night. They met outside the cat's house, this very house. The lessons were simple to teach, but hard to master. The leopard's body was large and clumsy while the cat's was small and supple, but in a matter of days, the leopard learned how to arch his back so his jumps were strong and forceful. He learned how to extend his claws, turning them into powerful weapons. And he learned how to crouch and crawl beneath the thickest bushes so he could hide from his prey.

After a month of lessons, the cat finally announced, "My friend, you know everything I have to teach you, and you have been a wonderful student!"

"I know everything?" asked the leopard. "You have nothing left to teach me?"

"No, my friend, I have nothing left to teach you. You have been the

most wonderful student." He paused for a moment. "Well, you have been my only student, but you were wonderful and learned quickly."

This was good news to the leopard—his teacher had no more to teach him. "And if there is nothing left for him to teach me," thought the leopard to himself, "then it is time for him to feed me!" His mouth twitched, and his stomach rumbled with hunger.

Suddenly, the cat was afraid. "Did you not eat tonight?" he asked, shaking. Instinct told him he was in trouble.

"No, I did not. And that squirrel in the tree looks very tasty. It is making my mouth twitch and my stomach rumble." Of course, the leopard was lying; it was really the cat that made his mouth water, but he wanted the cat distracted so he could pounce on him quickly.

"What squirrel?" asked the cat, pretending to look up into the tree. But truly, his eyes were on the leopard.

Thinking the cat unaware, the leopard extended his claws and opened his mouth as he pounced; and the cat, which was prepared for the attack, leapt into the tree and scaled it to its highest point. The leopard's teeth closed on wood, and he roared as splinters sliced into his mouth and tongue.

"Help!" screamed the cat, but to the world it sounded like a hateful screech.

The leopard let out a bone-chilling roar. "You tricked me," he screamed.

Fear left the cat; quickly, it was replaced by anger. "I tricked you? Of course, I tricked you. I taught you everything I knew except how to climb trees, you fool. And thank Olófin I saved that for myself, or else you would be chewing on my meat instead of this tree!"

The little girl clapped her hands, and hugged her brother joyfully. "Our cat is smart!" she said. "He tricked the leopard and saved his own life!"

The boy scratched his head. "That doesn't explain this," he said, looking down at the rug. "How could our small cat kill such a large animal and make a rug from it?"

"There is just a bit more to the story, children."

The leopard made such fierce roars, and the cat such bloodcurdling screams, that I grabbed my machete and ran out into the darkness.

Surprise was in the faces of both children.

Yes, that's right. I went after the leopard! The moon was full, and there was more than enough light to see the evil leopard clawing at the tree, trying to get to my pet in the branches above. So intent was he on killing my cat that I was able to sneak up behind him, undetected, and when I was close enough . . . well . . . that's not for small children to know. But that is how we now have a leopard skin rug.

"There is a moral to this story, children. Never tell your secrets to anyone, and never teach another all that you know. For no matter how much good you do for others, in the end, most pay you back with evil. Now, off to bed, and goodnight."

The Pact between Orishaokó and Olófin

Orishaokó was the first of Olófin's children to discover his innate ashé; he was a skilled farmer, able to turn rocky, untamed land into fertile fields. With his ox and plow and his farming tools in hand, he redesigned the earth's landscape a little bit at a time until it yielded bountiful crops. Orishaokó had an abundance of food.

While Orishaokó labored, the other orishas rested; the earth was pristine and full of mystery, and lazily, they explored the world wantonly. It seemed that was their only purpose in life, while Orishaokó worked feverishly. Olófin fed all the lazy orishas; every day, he produced huge, lavish feasts to nourish his children. Finally, weary of the burden, Olófin came to Orishaokó to ask his help.

"Orishaokó," he said, "I am old and tired. Since we all came to the earth, feeding the orishas has been my job. I have harvested the fruits that grow in orchards and the berries that grow wild in the forest. I have gathered herbs and slaughtered animals, and no one helps me. You, son, have a natural ashé for making the earth bountiful, and in a single season, you grow more food than I can provide in a year. Please, feed the orishas so I can rest."

"There is a time to plant, and a time to harvest," Orishaokó said. "There is a time to give, and a time to receive. There is a time to work, and a time to rest. There is time in this world for everything that needs to be done, and there is time to do everything. My brothers and sisters are lazy. They do nothing. Why should I feed them?"

"You are a prodigy among them all, Orishaokó. You found your ashé quickly. They have no idea what their powers or purposes are yet. In time, your efforts will be rewarded."

Orishaokó took a deep, indignant breath, and held it for a moment. Then he blurted out, "It's not fair!" He stammered like an angry, spoiled child. "Every day since the world began, I have labored and I have toiled like a slave making this world beautiful. They enjoy its beauty, and I get nothing back. I have plowed the fields until the soil was mud from my own sweat! And they, in their laziness, sit back and do nothing. And now I am to feed them, when they can't give me anything in return?"

Olófin smiled one of his deep-knowing smiles, and reached out to the stammering orisha. "Give me your hand," he ordered, but gently. Orishaokó reached out his right hand. "You have many fingers on this one hand. But none are the same as the others. The thumb is not like the index finger, and the index finger is not like the pinkie. But each digit has ashé; and if all five work together, the hand can do incredible things!"

Orishaokó stared at his hand while Olófin continued, "Each finger has ashé, a talent; and all that ashé must come together if great things are to be done. Each of my children is like a single finger. And all the fingers are children of the same hand; none can separate if great things are to be done."

Orishaokó pulled back his hand and challenged Olófin, "But these are my fingers doing the work! The earth has taught me that nothing comes for free. Everything has its price. My sacrifice in this world is my labor. What will their sacrifice to me be?"

"Orishaokó, I have made up my mind. While everyone is alive and has a body, you will feed them and nourish them. You will do this for no reason other than I tell you to do it. But know this: At the end of life, when the dead are put to rest, you, who are the life of the earth, will feed on them. Just as all is nourished by you in life, you will be nourished by their death, and the earth, from which their sustenance and your ashé come, will be reinvigorated when it feeds on their flesh."

Thus was the pact between Orishaokó and Olófin born: He feeds all beings in life, and they feed him through death. When at last the body is laid to rest in the earth, he rises up and consumes it.

The Tail (Tale) of the Little Monkey

The little monkey was a foolish creature, but he was not stupid; and he knew that if he were to prosper on the earth, he had to see the diviners and make ebó. Sitting at the mat, he watched as the elder, wizened priest cast his cowries again and again, and he was excited when he said finally, "Maferefún Elegguá!"* If you hope to prosper on the earth, and tell your tale to your great-grandchildren, you must make ebó to that orisha."

"And what might that ebó be, wise man?" asked the monkey.

The diviner detailed the ebó to the monkey carefully, and the monkey, having faith, made his ebó quickly. Before he left, the diviner told him, "You must remember that in life, a good thing is often paid for with a bad." The monkey scratched his head; he did not understand the proverb. Undaunted, he then set out to find his luck and fortune in the world.

As he traveled, he was lucky enough to find a banana tree filled with a rack of ripe fruit. He was hungry and pulled the fruit down so he could eat. Another group of monkeys came along, and when they saw the monkey eating by himself, they asked, "We are starving, and you

---

Maferefún Elegguá is a Lucumí phrase meaning "Praise be to Elegguá."

have the last bunch of bananas from this tree. Will you share with us?"

The monkey agreed, and he offered them some fruit. Quickly, all the monkeys grabbed what they could, and they fled high into the trees, laughing.

"You took all my bananas!" the little monkey screamed after them.

"That's life," they laughed. "One good thing is paid for with a bad thing." They swung out of sight before the little monkey could answer. Thankfully, he had eaten enough before they stole the fruit that his hunger was abated.

The little monkey continued his travels, and he met an ox tied outside a slaughterhouse. The ox was old, and he hung his head as if he had the weight of the world on his shoulders. "Ox!" cried the monkey. "Why are you so sad? Why are you tied up outside of a slaughterhouse when you should be tied to a plow, and tilling the fields?"

"I am here because I am old," said the ox. "All my life I have served my master, and I have pulled the plow through the fields from sunup to sundown. I never missed a day's work; even if I was sick, I pulled that plow because that's what my master wanted me to do. But now I am old, and because I am too old to pull the plow, I am here to be killed."

"Killed?" screamed the monkey. "That is not fair. You worked all your life and this is your reward?"

"Remember this if you remember nothing else: A good thing is paid with a bad. That's just how life is."

"Nonsense," said the monkey. "I will save you, and you can run free!" Quickly, the little monkey used his tiny hands to undo the knots in the rope. Soon, the ox was free. "We can run into the forest and hide!" he said, jumping up and down with excitement.

He turned his back to the ox and started to run when a sharp, piercing pain burned his tail; the ox had caught it in his mouth, and flipped the monkey high over his head. He landed on the ground with a hard thump. "Why did you do that?" the monkey cried.

"Because you were standing in my way," he said, barely looking over his shoulder. As he lumbered off to the forest, he yelled out again, "A good thing is paid with a bad—that's just how life is. Remember that, if you remember nothing else."

The monkey sat there in disbelief, rubbing his throbbing tail. When the ox was out of sight, he stood up and walked into the forest himself.

A few hours later the monkey smelled blood and death in the forest, and in fear, he scaled the highest tree. He clung to its branches, shaking, while he looked at the brush below. It was then that he noticed the mutilated body of the ox, half-eaten and discarded like trash. "I gave him a good thing, his freedom," thought the monkey, "and he found a bad thing, his death." He looked a little farther ahead, and saw the bodies of the monkeys who stole his bananas; they lay broken and bloody on the forest floor. "A good think is repaid with a bad thing . . . again." For quite some time the monkey hung in the branches, pondering those words. When he was convinced the murderer was nowhere near, he jumped down from the tree and kept walking through the forest.

The monkey walked for hours when he heard a soft growl followed by a whimpering mew; he stopped and listened. The sound seemed to come from the earth itself. "Who is there?" he asked, and listened as he heard an animal crying.

"Help me," it called out weakly.

The monkey walked carefully, looking into the bushes and up at the trees. "Where are you?" he asked.

"Down here," said a weak voice. The monkey stopped and looked down. He almost fell into a huge, gaping hole, and there at the bottom was a leopard. "I fell in this trap," he said, "and I can't get out." The monkey saw that the hole was filled with sharp spikes, and by some miracle, the leopard had avoided them all in his fall.

"Don't worry, I'll save you!" promised the monkey.

There was a tree close to the hole, and its branches reached out in the air over it. The little monkey reached up and pulled on the branch, but no matter how hard he pulled, he was not able to reach the leopard with it. "I have an idea," said the giant cat. "If you hang from the end of the branch with both hands, your weight will pull it deeper into this hole; and then, if you let your tail down, I can grab it with my mouth, and you can swing me out of the hole."

The monkey saw the wisdom of the leopard's plan, and carefully, he extended his tail into the hole. The leopard grabbed onto it with his mouth, his teeth grazing the skin. "Ouch!" cried the monkey; and quickly, he swung the tiger out of the hole and onto the ground. The leopard let go, and the monkey rubbed his bleeding tail.

The smell of blood was too much for the leopard, and with a hungry growl, he lunged for the monkey, both front paws extended to grab him with his claws. But he missed, and again the leopard fell into the hole.

"You tried to kill me!" the monkey cried, swinging higher into the braches while the leopard leapt and bit at his tail. His mouth closed on air, and he fell back into the trap, slicing his skin on a spike as it narrowly missed his torso.

"No," cried the leopard. "I was not trying to kill you. I was trying to hug you out of joy for saving me. But that was foolish, and I'm trapped again. Please . . . help me out! I won't hurt you, I promise."

The foolish monkey began to scale down the tree to help the giant cat once more when Elegguá himself emerged from the forest. "Monkey?" he asked. "What are you doing?"

"I'm trying to save the leopard. I pulled him out of that hole once, but he fell in again. He's not too bright!" taunted the little monkey.

"Neither are you, little one," said Elegguá, smiling. "For haven't you learned yet that good things are often paid for with bad? You made ebó to me, and that's why you've made it this far with your foolishness, but I'm telling you, monkey, that if you pull that leopard out again, I'm going to let him eat you."

Those words frightened the monkey and convinced him that he was being foolish. He jumped down from the tree and landed at Elegguá's feet, and together, the two of them walked off in the forest. The leopard roared in anger, but he was trapped, and in time died of thirst and starvation.

What happened to the monkey after that? He learned to let people suffer their own follies, and he spent his days swinging from tree to tree, far above the cares and concerns of the world. He lived long enough to have children, grandchildren, and great-grandchildren, and he made sure to tell each generation his tale so none of them would suffer as he did.

And that is the tale (tail) of the little monkey.

Obatalá Rewards Odé

The afternoon sun sailed high in the sky, but in the forest, with the thick branches and foliage of ancient trees blocking the sun, it seemed twilight as Odé tracked his prey in silence. The damp forest floor held a leopard's footprints, and they were fresh; wetness from the earth was only beginning to seep into their borders. The air was humid and sticky, and Odé broke into a sweat; he wiped his brow with the back of his hand as he stared ahead into the woods, but his hand was as wet as his face, and he only smeared the sweat into a thin sheen on his skin. He was tense; every muscle in his body felt tight and contracted as he walked carefully, avoiding thin twigs and dry leaves whose crunching underfoot would betray him.

It was then that he saw the leopard that left the footprints in the dampness—it lay lazily in a ray of sunlight breaking through the canopy overhead. Odé crouched, and slowly, he loaded his crossbow with a single arrow whose head was thin and razor sharp. He inhaled as he pulled back on the cord and held his breath as he took aim. He didn't exhale until the arrow was slicing cleanly to its mark.

The leopard's head arched back in pain as the arrow stabbed his chest; and then, it fell in a crumpled heap. It was dead.

Odé exhaled and smiled. He never missed his mark.

The hunter spent the next hour skinning, gutting, slicing, and quartering the animal's meat. When he was done, he wrapped everything in the pelt and went to see his orisha, Obatalá. Odé gave a major portion of all his kills to that orisha, for Obatalá was an old man, too old to hunt for himself. And of all the orishas on the earth, Odé loved him the best, as if he were his own father. "Obatalá will be pleased," he thought as he walked to his house.

Together, Odé and Obatalá sat on the orisha's front porch, sipping refreshments his servants brought. Obatalá was an old man, and stooped under the world's weight, but there was something fresh about his face. True, the onyx skin was wrinkled and creased, and even his creases were wrinkled; and his hair was as white as sheep's wool. But his eyes sparkled with a youthful energy, and Odé knew it was the ashé of all creation that flowed in his veins, keeping his mind as youthful and sharp as it was in his youth, and his body as healthy as a teenager's.

"Odé," said Obatalá, smiling, "as always, you are quite generous. You bring so much fresh meat to my house. Do you ever keep any for yourself?"

"Of course, father!" he said, grinning like a small child just complimented on a job well done. "I spend all day in the forest hunting. My meat-house is stacked with fresh, salted meats. I can only eat so much myself! It makes me happy to take care of you like this."

"You are more thoughtful than my own children, Odé." A shadow crept over Obatalá's face for a moment; it seemed to darken with sadness. But before Odé could say a word, Obatalá shrugged it off and asked him, "Will you be going to the white festival in town this weekend?"

"What white festival, father?"

"This year, everyone in town is gathering for a festival, and the theme is my personal favorite—white cloth." Obatalá gestured to himself with open palms, fluttering his hands from his neck to his waist. Odé smiled; Obatalá was always immaculate in his whites. "Surely you don't spend so much time in the woods hunting that you don't know about it?"

"No, I didn't know."

"Well, you must go! And take some of the fine animal pelts you cure and tan in your spare time. You could sell them for a ransom! They are so flawless and well-preserved."

Odé smiled and looked to the west. The sun was setting. "It's late, father. I need to go home."

Obatalá rose and embraced the young man. "May God bless you in all you do. And don't forget about the festival. It is unseemly for you to be in the forest all the time. Have some fun!"

Odé promised he would, and left. Obatalá pursed his lips and sighed as his friend left.

The day of the festival came, and Odé dressed himself in his best whites. Unfortunately, his best whites were among the worst of his ragged clothes, and as he looked down on himself, he frowned. "Everything I own is ruined by stains from the animals that I kill. I have nothing nice to wear." Still, Odé thought it would be fun to spend a day in town among friends and acquaintances, so he left his small hut and walked to the festival.

On a small hill overlooking the village, he stopped. Even though he was still some distance away, he was close enough to see all the villagers dressed in their finest whites. Under the brilliance of the sun, they glowed with a clean, fresh light. He sighed.

"Why do you sigh, Odé?" asked Obatalá.

Odé jumped at the sound of his voice. Only moments before, he was alone. "I can't go there, Obatalá. Look at them." He gestured toward the town and all the people garbed in fresh, white linens. "Their clothes are so nice. And mine," he said, gesturing to himself, "are ragged and stained with blood. I'm just going home."

"Wait." Obatalá put his hand on his shoulder, and Odé froze where he stood. The orisha's touch sent a powerful current coursing through his body; each hair stood on end, and his skin tingled. Although he'd never felt that before, he knew it was ashé, and he knew Obatalá had plenty of it. "You have always taken care of my needs. Never have you asked anything in return. Now let me take care of you."

What happened next was a mystery, and not even Odé could remember the words Obatalá uttered, or the gestures he made; he did remember that for a moment, there was a blinding white light, and the world ceased to exist before him. Then he was standing in the center of town, and everyone at the festival was gasping and laying their heads on the ground in reverence.

And when Odé looked down at himself, he could not stand his own brilliance; he wore fabrics so fresh and so white that they had to be made from the same stuff as the sun, and they glowed with a bright, fiery light that could only be supernatural. From the hems of his collar to the hems at his feet, the fabrics were studded with crystalline stones that gathered the light, and winked as stars.

For that day, Obatalá had imbued his friend with ashé, and at the white festival, there was no villager better dressed than he.

5

Oché

Five Mouths on the Mat

*The poverty of a diviner does not kill him; the suffering of
a diviner brings wealth; and the troubles of a
diviner always have happy endings.*

It is said that when creation stood on its final threshold, Olódumare
looked down on Earth from Heaven and wondered, "What more can
I give to the world?" He looked at its vastness, the beauty of all things
made, and Oché sprang from his thoughts. He smiled. The world was
complete. Being the last odu to arrive on Earth, Oché is the youngest;
and yet it is the sweetest, the most powerful. It was born from Unle
(eight mouths), and it is found in all the sweet river waters born in
the world. In the body, it rules perhaps the most important part—the
blood, the heart, for these veins are the true rivers of the body. It is
for this reason that when the odu opens on the mat most diviners will
quote this proverb: "Oché is the blood that runs through the veins." Its
influence is strong, and life cannot exist without the ashé it embodies.
Oshún owns this odu; and one feels her influence in all its composites.
Even if no direct mention is made of her, even if no ebó is marked for
her, diviners direct their clients to propitiate the owner of life's sweetness. For in the end, it is Oshún and the odu Oché that brings us all
that Olódumare forgot to give.

It should come as no surprise that every story presented in this chapter focuses on Oshún in some way. I chose to begin my stories with one I titled "The Birth, Death, and Rebirth of Oché." Even in the virtual Garden of Eden created by Olódumare, which we know as Ilé Ifé (the land of expansion), life was hard, so hard that the one thing of true value—love—was forgotten as both mortal creatures and immortal beings sought to propagate life. Life without love is meaningless; and it took the world's death rattle to remind everyone that not only was life worth living, but also it was love that made life worthwhile. The orisha Oshún and the odu Oché control these things. We learn these same lessons, and more, in relation to the odu Oché in the stories "How Oshogbo Became Dedicated to Oshún" and "How Oshún Came to the New World." When first born, no one believed that Oshún had any worthwhile ashé. They saw her beauty and grace, but none realized those qualities housed the potential to change the world. Quickly, everyone learned her strength.

Finally, in this chapter I had the chance to examine a concept, mystifying to most, that comes in any composite of Oché. Often, diviners tell their clients, "You promised Oshún something, and now she wants it." This is a theme repeated throughout most of Oché's composites. In my own spiritual work, I have delivered this message many times; and each time, the client scratches his head, unable to figure out exactly what it is Oshún claims. If Oshún is nothing else, she is mysterious; and more than that, she is a literal orisha. She takes people at their word. The concept of owing something to Oshún comes from a series of patakís that I call the "Cosita-Sagas."* The word *cosita* is Spanish, and translates into "something," or "a little something." As a literary figure, she is a tragic creature; and in exchange for deliverance from disasters suffered by both her suitors and her family, each promised "a little something" to Oshún or to various riverine spirits.

When demanded payment, the little something being Cosita herself, most refused to make good on their promises, and they suffered

---

*There are no less than a dozen Cosita stories found in the corpus of Oché. Space constraints limited me to telling only two of them.

or died. It was only when Oshún confronted Cosita's father to make good on his promise that he delivered his daughter into Oshún's hands, and Cosita fearlessly resigned herself to a life of servitude. While the father grieved, the daughter went happily—for what greater joy in life can there be than to serve the owner of all sweetness and richness on the earth?

Many know of Oché as the youngest of all the odu, yet it is one of the most powerful, the most awesome; in its grasp are all things bittersweet. For while Oshún is the sweetest of all the orishas, one must remember that she can be both the most antagonistic and the most horrible to offend. Crying profusely, she expresses her joy, happiness, and love; laughing, she forebodes all things sinister, displaying her displeasure at mortals. Oshún is the youngest of the orishas. She is tiny and fragile to behold. So it is with this odu. Yet Oshún is the strongest and most powerful, having learned to wield those things that make life bearable like a double-edged sword. Make her proud, spoil her, and give her the due that she deserves, and Oshún gives freely of her blessings. Make her angry, scorn her, and she withholds those things that make life sweet; there is only bitterness left. It is the same with the odu Oché. Be not fooled by this letter's youth. Under its influence, all things small become great and powerful, and under its effects, even the strongest men fall.

The stories told in this chapter teach us those things, and more.

The Birth, Death, and Rebirth of Oché

There was a time when creation stood at its final threshold; Olódumare, exhausted, looked down on his work. There was crystal blue water and lush green earth; there were towering mountains and yawning canyons. Day and night, darkness and light, white clouds and crystalline stars— all these things filled the world. Everything was beautiful. Still, unfulfilled, Olódumare questioned his work. He contemplated his creation's vastness, its raw, primal beauty, and thought to himself, "What more can there be? What else can I create?" He looked at the spirits who had helped him create, the fifteen odu and the orishas who were born of them. They could do little more than marvel at what God's hands had wrought. Once again, Olódumare looked down on the earth and tried to see his masterpiece as if looking at it for the first time. As he gazed, love welled up in his heart, although he understood it not, and so enormous was its ecstasy that it poured forth all over the world. It was sweet, fresh; his divine love birthed the life-sustaining water, forming a wild, rushing torrent that surged over the earth. His love filled the small valleys, long rivets, and cracks in the uneven land. As these fresh waters gathered, they became the mighty, swollen rivers, the tiny, bubbling brooks, the muddy creeks, and powerful waterfalls that rushed and thundered over the terrain. Oché had come into being. From Oché came a single orisha: Oshún. Both were delicate, gentle, and afraid; yet both were sumptuously stunning, and all the spirits on Earth and in Heaven marveled at their beauty. None realized, however, that their elegance masked the most potent energies in the world.

For after the birth of Oché and Oshún, one by one the remaining spirits (orishas, odu, and humans) settled on Earth, and all flourished. Oché and Oshún were still fresh, their ashé enlivening everything. In spite of this, everyone learned that life on the new world was hard: There was much work to do. Daily, everyone toiled; no one took time to reflect on creation's beauty; no one took time to rest, relax, or contemplate life and its meaning. There was only one thought, one purpose: to do what had to be done so life would continue. Oshún and Oché were thought to be too delicate, too tiny, to do anything useful, and they languished in loneliness. Denied worship, adoration, or even acknowledgment, Oshún and Oché slowly withdrew from the world, and neither flowered to their full potential. Alone and isolated, Oshún grew ill and weak, and Oché, not knowing what to do, collapsed in on herself. The sweet, life-giving waters receded into the ocean; they no longer rained down from Heaven. Earth dried up. Life withered. Olódumare looked down in despair. So great and vast were his gifts that he could not bear to see them spoiled; yet because the orishas and odu were his emissaries on Earth, he could only wait and watch to see how they would husband the world. Olódumare had given all he had to give; and in sadness, he turned away. His final creation, his greatest gift, was unloved.

Of all the orishas, it was Oyá who felt creation's death rattle reverberating in the earth; the ashé to feel the moment between life and death was hers, and she felt that moment approaching. Others were too busy working to realize creation's fabric was unraveling. The material world, her marketplace, was about to take its last breath; she felt it dying. To Shangó she ran. He was a diviner by birth; it was a right given to him by Olódumare. Yet Shangó had not exercised his right. He had not opened odu, and no one had made ebó on the earth. Oyá, who knew that the secrets of life and death lay within the shells, implored him to divine. Only then did Shangó gather his divination tools, and he went to what had become Oshún's deathbed. For the first time in his life, he prayed to Olódumare; he prayed to all the orishas and the spirits who inhabited the earth. He called upon all the odu and the spirits who were resting at the feet of God himself. Olódumare's face turned again toward the earth; love was welling up in his heart once more. All the odu came, hoping to be the one sign that would open first on the earth, to heal and sustain all that God created. All, that is, except Oché. As Oshún withered and lay dying, so did Oché; the sign did not hear the prayers Shangó uttered to Heaven. There, with the entire world withering, he cast the shells for the first time. Olódumare's love opened Oché one last time; the last odu created became the first to open on Earth. Again, cascades of fresh water poured across the earth; that which was dry became wet; those that thirsted were sated; places that were brown became green. Shangó marked ebó to Oshún in Oché, and the entire world paid her homage. Her eyes fluttered open. There was power and strength in them. It was then that the world began to comprehend her place in creation.

How Oshogbo Became Dedicated to Oshún

If paradise were said to exist on Earth, its name would have been Oshogbo.

For the city was built safely away from the wars and plagues that affected the rest of the Yoruba nation; it was bordered by a sweet river that never ran dry, and it sat on land so fertile that the crops sprang from the soil overnight and ripened in half a season. The forests were filled with fruit trees and wild berries, and never was a predator to be found in its deepest heart. So plentiful were its animals that hunting was a pleasurable and profitable pastime, and fresh meat graced every table nightly. The roads that ran through it connected the most vital trade routes of the vast empire, and money and goods flowed freely through its borders. People lived long, happy lives, untouched by sickness; and when old age came, they died peaceful deaths.

Still, no one was happy. In spite of their wealth, health, and abundance, no one who lived in Oshogbo could conceive a child. And that made all the married couples feel as poor as paupers.

The king, too, felt the unhappiness of his people; for he had multiple wives, and each remained barren. With no child, the blood of Odúduwa would perish in his own veins; and with no child, he had no heir to his kingdom. He sat in his chambers one night, lamenting his own inability to father children, and thought, "In spite of all our abundant blessings, we are cursed. I must speak to the diviners about this."

The next morning, he did just that.

It was Elegguá himself whom the king consulted that day; he found the orisha sitting in his hut, happily singing to himself. For quite some time, Elegguá ignored the king's approach, and when the monarch finally cleared his throat in annoyance, the orisha looked up and feigned surprise. "My King!" the orisha said, smiling so big his face seemed stretched out of proportion. "What brings you to my humble home?"

"Elegguá," the king said, "everyone in my kingdom is unhappy. I need you to divine for me."

The orisha smiled even wider; it was an impossible grin for such a small face. "Unhappy? But Oshogbo is one of the most prosperous towns in the Yoruba Empire! Why would anyone who lives here be unhappy?"

"Because they think we are cursed. No matter how hard anyone tries, none of the women conceive. Everyone is unhappy because no one can have children." The king was silent for a moment, and when Elegguá continued to stand there and smile, he continued, "And I, too, think we are cursed. We need help."

Elegguá sat on a thick mat, scratching his chin. For what seemed an eternity he sat there silently, while the king waited. And when the king grew impatient and began to speak, Elegguá held up his hand to silence him, and thought some more. Finally, when half the day was gone, he said, "That is a problem, indeed. The only way to solve that problem is to go to the orisha who controls conception itself."

"And who might that be?"

"Oshún," said Elegguá, "you need to petition Oshún. You and everyone in the town. Make ebó to her, and I'm sure she will help all of you."

That evening, all the people of Oshogbo gathered at the riverbank; with them, they brought all the foods they knew Oshún loved: honey, *ochinchin* (a dish made with eggs and shrimp), sweets, and candy. The priests stood at the river's edge, ready to make sacrifice with all her favorite animals—castrated goat, five yellow hens, five pigeons, and a guinea hen—when the king himself kneeled by the river to petition Oshún.

She rose from the river when he called her name; at first, she was a wet, watery creature, but she stepped on a single dry stone that jutted from the fresh water, and slowly her flesh took form. She was lovely.

"Why have you all gathered here?" she asked. "And what is this? Did you bring me offerings and sacrifices?"

The king put his head to the ground in reverence, as did the priests, and all the people who gathered. Carefully, Oshún walked among them all, blessed them, and bid them to rise.

"Yes, Oshún," said the king. "We brought you offerings and sacrifices. Elegguá sent us, and we need your help."

"What could you need my help with?" asked Oshún. "You are the people of Oshogbo, and your kingdom is among the most prosperous in the empire! What more do you need?"

"Children," said the king. "All the wealth in the world is nothing if one does not have children. Our wives cannot conceive."

Oshún smiled. "That is true," she said. "All the wealth in the world is as nothing if one does not have children. Bring me your gifts and sacrifices, and I will bless all the women in Oshogbo with children. But . . . there is more that you must do."

"We will do anything," promised the king.

"You must all worship me, and never forget me. This is my town now, and I am to be treated as your queen. Your favorite, most loved, most adored, and most desired queen."

The king promised that it would be so—Oshogbo would belong to the orisha Oshún. The priests made their sacrifices, and soon, all the women became heavy with children. The town of Oshogbo became a happy place.

At first, it was easy to remember Oshún; as women's bellies ripened with life, everyone marveled at the miracle of conception, and when labor pains came, women cried to Oshún for relief and safe delivery. Hundreds of healthy babies were born in Oshogbo within the year, and as women suckled their children at their breasts, from time to time they remembered to take offerings to the river. "Just as your river never runs dry of water, never let out breasts run dry of milk," they pleaded. Oshún blessed the breasts of each mother, and no child went hungry or thirsty.

Every year it was just like this, but when women had many children running after their skirts and suckling at their breasts, and when fathers were busy providing food for their ever-growing families, the promises they made to Oshún were forgotten. If a mother poured honey into her water once a year, it was a terrible burden for her. Oshún noticed this, and in time grew sour. When the women's wombs went dry, no one cared; each mother had more than enough children for which to care, and if their bellies were flat, it pleased them.

Elegguá found Oshún sitting on her riverbank early one afternoon; she looked bitter and angry. "What is wrong, Oshún?" he asked her. "It is not like you to have such a bitter face."

She heaved a deep sigh; it lifted and dropped her ample breasts sharply. Pursing her lips, she turned her head away from the orisha, and then looked at him again to stammer, "I gave the men and women of Oshogbo everything they asked for. Everything!" Her voice echoed against the trees. "And now that they have what they want, they forget where the blessing came from." Her bitter face twisted up, and a single tear slid from her eye. She wiped it away, and laughed wickedly. "Oh, those ungrateful humans!"

"People are like that," said Elegguá. "In time, they'll come back to you for help again. It is always the nature of mortals to want more."

"And do you really think I will help them, Elegguá?"

"You won't want to help them. But you will. It is the nature of the orishas to help mortal beings."

"Oh, I'll help them," she seethed. "But I'll help them on my terms, and not theirs."

"Of course," said Elegguá. "Your ashé is your own, and is a gift to you from Olódumare. Whenever you help mortals, you always help them on your own terms." Elegguá sat beside Oshún and laid his head on her shoulder lovingly. "But don't let them make you bitter. Humans are still evolving. One day they'll learn. There is hope for them yet."

"You have too much faith in them, Elegguá."

"It's not that I have faith in them, Oshún. I can see everything: past, present, future. I know their potential. Maybe one day, they will surprise us."

Oshún smiled sweetly. She started to speak, but Elegguá interrupted. "Besides," he said, "something terrible is coming to Oshogbo. A terrible plague that will sicken all the children almost overnight. When it comes, Oshún, only your ashé can cure them. And that's when you can make them remember exactly who you are."

They spent that evening together, watching the river flow off to the ocean, until well after even the moon set over the horizon.

A few weeks later, the plague came. One by one, the children fell ill, their skin hot with pox and fever. "It will pass," thought the worried parents. As their children lay ill in bed, soiling the sheets with sweat, they became worried; and when the first child died, there was panic.

The king went to see Elegguá that day. As always, he was alone, singing happily to himself. This time, however, the king did not wait for Elegguá to take notice of him. "Elegguá!" he said, his voice strong and commanding. "There is an emergency, and we need your help."

Elegguá wasn't smiling when he turned to the king. "I know. There is a plague, and all your children are dying." His voice was dry, as if reciting items from a shopping list.

"You know? Why haven't you helped us?"

"Until now, you haven't asked for my help. And now that you have asked, I can't help you."

"If not you, then who?" wailed the king. "Even my own children are sick, and they are dying!" Desperation and sadness made him sound like a whining child.

Elegguá dismissed him with a wave of his hand. "The only orisha who can help you now is Oshún. You remember her? The orisha you forgot when you got what you wanted."

The king was stunned, and he thought, "When was the last time I visited Oshún to make ebó? When was the last time I thanked her for her blessings?" He counted the years, and his jaw went slack. "Olófin forgive us. We have all forgotten her."

"Yes, and you must remember her, and quickly, before all your children die."

It was early evening when the king and his priests assembled all the villagers at the riverbank. In their arms, parents held their children; and sadly, the priests began the chants and sacrifices to propitiate the orisha. As honey and blood dripped into the river, Oshún arose; her gaze was stern but loving. "This is all I wanted from you," she said. "This is all I ever wanted. Your love."

Slowly she walked among the mortals; they lay on the earth in reverence, the limp bodies of their children beside them. She blessed them and cleansed the children. As her ashé flowed into them, the fevers subsided, and the pox healed. "From now on, this will be my sacred day in Oshogbo. Every year, everyone is to assemble and worship me, for I am the one true Queen of Oshogbo. And when the time comes that Oshogbo forgets me again, I swear with Olófin as my witness that my river will flood your city, and you will lose forever what all of you have worked so hard to build."

And since that day, Oshogbo has never forgotten Oshún; and every year on that same day, they gather at the river's edge to worship her and thank her for all the blessings she gives.

How Oshún Came to the New World

Many centuries ago, the orishas lived only in Africa, the cradle of civilization and the mother of all our races. Yet came the Spanish, the whites, to the holy continent, and with them they brought the evils of a modern world. Many of our priests and priestesses in old Oyó became corrupt when they saw the wealth that these men brought, and they were told that they could exchange the symbols of their orishas, the diloggún, for the wealth of gold. "We can wash our spirits anew," they rationalized, "and have the wealth that these strange men bring, for surely this is the will of our gods." In ignorance, they went to the ships and lay down their sacred implements for the precious metals that the traders carried; yet instead of receiving gold coins as they had been told, they were given iron shackles and taken prisoner over the sea. No one heard from them again. Then the slave-lords returned once more, and this time they offered the village chiefs gold in exchange for the strongest and healthiest of their peoples. These, too, were forced into submission and taken away over the bitter seas. Finally, having weakened the tribes through their own greed and sin, the traders returned once more and uprooted what they could of the empires, using their weapons of war to force those who were unable to run into submission. Thus did the evil of slavery begin with greed and lies, and thus did it continue over the centuries.

Many of the orishas came with their priests, either secreted in their hair or bellies. Some that could, sailed through their elements: Obatalá in the sky, Shangó in the storm, Aganyú in the volcano. Others were already there, in Cuba: Orúnmila and Elegguá who are everywhere and know everything, and Ogún, who rests deep in the earth wherever there is iron. Yet one orisha could not leave: Oshún. She lived in the sweet river waters of Africa, and tried in vain to follow her people over the ocean. Yet she could not, for when the river met the seas the fresh waters became salty, and therein she could not travel. So she went to her sister Yemayá and called her, begging, "Sister, where do my people go? Why can I not follow?" And tears slowly slipped down her face, tears of sadness and anger.

"Sister," said Yemayá, "our people are being stolen away to a place called Cuba, and those of us who are able are going with them in spirit to watch over them, to protect them as best we can. Some of us are already there, for our realms extend to theirs. Others are carried in the bodies of the priests and priestesses, for their faith in us is great. Yet you, sister, cannot go. Your followers have traded their diloggún for iron out of greed for gold, and your river ends at the sea. I am sorry."

Yet Oshún knew that her sister Yemayá was very powerful, being the mother of all the orishas. And she knew that if she truly asked, her sister would find a way to carry her across the seas. "Sister, I am sad; I am angry. Yet I forgive those that have brought this evil. I forgive those that have acted in greed. I want to be with them, to protect them, to make their lives sweet. How can I go to Cuba?"

Yemayá thought for a moment and smiled, "You are fresh water nourished by my rain: fresh water. You will travel with me to Cuba through the sky, in the rain with your lover, Shangó, and with the blessings of our elder Obatalá."

Again Oshún shed tears of joy, and she asked, "Sister, what do the people in Cuba look like? Are they like us with dark skin and curly hair?"

"No, sister, they are lighter; some are brown and others are white. They do not look like us."

"I have another wish, my sister. I want to look not only like our people, but also like theirs. I want to show all the beauty of the orishas, and the evil that they have wrought on our people. I want to show them all that life can be sweet, that there can be harmony, that there can be love. I want to show all that will adore us the gifts of Oshún."

Yemayá smiled as she straightened Oshún's hair and lightened her skin; she became the most beautiful of mulattos, yet retained her African features. She was stunning, voluptuous. "This is only illusion, my sister. Those that look upon your beauty will see those things that they find most beautiful. Through you they will learn that no matter the hardships, the bitterness in life, it can be sweet if they honor you and what you represent: love for all peoples and love for the orisha." And with those words Yemayá took Oshún into herself, into the rain, and together they traveled to Cuba to watch over the Yoruba race. Yemayá was their mother and helped them to adapt, to survive, to grow, while Oshún taught all that despite the bitterness in their lives, there could be sweetness. Thus did all the orishas finally come here to the New World: thus have they been worshipped by all.

A Foolish Merchant's Tragedy

The caravan lumbered slowly over the uneven terrain while bandits lay waiting in the forest. Inside the main cabin sat the rich merchant. Lazily, he lay back in his seat, watching the trees slip by slowly. For a moment, he thought he saw something strange in the bushes, a bit of movement from something larger than an animal; and he strained his neck as he pushed his head sideways against the window, trying to look back and see what it was. But they were traveling steadily, and he was unable to look behind.

And then, they struck.

Arrows flew through the air, striking the merchant's horses; with barely a sound escaping their bridled lips, they fell down dead, and they threw their riders from their backs. Those who did not die in the fall got up and ran—they were servants, not warriors—and soon, the merchant was alone with the dead. It happened too quickly: One moment, he was comfortable inside the coach, and the next, he stood surrounded by the dead. He stared in disbelief.

The bandits came armed with knives and machetes, and quickly they loaded up the merchant's wealth and were gone on their own horses. The merchant was alone—terribly alone.

With neither horses to ride nor men to guide him, he walked through the forest, stunned, and by nightfall he felt thirst, and then hunger; and when his throat burned from dryness, he crawled like an animal in the darkness. That was when he spied the men sitting around a campfire, and beside them was a cesspool; they were the bandits who robbed him, only in his delirium, he didn't recognize them.

As thirsty as he was, he crawled into their midst, and all the men went quiet when they realized this was the man they robbed. "Please," begged the merchant, "I was robbed by bandits, and I have been lost in the forest for hours." The men laughed when they realized he didn't recognize them. "Please, help me drink from this pool."

"You want to drink from this?" asked one of the men, staring at the fetid waters. It was so foul it smelled sulfuric, like rotten eggs, but to the merchant, it seemed the sweetest of waters.

"Yes. Please. Help me." He lay on the ground, reaching futilely for the pool, and one of the bandits, feigning kindness, dipped a gourd into it. He looked away with disgust as he held it to the merchant's lips, and everyone's mouth dropped in disbelief as he drank and begged for more.

The bandit was happy to oblige. Several gourds later, they loaded up their horses and galloped away into the night. "Please, don't leave me here to die!" the merchant screamed. But they were gone.

For just a bit, the man felt refreshed, and although he was exhausted, he was able to walk. By morning, the fetid water began working its evil; he felt his stomach roiling, and his head throbbing, and he leaned over a fallen tree to vomit. "I'm not well," he said to no one as fever boiled inside him. And then he screamed into the forest, "Somebody help me!" There was only an echo.

In delirium, he stumbled through the woods, sometimes walking, sometimes running, always falling after a dozen or so steps. When he came to the gentle river, he fell down on its banks and tried to drink, tried to soothe the nagging thirst, but every gulp of water came back up with a violent wave of nausea. "This is it," he said. "This is how I am to die. I will never see my love, Cosita, again." He thought of his fiancée whom he was to wed in a few short weeks, and he cried.

"Why do you cry?" asked a wispy voice. The merchant looked up, and with blurred eyes saw the spirits who lived in the river; they were hovering above its water, and they looked at him with a gentle concern that felt like love.

"I'm dying," he said. "And I will never see my fiancée, Cosita, again." The morning sunlight broke through the forest's canopy in rays; and each spirit hovered in its own ray of light. Their countenance was celestial. "If I am to die," he thought, "I could do no worse than die in their arms."

"Yes, you are dying," said one of the spirits. "But we know all the herbs that grow on the riverbanks, and we can save you. But you must give us something in return."

"I will give you something if you help me," cried the man, fighting the violent waves of nausea that were now just dry heaves. "I will give you something . . . anything you want . . . if you will just help me!"

"You will give us something?" the spirits asked; their voices merged as one otherworldly, ethereal sound. It resonated through the forest, and made the gentle river ripple with its strength.

"Yes, I will give you something. Just help me."

Quickly, the river spirits set about gathering herbs from the riverbank and they pounded them on a river rock until the juices flowed from their leaves. Their fingers and hands were covered in juice, and they offered these to the merchant; he sucked and licked them dry, and when the nausea subsided, bit by bit they gave him the pulp to chew and swallow. It soothed his stomach, quenched his thirst, and sated his hunger; and when he was comfortable again, he lay down to rest.

He slept deeply. His dreams were sweet—they were filled with visions of his love, Cosita.

When he awoke, it was night, and the river spirits encircled him. They smiled. "You are better now?"

The merchant stood up. He was better, but thirsty, and he went to the river's edge to drink. When he was finished, he said, "Yes, I am better."

One of the spirits stood in front of the rest. She put her hand on his shoulder, and said, "Good. Now you must do as you promised, and bring us Cosita. She will be very happy living as one of us."

The merchant froze. "Give you Cosita? I never said such a thing."

"Oh, but you did," insisted another spirit. "Before we healed you, you promised us something. And is not your true love's name Cosita?"

"Yes, but . . ." he stammered.

"And does not Cosita mean 'something'?"

"Yes, but . . ."

"Then you have a choice. Give us Cosita to live here among us, or give us your life back. You cannot have it both ways. You promised."

There, in despair, the merchant realized what he had done; and with love in his heart, and despair in his soul, he threw himself into the river; he drowned.

And that is how the foolish merchant met his end.

I Will Give You a Small Thing

There was no warning when the assassins came. Darkness fell, hearth fires burned out, and everyone slept as they crept through the village. Making no sounds to betray their presence, they slipped in through unlocked doors and unbarred windows, slicing men's throats mercilessly. As their women wakened, they slew them, too, and laughed as terrified children cowered in corners.

By morning, half of the village's men were dead, their families destroyed. The warriors set fire to the village and retreated into the forest. They took Cosita, the king's daughter, with them as well.

The king wailed and ripped at his hair. The village diviners tried to console him, but there was no soothing the king. "I will do anything to get my daughter away from them. Anything!"

"Will you make ebó?" asked the oldest, wisest diviner. "Will you propitiate Oshún for the return of your daughter?"

"I will do anything for Oshún if she helps me get my daughter away from those men. I will give her anything she wants: a little thing, a small thing, a big thing, a great thing. Something! Anything!"

"Oshún doesn't want anything. She only wants a small thing."

"Tell Oshún she will have it! But I won't give it to her until she helps me get Cosita away from those murderous men."

"Oshún . . . accepts . . ." said the wise man, his voice trailing off sadly. "Oshún will help you get your daughter away from the warriors, but you must give her a small thing in return."

The king sealed his promise with his royal word. It seemed as if the earth shuddered, or sighed. He didn't care; as long as his daughter was safe, that was enough for him.

Early that evening, he gathered what was left of his army, and went to reclaim Cosita.

It was the rainy season, and the swollen river churned furiously in its bed. The king's army gathered at the riverbank and watched the white rapids boiling and rolling over cragged rocks and boulders. From their horses, they shook their heads disdainfully. There was no safe passage; there was no way to cross. The king, in despair, slid from his horse and sank to his knees. He cried in front of his men.

"Oshún, my Queen," he prayed to the river, "If you can hear me, I need your help." He watched the river intently, and it seemed oblivious to his pain. "Oshún please . . . I will give you a small thing in return for your help, just like you asked. I promise." A single tear slid from his eye, dripped down his nose and fell into the river; its current slowed. Everyone gasped in amazement.

"My enemies stole into the village last night, and they stole my daughter, Cosita. She is all I have." His words were fervent, heart wrenching; and the great warrior cared not if his men saw him cry. "Please let us cross. I will give you something, a small thing, a great thing, something, anything . . . just please, let me cross your river."

At first there seemed no answer; but then, the crashing waters slowed and stopped. Quickly, all the water ran away and there was only a muddy basin. Slowly, the earth sucked up what was left, and the river-bed was dry. It was nothing short of a miracle.

It was even more miraculous when they found the assassins sleeping peacefully in the middle of the day; and with vengeful hearts, they slew them while slumbering. Cosita was bound, but unharmed.

Quickly, they stole Cosita away, the king embracing her strongly before they mounted their horses and galloped back to what was left of their own village. "We have to move fast, men!" cried the king, Cosita cling-ing to him as they rode through the forest. "I'm sure there are more warriors. Probably they were away hunting, and when they find their men slain, they will be after us at the village. We must be ready!"

They found the river savagely swollen; so flooded were its banks that the forest floor was swampy, and the currents curled upon them-selves, creating whirlpools where before there were only white rapids. Even the jutting rocks looked sharper, and the horses, in fear, reared up on their hind legs. "Sir," cried one of the king's warriors, trying to calm his bucking horse, "Something foul is afoot. The river has grown angry. There is no way to cross. We must prepare to fight here."

"And we will lose," said the king. They were too far away from their own turf; they knew not the land's layout here. They would be ambushed and killed. He dismounted his horse and tied it to a tree. Cautiously, he approached the river and knelt where the water muddied the earth. "Oshún," he whispered. "You promised to help us, and if we don't cross and get back to our village, most of us will die. Calm the river again, please."

"I will." An ethereal voice seemed to come from the river itself; it was loud and commanding, but sweet, and the horses snorted and whined, shaking their heads in fear. The king put his head to the wet earth in reverence, and all the men dismounted. Even Cosita slid down from the king's horse when a wet, watery figure emerged from the cen-ter of the rapids. Flat stones rose above the river, and as the figure took form, it walked across them regally. By the time its feet stood before the king's head, it had taken the form of an elegant woman—Oshún—and she bent over to bless the king, and bid him rise.

He stood fearfully. Few mortals gazed at the countenance of an orisha, and lived to tell the tale. "I will give you what you want, but please, you must help us."

"You promised me a small thing, and I want her now." Oshún looked over his shoulder and smiled at Cosita; she trembled where she stood.

"And you will have a small thing!" he promised. "Just let us cross your river safely."

"I want her now."

The king froze. "You want . . . who . . . now?"

"Cosita." Oshún smiled a warm, loving smile; but still, it chilled the king down to his bones.

"I didn't promise you Cosita!" he roared. "I would never give you my daughter."

"Oh, but you did," argued Oshún, but calmly. "Even before you began this journey, you promised me a small thing, and I agreed to help you for a small thing. At the river's edge, when you cried, you again promised me a small thing. And now that you want my help again, I am here to take a small thing. Is not your daughter named Cosita? Does that not mean "a small thing"? And did you not give your royal word? It is a bad omen to break your word to an orisha!"

Sadly, the king realized his own folly; and he embraced his daughter one final time before putting her hand into that of Oshún. Cosita's fear melted when Oshún held gripped her hand tightly; ashé flowed between the two, and Cosita knew only peace.

"Don't worry, King," said Oshún softly, holding his chin with her free hand. The same ashé that flowed into Cosita flowed into the king; and it felt like love. "In my world, there is neither pain nor sorrow. There is only pleasure and happiness. She will learn my ways, and how to serve me, and she will be one of the chosen few priestesses who will spend all her days caring for me. I will love her as if she were my own daughter."

Oshún walked with her over the rocks, and in the center of the river, both melted into the water. When they were gone, the river's waters receded, and the king and all his men were able to cross safely. Once they crossed, as the king feared, the remaining warriors rushed through the forest after them; but the river rose again and swallowed them up in its rapids.

Oshún had done all she promised, and more. Still, the king never recovered from the loss of his daughter Cosita and lived his days a very unhappy man.

6

Obara

Six Mouths on the Mat

Obara is like a double-edged sword—when brandished by the warrior, it frees the innocent from lies while threatening liars by the truth; and when plunged into the heart of the lie, someone always gets hurt, or dies.

Obara is a root odu simmering and seething with energy. Filled with multiple themes that sometimes seem at odds with each other, it is a difficult letter to understand, and it is problematic at best when divining for a client or godchild. Know that its apocalyptic pronouncements bring radical change to a person's life, yet it also centers on the creation and continuation of community as well as one's personal evolution. It bears witness to one's desire to grow, to evolve into something greater than the sum of one's parts. The growth and enlightenment brought here, however, are filled with tears and deception: Obara's cycle builds on itself, yet brings subterfuge. Just as sudden illumination in a darkened room brings temporary blindness, so can Obara's illumination bring spiritual blindness. Obara is also an odu of punishment, intrigue, and treason, and in this chapter, I chose stories illustrative of the letter from all these angles.

Obara punishes disobedience with the ultimate tragedy—death. In "The Farmer and His Ebó" we meet the man named Akinsa; he was desperate—drought had destroyed his farm. He lacked faith, but still, he went to see the diviners. In desperate times, people do things that are out of character in the hope that they just might help, and Akinsa came from a family of orisha worshippers who believed in both the wisdom of the diviners and the power of ebó. The orisha Elegguá put the diloggún on the mat for him that day. Akinsa *almost* completed his ebó, but his lack of faith and his own hunger were the final keys to his destruction. Simply, his despair got the best of him, and he was disobedient to the orisha's simple demands. One can assume, however, that the surrounding community benefited from his folly, for the rains did come, even though Akinsa did not live through the storm.

"The Best Food: The Worst Food" is my favorite pataki from the corpus of Obara; and in its varying forms, it is one of the best known among Lucumí adherents. Once, when discussing the spiritual implications of this odu, my own godfather told me, "The tongue can be a lion and it can devour you." We spent the evening discussing the implications of the tongue, and one's words, in relation to this family of signs, and by evening's end, he gave me his own recitation of this pataki. Over the years, I have heard many other versions recited by seasoned priests, and when I decided to include my version of this story in this chapter, I kept every version in mind as I wrote. If this parable tells us nothing else, it tells us this, "With the tongue, one can save or destroy the town—control the tongue."

Ochosi's presence in the odu Obara brings serious implications. For as one learns in the story "Ochosi Learns to Build a Trap," he is a cunning orisha, and his cunning is what helped humans evolve from simple scavengers to ingenious hunters. Yet the concept of traps is a theme central to this sign, and sometimes they are not physical traps built for hunting animals—they are spiritual traps built to imprison the immoral or unethical. Ochosi delivers justice blindly; the story "Ochosi's Curse" illustrates his indiscriminate nature when it comes to punishing crimes. The strong themes and morals of these patakís are painfully obvious.

I ended this chapter with a story puzzling to most Lucumí priests; and, indeed, at first it puzzled me. The title of this pataki is "The Story of Elegede." Years ago, back in the mid-nineties, I read a short version of this patakí in a handwritten notebook belonging to a deceased priestess of Yemayá. She was initiated at a young age (her son said she was made to her orisha about the age of ten), and she died at the ripe old age of eighty with no godchildren.* The story was written in Spanish, of course, and with her son's help, I translated it, among others. In the fragments she recorded, she wrote that the orisha Shangó gave a servant named Elegede to Oshún Ibù Olólodí as a wedding gift. Those familiar with that avatar of Oshún will know that she was Orúnmila's wife. In her handwritten fragments, it was noted that Elegede had a lustful heart, and she wanted to be one of Orúnmila's wives. He, however, had eyes only for Oshún.

Those who read my previous book *The Diloggún* might remember this brief passage from chapter 7 (about Obara) in which I wrote: "It is said that Shangó gave the ownership of all calabazas to Oshún in exchange for his use of this sign [Obara]. Since then, this sweet river orisha uses calabazas to prepare and store her most powerful spells and trabajos, and within the pumpkin she hides all of her wealth."†

It was only a few years ago that I learned the name Elegede was not so much a name as it was a Yoruba word. On a whim, I downloaded a Yoruba dictionary and looked up the word *elegede*. There was a listing for that word, and it meant "pumpkin." For as the fragments continued in the elder santera's handwritten notes, Elegede betrayed Oshún, and Oshún, in a moment of anger, killed her accidentally, burying Elegede's body to hide the murder. Suddenly, the lore behind Shangó's gift and Oshún's ownership of pumpkins (and all manner of calabazas) took on new meaning. Shangó gave Oshún a handmaiden; however, how an inanimate object could function as a servant was a mystery to me.

The final piece of the pataki's puzzle fell into place when I became

---

*The reason why this santera never had godchildren was simple—in itá, she had the odu Oché Meji (5-5) in both Elegguá and her crowning orisha, Yemayá. Oché Meji is an odu in the diloggún prohibiting olorishas from certain religious functions. In her case, it meant that she could never have religious godchildren. Still, she recorded meticulous notes regarding both odu and patakís that filled several handwritten notebooks.

†Ócha'ni Lele, *The Diloggún*, 261.

acquainted with a Yoruba student at Rollins College in Winter Park, Florida. He filled in the remaining fragments of the story that I was missing. He was born and raised in Ogún State, Nigeria, and came from a family boasting an ancestral Obatalá shrine more than 600 years old. He knew the story of Elegede and told me, "Elegede was once a woman. She was Oshún's servant. She tried to steal Orúnmila from Oshún by telling him she hunted like a man. While the entire compound was out at night looking for Oshún, she came home and found her servant riding one of her favorite horses. There was an accident, and Elegede, she fell off Oshún's horse. She broke her neck in the fall. Because there were no witnesses to the accident, Oshún buried her, and eventually pumpkins grew from her grave. That is why our word for 'pumpkin' is *elegede*. And that is why we still refer to the *elegede* as being Oshún's servant. Because in her human form, she was. And in her inhuman form, Oshún still found use for her to store her treasures."

The reassembling of all those fragments makes up the final story in this chapter, "The Story of Elegede." Of all the patakís presented here, I am most proud of this one.

Drama, punishment, intrigue, death, and wealth—all these are themes of Obara, and all these are found in its patakís. For, truly, Obara is like a double-edged sword—bringing light and evolution to those who are noble, and darkness and death to those who are ignoble. If one knows nothing else about this odu in the diloggún, one should know that.

The Farmer and His Ebó

Akinsa leaned against his plow under the hot, broiling sun; he coughed, choking on the dust its blade kicked up. "No rain in days," he said to his oxen. They, too, were sneezing and snorting in the dusty air. He looked up at the sky. "Doesn't look like there will be rain for days." The drought was wilting his crops, and with them, his hopes wilted as well.

He gave the beasts a whip with the bridle. Grudgingly they walked, pulling the plow behind them. Dust like powder floated in the air. Akinsa sighed. "Why do I even try?" he asked himself.

Later that night when he was washed and rested, Akinsa knew that if something didn't change with his luck, he would starve. His pantries were empty. His crops were dying, almost desiccated in the fields. As a last resort, he decided to see the diviners and make ebó.

Akinsa knew his neighbors went to the diviners frequently; and as a child, his own parents saw the priests infrequently to improve their luck. He, however, did not have his parents' faith in them. For every problem they solved, there seemed to be yet another waiting for them the next day. It was never-ending. It was Elegguá himself who divined for the farmer that day, and although he listened to the orisha, in his own head he argued every word uttered. When Elegguá told him, "The drought is ruining all you have," he was perturbed.

Akinsa told Elegguá, "The drought is ruining everything for all the farmers. Tell me something I don't know."

"You came here to improve your luck and the orishas are offering you an ebó."

"What might that ebó be?" Akinsa asked.

"All they want is a plate of cooked food. They will improve your luck if you do that, and have faith."

Akinsa promised to make ebó, and he left.

At home, Akinsa cooked. All he had were a few small steaks, and he broiled these gently. He prepared beans and rice, the last he owned. Savory aromas filled his kitchen. Akinsa was hungry, and he knew that after this food was served, it might be days before he had more to eat.

Then Akinsa looked out his window, at the glaring sun and the dusty fields. He saw the crops lying flat against the earth, dead, and looked at his oxen fenced in by the barn, with no grain. "Even if I make ebó," he thought, "there is no relief for my problems. My crops will still be dead. Even if the rains come tonight, they won't be reborn. My oxen need food, and without my crops, there is nothing to feed them."

He went outside, screaming to the heavens. "All your diviners are liars!" So still was the air that there was no echo. He waved an angry fist at whatever gods might be listening. "Liars, all of them! And you yourselves are no more powerful than mortals! Ebó does no good. How will you bring my crops back to life? How will you feed my animals? How will you feed me?"

Akinsa stormed back indoors; he was enraged and hungry. He grabbed a fork and knife and started to eat the steaks. "This is ebó!" he said with his mouth full. "I am feeding myself as ebó!"

Still shaking with anger, he took a deep breath as he swallowed. A piece of meat lodged in his throat; he couldn't swallow; he couldn't cough.

That day, Akinsa choked with anger and despair in his heart. As he fell to the floor, through his window he caught one last glimpse of the sky outside. It was darkening, as if to rain.

The Best Food: The Worst Food

Obatalá sat on his throne, listening to the stories the orishas told him about his favorite son, Shangó. One by one each spoke in turn, and as the afternoon wore on, the stories became more outrageous. The elder orisha fought to keep his eyes open; the lies and embellished half-truths wearied him more than they angered him.

"Obatalá! Obatalá!" Oyá shook his knee briskly. He realized he had nodded off. "It is obvious you are tired, Obatalá, but we need to know what you are going to do about Shangó."

He looked at her sadly. "I will speak to him." It was all he said.

The orishas left Obatalá's palace early that evening. None of them were happy.

When the last orisha left, Obatalá sent his servants to find Shangó. "Bring him to me quickly," he ordered. "I need to speak to him tonight." They went looking for the orisha as told.

It was late when his servants brought Shangó to the palace. Obatalá was pacing in his throne room, lost in thought; he was so distracted he barely noticed Shangó enter.

The young orisha prostrated himself at Obatalá's feet. Gently, his aged hands touched Shangó's shoulders and lifted him from the floor; the two orishas embraced like father and son. "Father," said Shangó in his ear, "Why have you called me this late? Is something wrong?"

Obatalá grasped his shoulders firmly, holding him at arm's length. "We need to speak."

There was a touch of worry in Shangó's voice when he asked, "Have I done something wrong?"

Obatalá sighed heavily, and still embracing the orisha with one arm, walked him to the window. Together, they watched the darkening world outside as Obatalá spoke. "Shangó, you were quite young when I gave you ashé and made you the king of a vast kingdom."

He nodded his head. "I was. I didn't think I was ready to be king, but with you at my side, advising me, I think I have done quite well." He threw his shoulders back so his chest protruded proudly. "I have made Oyó the richest kingdom in the world. I have expanded our borders, acquired tributaries, and made treaties with kingdoms far beyond ours. Even our enemies respect us, and no king dares intrude on that to which we lay claim. I don't think our people have ever enjoyed such wealth in the world."

"There is more to being a king than expanding territory and creating wealth, Shangó."

"What else is there?"

"Shangó, I gave you your ashé because, in my eyes, you were a noble young man above reproach. You did everything for not only your own good, but also the good of others. Something changed as you got older. You worry about money, war, and conquest. And you no longer care about your own reputation. All afternoon my chambers were filled with orishas, and each was complaining about you and your behavior. Without a good reputation, you won't have the goodwill of others, and without their goodwill and respect, your rule will crumble slowly."

"Obatalá," Shangó said, his voice strained with worry, "What have the others said about me?"

Sadly, Obatalá told Shangó everything the orishas said.

"None of that is true!" Shangó roared, his voice shaking the palace walls. "Most of those things are lies, and those that aren't lies are embellished half-truths. Father, I would do nothing to hurt this kingdom. I would do nothing to hurt you. Tell me you don't believe them!"

"I don't." He looked out the window; it was dark, and his reflection stared back at him. "Shangó, I want you to prepare a huge feast for me as ebó. We will invite all the orishas as our guests."

"What should I serve you as ebó, Obatalá?"

"Prepare the best food in the world."

A few days later, all the orishas gathered around Obatalá's banquet table. Shangó stood at one end and Obatalá at the other, with all the orishas seated at the broad sides; they watched, hungrily, while servants brought huge, covered dishes to the table. With the feast assembled, the servants stood back, waiting for Shangó's command. Obatalá said, "Shangó, there are so many covered dishes here. Just a few days ago, I asked you to prepare the best food in the world as ebó. On what do we feast tonight?"

Shangó nodded to the servants, and as they came forth to uncover the dishes, he said, "Roasted beef tongue, father."

"We feast on beef's tongue?" Obatalá asked. "Why do we feast on beef's tongue?"

"Because good ashé is the best thing in the world, and the tongue is full of ashé!"

Everyone thought about Shangó's words, and they all agreed: The tongue is full of ashé. "Ashé!" they all said at once, and everyone feasted.

A few days passed, and still, the orishas came to Obatalá with lies and embellished half-truths about the youthful Shangó's exploits. Wearily, Obatalá called Shangó to his palace again. "The orishas still speak poorly of you, Shangó."

"What am I to do? I cannot control their words."

"No, you can't," the elder orisha agreed. "But you can make another ebó. Prepare a feast in my honor, but this time, prepare the worst food in the world."

✐✐

A few days later, there was another feast. As before, Shangó and Obatalá stood at opposite ends of the banquet table while the orishas sat at its broad sides; the servants brought great covered dishes of food, and waited for Shangó's command. "Shangó," said Obatalá, "tonight I asked you to prepare the worst food in the world for all of us to feast on."

A cry rose up, Oshún's voice rising about them all. "We are feasting on the worst food in the world?" she asked, exasperated. "We are kings and queens. Why would we feast on something so awful?"

Obatalá held his hand up to silence her. "Shangó, what are we feasting on tonight?"

"Roasted beef's tongue," Shangó said with a wry smile on his face. He was looking directly at Oshún. She held both hands over her heart.

"Shangó, did we not eat that just a few days ago?"

"Yes, we did," he answered, smiling.

"And if beef's tongue was the best food in the world, why, today, is it the worst food in the world?"

"Tongue is the best food, and tongue is the worst food. For a good tongue will save us all, and a bad tongue will destroy all that Olófin created!"

All the orishas hung their heads in shame: To themselves, each recounted the lies they told Obatalá about Shangó, and realized their own tongues, and not Shangó, were destroying the kingdom.

In silence they ate; never again did they falsely accuse Shangó to Obatalá.

Ochosi Learns to Build a Trap

There was a time when humans were no more than scavengers; they scoured the forests and the plains for food. Sweet, sugary berries and soft, ripe fruits; leafy green herbs and thick roots; soft mushrooms and firm, wild vegetables: these were the things they lived on. As a food supply, it was unpredictable. Periods of drought made food scarce, as did heat waves and cold winds. Sometimes the berries didn't ripen, and fruit rotted on the tree. Humans were forced to feed on what they could find, and the orisha Ochosi knew there was a better way.

For humans were meant to be hunters, and feed on the meat of the kill.

Ochosi himself was never a hunter; he knew not how to handle weapons. Yet the orisha was brilliant, and watched as nature's predators captured their meals. They all used sharp teeth, long claws, lightning-fast speed, and superior strength to capture their prey. Ochosi had none of this, but he had one skill none of the animals had: intelligence.

Night and day he labored, using that intelligence to create the world's first animal trap.

His first one was quite simple, little more than a firm basket with one side held up on a forked stick. To the stick was tied a long string. On the dirt under the basket, he scattered a handful of seeds as bait. Satisfied that his trap was ingenious, he unraveled the string many yards away from the basket, covering it with twigs and leaves as he walked. Finally, he hid in the brush, still in sight of the primitive trap. And he waited in silence.

Two birds spied the basket as they flew overhead, and swinging by for a second look, they saw the scattered seeds. Cautiously, they scanned the forest brush for predators. So well hidden was Ochosi that they missed him in the brush. Convinced they were safe, the two birds landed, and started pecking at the seeds. Ochosi pulled his string, and the basket trapped the birds.

That night, Ochosi roasted his kill, and it was delicious.

For weeks the orisha built bigger and bigger traps; and after trapping all manner of small prey, he set out to catch bigger animals, such as the leopard. For that he dug a huge hole in the earth, and at the bottom of the hole, he put several long wooden spikes. He covered the hole with thick branches, and threw smaller leaves and twigs on top of that. As bait, he threw the carcass of a dead bird, one of the animals caught with his smaller traps, in the center. Ochosi then climbed high in a tree, and waited for a leopard to pass.

It took quite a few hours, but in time the scent of rotted flesh traveled through the woods, and attracted not one, but two leopards. They saw the bird sitting on the forest floor, looking as if it were asleep. Hungrily, they circled the bird, still outside the trap's reach, but then both roared in unison and, at the same time, pounced on the bird. The branches snapped; they fell in the hole and on the spikes.

Both died instantly.

"This is more meat than I can eat!" Ochosi could not contain his excitement at his luck. "And the skins will fetch a king's ransom!" He gutted, skinned, cut, and quartered the leopard, letting its blood run into the trap. "The smell of blood will attract more animals," he thought to himself. He reset his trap with branches, twigs, and leaves, leaving another small bird in the center as bait; and he went into town to sell his meat and pelts.

When he came back, there was another leopard lying dead on his spikes.

Every day went just like this: Ochosi returned to his trap early in the morning, finding another leopard dead. He skinned, cleaned, cut, and quartered it, and then returned to town after resetting the trap. Soon, he was a rich man as all the people in nearby villages bought his meat, and all the kings purchased his pelts.

This was the birth of trapping animals in the world.

Ochosi's Curse

Sunrise: Darkness made one last stand on the earth, thickening in the sky as it braced for morning's onslaught. In the east, it shuddered, thinning and melting as the sun licked the horizon, painting Heaven and Earth with color. Darkness screamed, rolling to the west as the sun's fire brushed the forest with a muted, misty glow. Feeling the rising warmth, trees lifted dew-laden leaves toward Heaven, thirsting for light. The morning air stirred; breezes born with the first rays of sunlight skirted through the forest, lifting the scent of damp moss and wet earth. Slowly, the world awakened, wiping sleep from its eyes, and Ochosi stood, watching and waiting. He was alone, already focused on the sounds and scents rising around him. His muscles tense, his black skin glistening with a thin sheen of sweat, he listened as animals stirred from their slumber; and quickly, he chose his prey.

Muscled arms lifted his bow and arrow; they flexed, tensing the bow. Sharp eyes fixed on his target: a young pair of pheasants, oblivious to their fate. A deep breath, a narrowing of his eyes, and a quick snap of his fingers sent the arrow slicing into the heart of not one, but both; they fell with only a soggy thump.

The kill held no more excitement for him than that of any other game he hunted, but when he retrieved his prey, he saw their beauty. Long, silky feathers, full, rounded bodies, and wings that were both powerful and graceful. Never had he seen a pelt so fine. He thought of his mother, and how she would cherish game so graceful. Quickly he went home to stash his kill, and just as quickly, he sought out his mother.

While Ochosi was away from his home, an old, wizened woman knocked on his door. Finding no answer, she let herself inside; surely Ochosi would not mind. Hanging by his hearth were two of the most beautiful birds she had ever seen. It broke her heart that they were dead, but such was their grace that she could not help herself. There were two, she reasoned, and surely Ochosi would not mind if she took one for herself. She lifted it from its hook, and set back out into the woods, pausing only briefly to wonder if she should wait. But Ochosi would spend hours in the forest, hunting; she would return later that evening to see the powerful hunter. Her house was not far away, but the day was beautiful; she stashed the bird in her shoulder sack, and set off for a leisurely walk.

Ochosi came home; outside his mother's house, he had waited for hours. But she did not return. He then spent the rest of the day tracking game, but the forest had seemed empty, and not an animal or a bird did he spy. Darkness was coming, and with the fading sun, so faded his resolve to hunt. Tired and hungry, he was soon home. Once inside, his anger began to boil when he saw that one of his two beautiful birds was missing. An anguished cry erupted from his lips, shaking even the clouds in the sky; it seemed that the sun itself tried to hide from his roar, and darkness quickly rushed over the land. The same old woman who was at his house earlier heard this, and fear gripped her heart. "My son!" she gasped, running down the path that lead to his house. "He is in danger."

Ochosi's temper seethed; his arms tensed furiously as he gripped his bow and arrow. "My arrow will pierce the heart of the thief," he cried, and the arrow sliced the darkness, fueled with Ochosi's preternatural strength. The old woman never saw the arrow; she only felt its sting as it sliced her heart. "My son," she cried again as her life ebbed and blood flowed from her breast. And as she broke through the path, and collapsed at Ochosi's feet, the contents of her sack spilled on the ground; in horror, Ochosi saw his missing bird. His own blood coursed through his veins like ice water as he realized what he had done: he had killed his own mother.

The Story of Elegede

Elegede was dreaming, and it was sweet: Orúnmila held her in his arms. They were powerful, strong; and she felt desire rising like heat in her loins. He kissed her, and her body relaxed, becoming soft and pliable in his embrace. "I love you," he whispered in her ear. Elegede shuddered, and awoke.

It was like this every night. Elegede dreamed of Orúnmila while he lay in bed with his wife, Oshún Ololodí. "But not for long," she thought to herself, hugging her pillow and laying back in her bed.

The morning was still young when Oshún Ololodí awoke; and she lay still for quite some time, staring at a blank wall while the world of sleep and dreams faded from her thoughts. She took a deep breath, and called out, "Orúnmila? Husband? Are you awake?"

There was no answer.

Lazily, she rolled over. His side of the bed was empty. The sheets were rumpled as if he'd thrown them off carelessly, and she reached out to touch them. They were cold; Orúnmila had risen hours ago. "Orúnmila?" she called out. She heard quick footsteps coming down the hallway. They weren't her husband's footsteps.

The door opened after a quick, polite knock and Elegede stood at the side of the bed. "Orúnmila left early this morning, mistress," she said, bowing her body slightly in subservience. Oshún sighed and looked at her servant. She wasn't a pretty woman, but she wasn't homely, either; she was short, almost stout, but had a handsome enough face. Although she'd never married, she had wide, childbearing hips that some men would find attractive enough, but instead of marrying and serving a husband, Elegede chose to serve Oshún as a housemaid, and Oshún was happy to have her on her staff.

"When did he leave, Elegede?"

"He left hours ago, mistress, long before the sun rose. I packed his bags last night, and carried them to his horse this morning. He didn't want to wake you, so I saw him off for you."

Oshún pulled the covers up to her chin and closed her eyes. She snuggled back into her pillows and asked, "How long will he be gone this time?"

"At least a week, mistress." It was a lie. Orúnmila told Elegede he'd be gone only a night, and would be back in the morning; but Elegede was hoping Oshún would do something stupid, like go hunting. Orúnmila hated it when she went hunting. It was a man's pastime, not a woman's, and Orúnmila threatened to leave her if she didn't stop doing such manly things. "And then," Elegede thought to herself, "Orúnmila will be all mine." She felt a familiar fire burning in her loins; Elegede wanted his affections so badly it hurt.

"Good," said Oshún, "I needed some time to myself anyway." She rolled over on her other side, and that was the last thing she remembered before falling asleep again. She dreamt of the hunt.

Oshún slept until late in the evening, and when she rose, Elegede was busy preparing the evening meal. "Will you be eating in your room, Oshún?" she asked, plating the food for her.

"No, Elegede, I'm not hungry tonight. I'm going out."

"Out, mistress? This late? It's dark outside."

"Yes, I am going out," she said, and then, in a whisper, "I am going hunting. I need you to prepare my horse."

"Hunting!" Her voice was loud, surprised, and Oshún cringed at its volume. Everyone in the household would hear her. "I'm sorry, mistress," she said, almost a whisper. "But the forest is a dangerous place, especially at night, and you know how your husband hates it when you do such things. They are . . . unseemly . . . for a woman of your stature."

Oshún stood to her full height, her shoulders thrown back and her head held high. She took Elegede's chin in her right hand. "You let me worry about my stature, Elegede. And you worry about preparing my horse." With a flick of her wrist, she released Elegede's chin and she stumbled back just a bit. "I'll be ready as soon as I get my machetes. Hurry along, now!"

"Wait until Orúnmila hears about this!" Elegede thought to herself. "He won't be rid of Oshún and her manly ways fast enough!"

For hours, Oshún Olólodí rode her horse through the forest; she was not so much hunting as she was enjoying her freedom in the cool, moonlit night. A white owl rode on her shoulder, its head turning from side to side, an eerie 180-degree twist that delighted Oshún to no end. With one hand she held the horse's reins, and with her other, a razor-sharp machete, its hard steel glowing in the moonlight with an eerie, preternatural sheen. Moments like these were her happiest, and she lost herself in the shadows.

She let the horse stop at a riverbank so it could drink, and then, on the other side of the river, she saw the buck. It, too, was drinking from the water. For just a moment, Oshún's eyes locked with the deer's; she eyed it hungrily, and the deer eyed her fearfully. Then it broke into a fast run.

"Go!" Oshún cried, digging her heels into the horse's side. It took off into a fast trot, and still gripping the reins with one hand, she held her machete high, the rush of the hunt upon her. The owl took flight above the deer, and even when Oshún lost sight of the beast, she knew her owl could see it, and she followed its flight instead.

The deer ran fast, but the horse ran faster, and with Oshún following the owl's flight, the distance between them closed quickly. When her steed was side by side with the deer, she gave a final lunge, dealing a fatal blow as she brought her machete down on its neck. She stopped, letting out a great cry of triumph as the owl landed on her shoulders. "We are a good team," she said to the bird, and its only answer was a single "whoop" that echoed through the forest.

The owl fluttered back into a tree while Oshún made quick work of the carcass with her knives, gutting, skinning, and quartering the animal so it was easier to carry. When she was done, carefully she removed the antlers, her favorite part of the kill. She wrapped everything in the animal's hide and quietly rode home.

Not that she had to walk quietly into her own house. Her husband, Orúnmila, was away on business, teaching his *babalawos* (initiates) the secrets of Ifá, and divining for his many clients and godchildren all over the countryside. Oshún loved her husband, but she loved him even more when he was away. Orúnmila felt it was unsightly for such a beautiful woman, and the wife of a *babalawo,* to be out and about hunting like a man. But Oshún Olólodí loved the thrill of the hunt, and in truth, with her owl, horse, and machetes she was better than a man at running down and killing her prey. The hunt made her feel powerful, alive.

Still, there were servants, and she didn't want her servants ratting her out to her husband. So before she came inside, she slipped off her bloodstained hunting clothes, and in the river, with her owl keeping a lookout, she bathed and scrubbed herself clean. Only when she was dried and dressed did she dare go home.

She was startled when her servant Elegede met her at the door. "How was your hunt, mistress?" she asked.

"It was wonderful," she said, almost dreamily, as she handed Elegede the pelt-wrapped venison and antlers. "I think you should cook the meat for tomorrow night's supper. And have the antlers prepared for my husband. He loves them as much as I do."

"And when Orúnmila asks where it all came from?"

"Tell him you bought it at the market. That is what you always say, no?"

"You know he's right," the servant called out to Oshún as she walked to her chambers. She followed her briskly, still carrying the pelt. "It is unseemly for such a beautiful woman to be out and about at night, hunting."

Oshún turned; her voice was icy and terse when she said, "That is none of your business, Elegede. What I do concerns me and no one else. Do you understand?" Her demeanor was calm, but her eyes betrayed her anger. They bore into Elegede with a stare that was primal.

"Yes, mistress. Your secret is safe with me." She was trembling fearfully when she answered Oshún.

Satisfied with Elegede's answer, she said, "I know I can trust you. We are women, you and I. We all have secrets from our men."

"Yes," thought Elegede as Oshún walked away. "But only secrets are secrets."

Orúnmila returned early while Oshún Ołólodí was still sleeping; her late night hunt in the forest wore her out tremendously. But Elegede was waiting for her master's approach. For years she served the couple, and although Orúnmila had no love for the homely woman, she was consumed with desire for the elegant man. He was surprised when he saw Elegede by the front door, waiting for him.

"Did anything interesting happen while I was gone?" he asked as she took his bags from him.

"As a matter of fact, something interesting did happen, sir," she said. In whispers, she told Orúnmila of Oshún's late-night hunt. Orúnmila was not pleased.

Alone in their bedroom, Orúnmila woke Oshún gently. She smiled when she saw her husband sitting on the bed and reached out sleepily to embrace him. "You are home," she said, still groggy from her late night.

"Yes, and you are still in bed. Why are you sleeping so late?"

Oshún sat up, caressing her husband's head lovingly with one hand. "I can barely sleep at all when you are away, husband," she said smiling. Orúnmila smiled back. Even first thing in the morning, his wife was beautiful when she awoke.

"Perhaps the reason you cannot sleep is because you are out all night hunting?"

Oshún pulled her hand back, and froze. For what seemed an eternity there was silence between them, and then she stammered, "You know?"

Orúnmila stood up and looked out the window as he spoke. "We have talked about this so many times that I'm tired of speaking, Oshún. You are my wife. I am a priest, practically a king in this land. I know you grew up hunting; and I know there are few in the world more skilled with the machete than you. But it is unseemly for my wife to be out and about in the forest hunting like a man, and at night. You promised me you were done with your old ways."

She took a deep breath before she spoke. "How did you know? Did Elegede tell you?"

"Elegede is your servant, not mine. Why would she betray you?" Angrily, Orúnmila stormed from the room.

"Why would she betray me, indeed?" Oshún asked herself.

That same day, Oshún dressed and went to visit her sister, Yemayá Achabá. It was a long journey to her sister's house, but Oshún rode her horse hard and furious over the countryside. When she arrived, her clothing and hair were disheveled from the ride, but she did not stop to refresh herself before knocking on Yemayá's door. She was concerned when she saw Oshún's weary, ragged face. "To what do I owe this honor?" Yemayá asked her sister.

"I have problems at home," Oshún said.

"And you need my advice?" asked Yemayá. Oshún was proud; and if she were here, asking for her advice on problems at home, then those problems must be great indeed.

"I need more than your advice, Yemayá. I need your ashé. You are a diviner, and this is a problem that needs divination." Slowly, sitting beside Yemayá, she told her sister all that transpired—she told her about her hunting, and about how Orúnmila discovered the hunt when he returned home the next day. And then, she froze. "Wait," she said. "My servant Elegede told me that Orúnmila told her he would be gone for a week, and yet he was home the very next morning."

"And, of course, your servant knows everything that you do?"

"Not everything," said Oshún, frowning wickedly. "But she did know I was going hunting. I had her prepare my horse, and she was waiting for me when I returned home."

"You may have discovered the rat yourself," said Yemayá. "But, you're right—we should divine. The oracle will tell us everything going on that you don't know about." And there, on that late afternoon, Yemayá cast her shells on the mat and told Oshún everything she needed to know.

Riding her horse back home, Oshún was so lost in thought and anger that she barely noticed how late it was. The skies were darkening, and red eyes peered from the forest; hungry growls broke the silence. Oshún felt no fear; she was strong, powerful, a predator in her own right, and nothing frightened her. *"Of course, it all makes sense,"* she thought as the cold night air ripped at her hair; the horse was galloping faster and faster, driven by the tense digging of her heels into its sides. *"Elegede is a young woman still, and never has she had a man that I know of. Of course she wants Orúnmila for herself. He is, after all, very handsome."*

Her blood was hot as she raced home, and when she arrived there, she jumped off her horse so quickly that it was startled and almost fell. She burst into her own home, the door slamming hard against the wall, leaving a dent. "Elegede!" she yelled; her voice made the walls vibrate. "Orúnmila!" There was no answer. The house was silent. Quickly she ran from room to room, but the house was empty. Her anger quelled itself into confusion. "Where is everyone?" she yelled again, this time knowing there would be no answer.

She ran back outside to the stables, where Elegede spent much of her free time brushing and pampering the horses. "Elegede!" she yelled. Again, no answer, but she saw that all of the horses were gone. And then, she heard a gentle gallop coming around the side of the house. She ran to the sound, and saw Elegede casually riding one of her own horses.

"Elegede!" she yelled, running up to the horse and grabbing its reins. "What are you doing on my horse? Where is Orúnmila?"

The servant smiled. "He is out looking for you, mistress, as are the rest of the servants."

"They are out looking for me? Why are they looking for me?"

Again, Elegede said, "They are all out in the forest, looking for you. Your husband is very worried." She pursed her lips and shook her head from side to side, as if Oshún were a child and should be ashamed.

Oshún's eyes narrowed into slits as her grip on the horse's reins tightened. "And why is my husband looking for me, Elegede?"

She smiled an evil smile. "Because you have been gone all day and most of the night, and he thinks you have been out hunting."

Oshún stood back, still holding the bridle. "And why would he think that?"

"Because I told him that's where you went."

Anger flashed red behind Oshún's eyes, and the world seemed to dim; still, she held her composure, and only shook a bit when she asked her servant, "Why would you tell him such a thing?"

Elegede loosened her own grip on the horse's reins, and crossed her arms across her breasts arrogantly. "Because you don't deserve a man such as Orúnmila. You spend all your time looking for ways to sneak out into the forest at night, to hunt. You act like a man. You dress like a man. He needs a woman to love him and bear him children. He needs me, and not you!"

Her words stung, and Oshún broke. In a movement so quick it seemed a blur, she pulled a short knife from the waist of her pants and sliced the horse's flesh. It was a superficial cut, nothing mortal, but the beast bucked in fright and pain; Elegede, who was not holding the reins, flew off the horse and landed headfirst. Wildly, the horse galloped away, the cut's sting driving him mad; and Oshún saw, emotionlessly, that Elegede's head lay at a morbid angle. Her neck was broken.

Oshún buried her with no more concern that that of a dog burying its own waste.

Later that night, Oshún was sleeping peacefully in bed, more peacefully than she had in weeks when her husband woke her up, angrily. "Oshún!" he said, his voice firm, "Where have you been? We've been out all night looking for you."

Sleepily, Oshún lifted herself up on one elbow and smiled innocently. "If you must know, husband, I have been at my sister's house all day. It is a long journey, and I got home late. No one was home to tell me what was going on. What was I to do? I went to bed."

Orúnmila drew in a sharp breath. "Did you not notice all the horses and servants were gone?"

"I did. And that's exactly why I didn't know you were worried about me. Everyone was gone. So I went to bed."

"Were you hunting again?" he asked, angrily.

"No, I was at Yemayá's house. Send a servant in the morning to ask her if you will. Send Elegede. I don't care."

"Elegede is not here," Orúnmila said. "She separated from the group last night while we were looking for you, and she's not home yet."

"I'm sure she'll turn up," Oshún said. "Now, can I go back to sleep?"

Orúnmila left the room. He waited for Elegede to return. He wanted to know why she would say Oshún was out hunting if, indeed, Oshún was at her sister's house. When morning came and still she did not return, he was worried.

Orúnmila sent a servant to Yemayá's house that morning; and he returned with the news that, yes, Oshún spent all afternoon with her

sister. By late evening, the horse Elegede rode returned, and when everyone saw it returned alone and with a gash in its side, they all feared the
worst for the servant. The next day everyone searched, and when no
sign of her was found, they mourned Elegede as one of the dead. Oshún
feigned sadness, but inwardly, she was pleased.

And days later, in the spot where Oshún buried her servant's broken body, a vine poked through the soil. She regarded it curiously, and
watched as the vine grew daily, sprouting green leaves and finally fruit.
First, they were a golden yellow, and as they swelled and ripened, they
turned a delicious orange. It was the birth of the pumpkin, and it was
born of Elegede's treason, and Oshún's anger.

7

Odí

Seven Mouths on the Mat

While one might regret his mistakes and transgressions,
he must still bear the consequences of his actions.

In my first book, *The Secrets of Afro-Cuban Divination,* I wrote that Odí was born of the odu Okana, an energy I described as an expression of harmony and justice brought about through radical, harsh changes.* I expressed my belief that it was a seal to all things created by Okana's energy, and I wrote, "As a seal to creation, Odí ensures that what exists is here only by the will of Olódumare and the orishas; all that exists is either an expression of holiness or a force designed to allow that holiness to continue and manifest."† Yet there is another way to study the odu Odí, another way to view this seal—through sex and sexual activity. For Odí is an erotic odu, filled with carnal expressions of love as opposed to those emotional; it was she who taught flowers, insects, animals, and humans how to copulate and procreate. The great seal created to hold those creative energies in physical form is the orgasm. Since Odí ensures that what exists on the earth is an expression of Olódumare's will, that makes sex and its resulting off-

---

*Please read chapter 1 of this book for more about Okana and her stories.
†Ócha'ni Lele, *The Secrets of Afro-Cuban Divination: How to Cast the Diloggún, the Oracle of the Orishas,* 186.

spring (or lack of) holy, and sexual ecstasy itself becomes something divine and sacred.

Two of the stories chosen for this chapter examine Odí's sexual nature. "The Creation of Copulation" is a short piece describing why and how Odí came to Earth with the knowledge of sexual intercourse. Olódumare was mournful of the world's ephemeral nature, and Odí discovered how to keep the flesh firm in the material world. With God's permission, she brought that knowledge to Earth; it was a gift as beautiful and as dangerous as the fire the Greek Prometheus brought from Heaven. In "Where the Hole Was First Opened," sexual morality is the theme. Most initiates know various versions of this story—and they know it as an explanation of why we bury the dead. In truth, that is but a minor theme of this piece. It examines the importance of sex and sexual activity to a relationship, and it delves into the themes of adultery and indiscretion. And while it is true that the first hole for the dead was opened in the odu Odí for the odu Odí, the true morals are that one's body is sacred, not a vessel to be shared randomly; and the wages for lies and adultery are death.

I would like to point out that there are other versions of this pataki in which the characters are the orishas themselves. In those versions, Shangó is exchanged for the diviner Mofá, Oyá is exchanged for the wife Odí, Ogún is Oyá's secret lover, and the son's name is Elegguá. In some of these versions, the king who pronounces death and burial of the adulterous woman, Oyá, is Obatalá himself. Of course, the setting for this drama played out in ancient Oyó: Shangó and Oyá lived in the ancient kingdom as king and queen, and Ogún came from the outlying nations. With the orishas as the main characters of this sacred drama, priests and priestesses familiar with both our history in Cuba and the energies of Odí will draw conclusions that are more exciting from this story.

"He Who Fights Knows about War" was my final pick for this chapter about Odí. I chose it because its themes and messages are simple: In Odí, Ogún becomes something frightful, and because of this no one understands his suffering. This feeds his wrath, fueled by exhaustion and not anger. As he rampages through the world annihilating everything in his path he tells us, "Only those who fight know about war." It is a painful cry, a plea for understanding, but the human heart has no sympathy for the act of destruction; it has sympathy for only the suffering in its wake. It takes the powerful ashé of Elegguá to hold Ogún's mighty arm back; and it takes the cool nature of Obatalá to restore Ogún's balance. If Odí is known as a sign of nature, and Ogún is seen as a force of nature, then one understands nature's wrath—and that all things, even death and destruction, are eventual.

The Creation of Copulation

It was Odí who taught the world to make love.

Creation was complete; and the world floated in space, a brilliant blue and white jewel resting in black velvet, but as Olódumare pondered his work, his heart was heavy with despair. He knew that nothing in the material world would last forever, and his Earth was no exception. Exhausted, he pondered this, and Odí, in one sensual, fluid movement, went to his side. "You can rest, Olódumare," she said, her voice husky and soft. "I will see to it that life continues in spite of itself."

Olódumare was puzzled, but Odí went to earth. God stood still, and watched.

First, she went into the forest, and gently, she touched the plants and vines and trees with her fingertips. Lightly, she blew on their stems, and watched the flowers unfold. They were delicate and graceful, and soft scents filled the earth. "This is what you must do," she whispered, "if you are to live." Birds, bees, butterflies, and insects found the aromas appealing; and slowly, they explored the flower petals with the noses and mouths. Fruits ripened; flowers grew heavy, and seeds scattered across the earth. "This is as things should be," said Odí.

She found the animals lying in the fields; the forest scents were intoxicating, and they, too, rolled among the freshly scented flowers. Carefully, Odí knelt beside a female leopard, and with soft hands, stroked its belly with her red nails. It purred; it stretched and rolled on its back; and she let out a needy mew as her legs opened and back arched. Another aroma filled the air, the smell of heat, and the male leopards began to roar in the jungle. Soon, all the female animals were in heat, and the males mounted them.

"This is how things must be," said Odí, "if you hope to live."

Finally, Odí found a man and woman standing at the edge of the meadow; they were confused by what they saw—needy animals mounting each others' backs, rocking and rolling and crying out with ecstasy. "Watch," Odí told the male, "and learn."

Gently, she helped the woman lie on her back, and smiling, she lifted her legs so they were bent at the knees; and she spread them wide so her vagina spread like the delicate petals of a flower. As she lay there, smiling, Odí stroked between her legs, and a damp, musky scent rose from her most secret place. Odí looked at the man who looked at them both, and saw his penis rising; it was hard and strong, and she said, "That . . . goes here . . ." and she helped the man mount the woman.

She stood back and watched. Their confusion turned to need, and their need turned to pleasure, and soon all the men and all the women in the world were copulating as well.

Olódumare smiled in Heaven. It was not what he planned, but it was beautiful. The world became fruitful and multiplied that day. For Odí taught the world how to copulate, and the material world, in spite of its ephemeral nature, found a way to continue.

Where the Hole Was First Opened

It was early morning when Mofá opened his eyes. Thin rays of light filtered through the bedroom drapes, filling the room with a pale, soft glow. For quite some time he was motionless in bed, dazed after a night of sleep and dreams, and as these loosened their grip, he remembered where he was, and slowly, so as not to disturb her rest, he turned on his side to face his wife, Odí.

Carefully, Mofá propped his head up on his left hand, his elbow resting against the soft pillows, and he watched his wife breathe. Odí was still, but her chest rose and fell slowly with each breath. His eyes rested at her breasts; they were full and firm, stretching the fabric of her nightgown dangerously as they rose. He smiled, and reached out to touch them, but stopped before he did. As his hand hovered close to her, the difference in years between them was obvious: his skin was worn and wrinkled, hers smooth and supple. "Why does a young woman love an old man such as me?" he thought.

He frowned, but only for a moment as he looked at her face. Odí was beautiful. Her skin was a rich, deep onyx that mocked the darkest night, and in her sleep, tiny beads of sweat formed on her brow. In the growing morning light, they sparkled and shimmered, like so many tiny diamonds resting against black velvet. Her complexion was smooth, and her cheekbones high; her lips were full, and ripe, and soft. Gently, he kissed her on the mouth.

Odí smiled when she woke, and she stretched, arching her back and throwing her arms around her husband's neck. Gently, she raked her long, red nails across the back of his neck. He loved those nails more than anything else about his wife; when they tickled his skin, he shivered. "Have you been awake all this time, watching me sleep?" Her voice was husky and soft.

"I always watch you sleep. You're beautiful."

They lay there for quite some time, their arms and legs tangled, his head resting on her ample bosom. It was Mofá who broke the silence first. "I wish I could . . ."

"Shush . . ." she whispered, stroking his thick head of grey hair with her nails. "It's okay."

For months, even though Mofá was passionately in love with his wife, he was unable to please her as a husband should. "But it's not right. You have needs. I don't know what's wrong with me anymore."

"There's nothing wrong with you, and I have everything I need," she said tenderly, and he almost believed her. Mofá lifted his head from her breasts to kiss her again; and Odí raised her hips against him lustfully. It was a needy grind against his groin, but her desires were not for him. They were for her lover.

❧

Mofá and Odí had a son together, and every morning, he was the first out of bed and ready to start the day. This day was no different; there came a muffled knock at their bedroom door, and then a louder one when they did not answer. Odí smiled at Mofá, "Do you want to answer that, or should I?"

Mofá groaned as he pushed himself out of bed; carefully, he slipped his feet into his slippers, and tied a robe around his waist. "You stay in bed. I'll get him ready for his lessons." He leaned back to kiss his wife one last time, and opened the bedroom door to an anxious ten-year-old boy.

Alone in bed, Odí wrapped the sheets around herself tightly and leaned back against the pillows. She listened to her husband and son rushing to make breakfast, and she smiled. "Life is good here," she thought. Then, she frowned. "Well, life is as good as it can be here." With a deep sigh, she closed her eyes and thought of her lover. So long had she gone without intimacy that Odí had taken a secret lover; every day when her husband was gone, he would sneak in through the back and spend the afternoon with her, in bed. But she'd not seen him for four days, and Odí was worried. "Maybe I'll never see him again?" Sadly, she got out of bed and dressed.

"He might come today after all." It was a whisper, and wishful. Odí needed him badly.

It was early afternoon when he scratched lightly at the backdoor. Odí was sitting at her kitchen table, sipping her coffee; her long, smooth legs were crossed at the knee. Thoughtlessly, she bounced her right leg up and down rapidly in succession. When she didn't answer the door, he knocked, but softly, and she jumped when she heard it.

Quickly, before the neighbors had the chance to see him, Odí whisked him inside. Her embrace was needy and passionate, and he returned her embrace with an open-mouth kiss. He lifted her with his huge, muscled arms; for him her weight was effortless, and Odí thought, "My husband could never do this. He is too old." Swiftly, he carried her to the bed, her long, braided hair barely sweeping the floor. He laid her on her marriage bed, and there he took her like a wild animal, making her scream with both pleasure and pain.

But today was different from other days: Four days without him made her crazy, and the fire in her loins was hot. She rocked him like a tempest rocks a boat at sea. Soon, the screams were not her own; they were his, and the brutal, needy grunts and groans shook the walls as violently as they shook the bed. When they were done, Odí and her lover lay entwined, spent and panting like animals. Still gasping for breath, he said, "I can't do this anymore. I need you. All the time."

"And I need you." A single tear slid down her cheek. "I love my husband, and don't want to embarrass him by leaving him; but I'm in love with you . . . passionately, feverishly, hopelessly in love with you." He lay on his back, his hands behind his head so his chiseled body was stretched and tight; and she lay on her side, grinding her body into his side hungrily while she raked her nails against his neck and shoulders. Despair and desire made her crazy, and waves of pleasure erupted in her again. She cried out; and when she was silent once more, panting, she saw that her lover held a small glass vial.

"This is the answer to all our problems," he said, and he handed her the potion.

Odí looked at it, still stunned from the pleasure. It was a simple stopper vial with no markings. As her mind cleared, she swallowed, and asked, "Is this poison? Do you mean to murder my husband?"

"No, Odí. It is not for your husband. It is for you. Drink it." He took the vial from her and pulled out the cork.

She bolted upright, pulling the sheets around her chest. "You want to poison me?" Her face paled with fear.

Seeing her terror, he put the stopper back in the vial, and sat it down on the bed. "It's not poison, Odí. But others will think it is." She looked at him, still fearful but now puzzled. "Odí, it's a potion that will put you into a very, very deep sleep. Your breathing will slow, and it will be so shallow that your chest will not rise and fall. The sound of life in your chest, your heart, will be imperceptible. It will beat so slowly and softly that no one will hear it, not unless they listen for a long, long time. One vial of this and you will sleep for three days. On the fourth day you will wake up. And by then, you will be resting in the forest at the feet of the Iroko, left for dead. Mofá won't be disgraced. He will be mournful. And everyone will mourn the loss of his beautiful wife with him."

Cautiously, she picked up the vial and lifted the cork. She sniffed at the lid. It smelled faintly of almonds. "They will think I killed myself with poison," she whispered.

"Yes, and on the fourth day, I will come find you, and we can move to a new town. Start over. Be together. And just to be safe, you can disguise yourself. You can change your style of dress. You can cut your hair short." He stopped, biting his lower lip, and gently, he took her hands in his. "Just don't cut these, your long, red nails. They make me crazy. I love them."

They sat there for quite some time, and when the shock of the vial wore off, she rested against his thick, chiseled chest, his arms wound tightly around her body, with her nails gently tickling the skin on his arms. When the sunlight in the room began to mute and the shadows stretched, she turned to him. "Mofá will be home soon, as will my son. You're sure this will work?"

"Positive," he said. "I bought two vials of the potion, and tried one on myself." He paused, holding her hands in his. "Where do you think I was the past three days? The world thinks I am dead! When I woke up, I was alone in the forest at the feet of an Iroko; I unwound the cloth binding me, and walked away." He smiled. "I would rather hurt myself than you. And as you can see, I woke up, and I'm fine."

"I love you," she said, tipping the open vial against her lips. It was sticky and sweet, and she swallowed it all in one gulp.

"I love you, too," he whispered, kissing her on the lips. That was all she remembered before the room went dark.

He left her lying naked, tangled in the sheets with the vial still in her hands. He crept out the back door just as Mofá and his son were coming through the front. And he heard their screams when they found Odí crumpled and lifeless in the bed.

☙☙

It seemed everyone in town mourned the death of Odí.

Mofá was an old man, but sorrow made him all the more frail, and his young son had to help him walk. Mourners came to their home, leaving more food than the two could eat in a year. The funeral dirge was simple, but long; and by sunset on the third day, Odí's body was laid to rest deep in the forest at the feet of the ancient Iroko. Carefully, she was wrapped in white linen; and when her stiff body fell to the side between the tree's great roots, Mofá fainted. Their son wailed. Gently, the mourners carried both back to town.

Sunset the fourth day, as he promised, Odí's lover knelt at her side, gently cutting away the strips of white linen binding her body. When her eyes fluttered open, he greeted her with a kiss. Odí was confused. It seemed that only a moment ago, they were together in her bed.

They made love there in the great tree's roots, and before sunset, the two set off to make a new life in a new town. Odí cut her braids; her hair was short, and she dressed as a pauper. She took up work in the local marketplace selling okra and other vegetables that she grew herself in her garden. Her new husband was a laborer, the reason for his well-muscled, sleek body, and although she lacked many of the luxuries she had with Mofá, she was happy with her new life.

Mofá, as well, moved on. Without his wife, his young son took up many of the household chores; and the old man did what the son could not finish. Still, Odí was always in his thoughts, and his heart. His love was pure; and no matter how many women came to court his affections, he only thought of one woman—Odí.

After months of mourning, Mofá was ready to go out into the world again, continuing his work as a diviner; and in time, it happened that he was called away to a neighboring town to divine for the village's king. Since there was no one at home to watch his ten-year-old boy, Mofá took his son with him, and when they arrived in the village, he gave his son money and told him, "Go to the market and wander there for a spell. When the sun starts to set, I want you back here at the king's home. We will leave town together tonight."

It was late afternoon when the young boy heard a voice like his mother's in the market. Over the din of the crowds, she was yelling out for buyers to come check her produce. "I have the finest okra in the village!" she yelled out; and he saw her holding up handfuls of the vegetable as she yelled.

When he saw the red nails, he thought he'd faint.

Slowly, with a gnawing pit in his stomach, the young boy walked up to the woman's booth; the closer he came, the more it looked like his mother. Her hair was short like a man's, but it was her face, her figure; and the red nails that stroked his head many a night as he lay down for sleep flashed and sparkled in the late afternoon sun. At the edge of the booth, with her back to him, he said one word. "Mom?" It was a plea, not a question; and the tears came from his eyes before she could turn and face him.

When Odí heard her son's voice, her heart broke, and then the broken fragments hardened; with fear chilling her skin, she turned and saw her son looking up at her, hot tears streaking his face. Trembling, Odí shook her head slowly. "No. What did you call me?"

"Mom?" His lower lip trembled, and his body shook.

"I don't know you, child. I am not your mother. Go home." She turned her back so the boy could not see her cry, and began to yell again, "I have the finest okra in the kingdom . . ."

Slowly, he backed away from her, and when the crowd closed around the booth and he could see Odí no longer, he turned and ran to the king's palace.

"Mom is alive!" he screamed as he grabbed his father's legs, hugging him tightly and trembling as tears came freely.

Mofá narrowed his eyes and stroked his boy's head lightly, and then, with great difficulty, he bent down on his aged knees and took the child's head in both of his hands. "What did you say?"

"Mom. Mom. She's alive." He stuttered and spit as he tried to get the words out.

The king walked to Mofá, putting his hand on his shoulder, gently.

"Is the boy okay? He looks as if he's seen a ghost. And isn't your wife dead?"

"She is," said Mofá, looking, puzzled, at his son.

"No, she's not!" The child screamed incredulously. "And she made me go away. Dad, she's alive. I saw her selling okra in the marketplace."

The king called his wife; and when she came, he put the boy's hand in hers. "Watch him," he said. "The child has had a great shock. We're going to the market to see the woman that sells okra."

"But he *recognized me*," Odí insisted as her new husband stood at her side. She was shaking, trembling, and he held her head on his shoulder, rubbing her back lightly to console her.

"Are you sure it was your son?"

"He called me *Mom*!" Fear and sorrow turned her voice shrill. "I am supposed to be dead. Can you imagine how he feels?" Hot tears burned his shoulder as Odí cried.

He looked through the crowd suspiciously; while Odí mourned her son, he was worried that someone else might recognize them. "Then we're leaving this town tonight. I'll stay with you. We'll finish up here. And then we'll go home, grab our things, and move on." Odí lifted her head; her eyes were red and sore from crying. "We'll go so far away that no one will chance upon us."

Odí wiped her eyes with the backs of her hands; her red nails flashed brightly in the late afternoon sun. And then, she picked up a handful of okra and yelled, "I have the finest okra in the village . . ."

By horse the king and Mofá traveled: the king took his most trusted guards, and both were in the center of a heavily-armed caravan galloping furiously through the kingdom, to the marketplace. Villagers saw the royal entourage's approach; they grabbed their children and moved to the sides of the streets so they could pass quickly. It took little time for the group to arrive at the marketplace.

Over the din of the market, Mofá listened to the hawkers, and he froze when he heard his wife's voice, but faintly, "Okra! I have the freshest okra in the entire village!" Wearily, he sank down against his horse, covering his face with his palms. Tears slid down his cheeks.

"Mofá?" asked the king, "Is it your wife?"

Mofá's eyes were reddened when he lifted his head. "It sounds like her voice. But it can't be. She's dead. I watched as her lifeless body was wrapped by the priests; I was there when it was set to rest at the Iroko's feet. But that voice . . . it sounds like her. Maybe that is why my son thought it was his mother. But it can't be her."

"Are you sure?" asked the king. "Your son was . . . convinced . . . that it was her. Let us take a closer look."

As they approached the vender's booth, villagers moved to the side when they realized it was the king traveling with the royal entourage, and the woman at the booth was at first confused, and then pleasantly surprised when she saw the king on his horse. "Sire," she said, curtseying a bit in obeisance, "it is a pleasure to have you here. Have you heard about my okra?" Her new husband was turned away from the king, scanning the gathering crowd for signs of Mofá or his son. But the old man was so well hidden by the guards that he didn't see him sitting on his horse, his eyes burning with both sadness and rage.

The king dismounted slowly, and the guards pulled their horses to the side so he could walk through. "No, I haven't heard about your okra. But I am here on business."

"And what would that be?"

"What is your real name, lady?"

"My name?"

Mofá dismounted; and while Odí was distracted by the king's presence, he walked to the booth, his mouth hanging open in disbelief. "It is you?" he whispered. The man sitting beside Odí tried to stand, tried to run, but the guards dismounted quickly and detained him.

"What?" she asked, turning pale when she turned and saw Mofá standing before her. Both hands went to her chest, and slowly, she backed away.

"My son . . . our son . . . was right. It is you."

"I don't have a son," she stammered, and she watched as the crowd closed in around her booth. They were curious as to the king's business with her, and they were quiet, listening.

"You do have a son. We have a son together, Odí. I know it's you. The hair is shorter. Your clothes are raggedy. But your voice is unmistakable, and your long, red nails give you away. After twenty years together, did you think I'd not recognize my own wife if I saw her?"

"She's *my wife*!" hissed the man; he was struggling against the guards as they held him. "You're crazy, old man!" A fist pummeled the back of his head; it was one sharp blow, and he fell to his knees in pain. The guard twisted his arm behind his back, holding him down so he could not move.

"Is this true?" the king asked the woman. "Are you Odí? Are you Mofá's wife? And is this new man now your husband?"

She stammered.

"Are you sure this is your wife?" the king asked Mofá.

"I am sure."

The king motioned to his guards; quickly, they restrained the woman while the king addressed the town. "Good people, as you all know, Mofá is one of the wisest diviners in all the land. Months ago, his wife died, and she left behind a loving husband and a young son. And now, after months of mourning, Mofá and his son find her here, in the arms of another man."

Odí twisted free from the guards and fell at the feet of her lover; in surprise, the guard let loose of the young man, and they clung to each other fearfully while the guards encircled them both. "What is the punishment for adultery in our land?" asked the king of the growing crowd.

"It is death!" offered one of the villagers. Quickly, one by one, the crowd began chanting, "Death. Death. Death. Death."

"But what of my son?" whispered Mofá to the king. "What will we tell him?"

"We tell him that he was mistaken. We tell your son that the woman could have been a dead ringer for your wife, but simply, it was not her. He doesn't have to know anything more than that."

Mofá nodded his head sadly, and walked away.

Before sunset, the townspeople had stoned Odí and her lover to death; and to make sure the two of them stayed dead, instead of laying them at the feet of the Iroko, they were buried deep in the earth so they would never rise again.

And this is why we say, in Odí, that the hole (the grave) was first opened; and that the wages for adultery are death.

He Who Fights Knows about War

Growling like a hungry beast, Ogún crept through the streets of Ikoyi, slicing at the air with an iron machete as if clearing brush from the forest. His eyes were glazed with exhaustion and anger, and if he saw the fearful villagers cowering away from him, he did not care. Men grabbed their wives, women grabbed their children, and they cowered in allies and ditches as Ogún thundered by. He spoke, and his voice seemed like thunder in the clear afternoon sky, "Only those who fight know about war!"

It was a bad omen. When Ogún was heated beyond the point of reasoning, everyone knew war was imminent, and until blood ran, there was no cooling the orisha. The King of Ikoyi knew his people had to fight if they were to save themselves, so he went to Elegguá to consult. The orisha marked ebó. "If you want not only to win but also to survive, you must make ebó in the mountain," he said. "Obatalá is the king of war when it is fought for the sake of peace, and he will save you." The king agreed that he would make ebó. "But," said Elegguá, "your most powerful warrior is destined to lose his own life saving yours."

"Cesto?" asked the king. "Cesto has survived many wars. He is a brilliant warrior, and my best strategist. Are you sure he will die if he does not make ebó?"

"Is my name Elegguá?" asked the orisha.

The king told Cesto about Elegguá's words. He was not pleased. "Me? Die in a war?" Cesto asked. "That's absurd. I am the most powerful man in this kingdom. I am the fiercest fighter in the entire world!

I pity the man who tries to take me down; and I will keep you safe, King!"

"But Cesto, Elegguá said you would die saving me."

"Elegguá is a cheat and a liar. He does not know Cesto." He thumped on his chest with his fist, and walked away.

Elegguá heard everything; it was his nature to hear everything.

The King of Ikoyi made ebó in the mountain, and when he returned, the war began. Foreign armies invaded his cities, and the first arrow shot plunged into Cesto's chest as he tried to get the king to safety.

Cesto was dead. Elegguá walked to his lifeless body and said, "Now tell me that I am a cheat and a liar!" He walked away from the stunned king, whistling happily.

Still, the king had made ebó, and before the day ended, the invaders lay slain.

As the sun set, an exhausted Ogún walked through the streets calmly, his machete hanging limply at his side. As he walked, he said wearily, "Only those who fight know about war."

If the king knew nothing else that day, he knew about war.

8

Unle

Eight Mouths on the Mat

Teach me how to divine so that I may know how to divine. Teach me how to appease the orishas so that I may appease the orishas. Teach me how to prescribe sacrifices so that I may prescribe sacrifices. For wisdom is all that I am seeking, and this wisdom will be my wealth.

Having opened with eight mouths on the mat, the ritual of diloggún becomes a solemn but joyous occasion. The reading transcends to a time marking not only the beginning of creation but also the dissolution of all things. To borrow a metaphor from the Christian faith, one might call this odu the alpha and omega; it is the father of the odu, spiritually speaking, and its power is transcendent. Babalawo Fa'Lokun Fatunmbi writes of this odu, "[It is] the primal impulse for expansion, evolution, and ascension . . . a way of knowing that involved the whole being and not just the intellect."* This letter is the eldest of the elders, the raw energy expanding and awakening in the east, and it is the path by which all spirits began their descent to Earth. Its primal stirring created light, holy and infinite, a white fire consuming that void. Its

---

*Awó Fa'Lokun Fatunmbi, *Awó: Ifá and the Theology of Orisha Divination* (New York: Original Publications, 1992), 138.

movements birthed the Irunmole, those orishas who sprang from Heaven with Olódumare's first thoughts. In short, Unle is life, and life is Unle.

The oral corpus of the root odu, Unle, contains no less than one hundred patakís detailing his works as a mortal, earthbound creature. Most of our knowledge of this odu's ashé comes from these stories. Choosing those I felt most vital to illustrating this pattern's importance to the diloggún was no easy task. Unle had no earthly parents; he was a direct emanation of Olódumare, a creature born with the ultimate gift of wisdom and divination, and I felt this was the most important message to relay through my writing. Unle simply was not, and then he was; and he found himself sent to Earth with one purpose—to help the world overcome its inherent osogbo, the misfortunes that plagued humanity for no other reason than to create torment and discord. Torn between wealth (owó) and wisdom (omá), as most fleshly creatures are, he was taught by Elegguá that the true path to wealth was education, for education brings wisdom. Armed with a superior spiritual education, Unle found that owó (a jealous mistress by all means) sought him out jealously as he pursued omá exclusively.

In my opinion, this is one of Unle's greatest teachings, and one that not only the Lucumí but also the world at large should emulate.

Of course, no discussion of Unle is complete without a brief examination of Obatalá and his (or her) role in this family of odu. Like the odu Unle, Obatalá's only concern was the nurturing of the world and the human race, both of which he had a heavy hand in creating. Obatalá is an orisha teaching us the value of selflessness and self-sacrifice, and selflessly he sacrificed himself through both hard labor and a sense of duty toward all Olódumare entrusted to him. The story "Obatalá Eats Heads" has a macabre tone in its title, but it shows how, through hard work and sense of purpose, one can evolve and rise above the toil of existence to become king. It is here that Obatalá found his true purpose— to be the ruler of all the orishas in Heaven, and his selfless sacrifices rewarded him with the keys to the Kingdom of Heaven.

Hard work, selfless sacrifice, and an undying sense of duty are the very things that push us beyond our station in life to true greatness.

If the patakís of Unle teach us nothing else, they teach us that hard work, a superior education, good character, and a willingness to do what Olódumare has given us to do reap rewards beyond our greatest imaginings. Each of the stories I chose for this chapter illustrates these things, and more.

Unle Is Born

It was early morning, but still night, and Olódumare was alone, standing motionlessly on a balcony overlooking both Heaven and Earth. His eyes were closed to what lay before him: His mind was focused on things in other worlds. So deep was his concentration, so motionless was his body, that he seemed a black marble statue, permanently poised over creation. A light breeze lifted the diaphanous robes swathing his body; they filled the room behind him with their fullness as they twisted and turned in the night air.

God took a deep breath and opened his eyes as if he had only blinked. He lifted his arms to the sky and felt warmth as the sun rose above the eastern horizon. The sun, the body of Olorún, as it had for thousands of years, trailed above, slowly dispensing ashé throughout creation.

"As above, so below," he whispered, knowing that as Olorún spread ashé through Heaven, he was also spreading it on Earth.

Olódumare, unmoving, again seemed a marble statue on his balcony as he delighted in the warmth on his face. The muted morning light made his black skin seem phosphorescent and rich.

Then came the predictable morning knock at his chamber's door: Every morning, there was a knock at his door, some new soul who yearned to travel to earth, experiencing life. Today, however, this knock came earlier than usual.

In a single motion as fluid and effortless as breathing, Olódumare withdrew from his balcony, and seated himself in his throne. His light, gauzy robes were still drifting and trailing through the air as he extended a hand toward the door, and bid it open.

It was Unle, and the odu stiffened with awe as he stood in the

doorway and saw God for the first time. Sitting in state, his statu-
esque quality returned, and had it not been for the supple sheen of
his face, or the soft glow of omnipotence in his eyes, Unle would have
thought him a statue. But most impressive to Unle were Olódumare's
white robes. It seemed God wrapped himself in all that was pure and
clean, a tapestry of white light, not cloth.

For what seemed an eternity, Unle stood and gazed at his creator.
Ashé filled the room; it suffused everything in it and swallowed Unle
like a hungry beast. It was love, it was life, it was power, and it was
thick. He could barely move.

Olódumare smiled, and that simple acknowledgment brought tears
to Unle's eyes. Finally, he knew God was seeing him face-to-face; it was
intimate, like the love a father feels for his child or a woman for her
lover. Having no words to express the feelings welling up in his heart,
Unle, his head bowed in submission, approached the throne, and put
himself on the floor in reverence.

He felt strong hands on his shoulders; fingertips brushed him firmly
and sent currents of ashé through his body as the rich, elderly voice
intoned, "May you be blessed. Arise!" Strong arms lifted him, embraced
him, and for a moment Unle forgot he was Unle, and he was one with
Olódumare.

Gently, Olódumare broke the embrace, and Unle shivered. It was
loss, it was sadness, it was separation, and for a moment he couldn't bear
it until God spoke, "Why have you come, Unle?" It was an invitation to
speak, not a question. God knew everything.

"I have come to request my destiny on Earth." Unle's voice wavered,
and it ended in a whisper. A destiny on Earth meant a separation from
Heaven. Here, in God's presence, he couldn't bear that thought.

Olódumare touched Unle's chin firmly, and lifted his head so their
eyes met. "What would you like to do on Earth, my son?"

A thousand and one desires rose in his thoughts, but Olódumare's
voice plunged deep inside, pulling Unle's true destiny to the surface.
And before he could answer willingly, he found himself saying, "I want
to help others."

"How would you help others, Unle?"

Again, Unle thought of the many things he wanted to do; but again, Olódumare's question touched something deep inside him, and Unle found himself saying, "Teach me how to divine so that I may know how to divine. Teach me how to appease the orishas so that I may appease the orishas. Teach me how to prescribe sacrifices so that I may prescribe sacrifices. For wisdom is all that I am seeking, and this wisdom will be my wealth."

"Wisdom and knowledge are your grace. But what you accomplish with your long life and wisdom is in your hands. As a diviner, you will know how to avoid all manner of misfortune and bring all types of blessings to yourself. Use those gifts wisely."

Olódumare stretched out his hands, taking Unle's head into them. He felt a powerful ashé flowing; it was warm like fire, yet liquid like water, and he shuddered as God cried, *"Fun mi ashé lenu lati nsoro. Ashé tó, ashé bó, ashé bima! Ashé ishe'mi!"** His voice caused the very fabric of Heaven to rumble and shudder, and in his hands appeared a wizened, humbled head. It was Unle's new head, the one that would accompany him to Earth. Olódumare whispered, "Good luck, my son."

Unle was in Heaven no more.

There came another knock on Olódumare's door . . .

Unle remembered very little of that day in Heaven when he requested his destiny; the trauma of forced separation buried the knowledge of perfect love and union with Olódumare. To remember the loss would be too painful, and in his wisdom, God blotted it out. But he knew he always existed. He knew that as God unfolded, becoming self-aware, he was one of the first-born, and he knew that he had no mortal parents on Earth save Olófin. Unle knew, and remembered, that unlike the other odu who came to Earth before him, forced to endure mortal childhoods, their memories of Heaven erased by undeveloped brains incapable of holding even shadows of their former selves, he simply

---

*"Give my tongue the ashé with which to speak. Ashé is sufficient; ashé envelops all; ashé is born. Ashé, work for me!"

was a grown man. The natural law of birth did not apply to him.

As he pondered this mystery, the sense of separation from Heaven deepened until he could take it no more. Unle almost regretted being on Earth. He looked up into the sky and tried to see Heaven, but all he could see were white, amorphous clouds that rolled lazily through a backdrop of blue. As he strained to see beyond the clouds, to see his true home, Unle felt a familiar sensation welling up in his heart, a tingling that he could only describe as ashé. It filled him, and he realized that Heaven wasn't as far away as he thought.

He looked at the world around. It was like Heaven, but different; it was alive in ways Unle had never experienced. Everything had weight; Unle felt the weight of his own body, and tried to move. The act was . . . pleasurable. As his mind opened to the new possibilities the mortal world encompassed, Unle felt two forces at war with each other: iré (blessings) and osogbo (misfortunes). The iré in the world brought him joy, but the misfortunes he sensed brought him sorrow, and stained his pure heart.

"I can help all these people who live here," he thought, "with my skills of divination."

Unle walked; his mortal body felt alive in ways his heavenly body never provided. After some time, he felt a new sensation: thirst. He stopped at a river to drink. The current was slow, and Unle saw his own reflection. His face was that of a young man. "This can't be right," thought Unle. "This isn't the head that Olódumare gave me in Heaven."

Unle was confused, but he wasn't worried. He came to Earth by Olódumare's grace with a working knowledge of divination and ebó. He knew how to help people overcome misfortune and lock in blessings. He set out to do just that—help people overcome the misfortune in their lives, and evolve. He had faith, and with that faith he knew all things in his life would work out in time.

Unle's Ebó to Elegguá

Unle knew of the orisha Elegguá. He was on Earth, but immortal, and he was young, yet as ancient as the first stirrings of the universe itself. Elegguá was the witness to all things, the one orisha who was with Olódumare when he first awakened in Heaven and began to create. Unle sought Elegguá at the crossroads that separated Earth from Heaven.

The orisha knew Unle was coming. Elegguá knew that Unle was coming to make ebó. The odu found him there, waiting, and he pampered and plied him with gifts of fruits and cooked foods that he made with his own hands. For what seemed an eternity, the orisha did not speak. He ate and ate. Ate and ate. Ate and ate. Finally, when he was sated, Elegguá looked to Unle and smiled.

"What do you want?" he asked.

Unle prostrated himself before the orisha, and as he bid him to rise, Unle embraced Elegguá and said, "Life is hard, and I want to be prosperous. How may I ensure the blessing of owó in my life?"

Elegguá smiled. "Owó is a jealous master," he said, his eyes narrowing in thought. "He is always jealous of Omá. Ignore Owó for Omá. Follow and pursue Omá relentlessly, never looking back for Owó. Owó will follow you, Owó will watch you, and Owó will try to seduce you with her gifts. The more you ignore her, the more she will offer and throw in your path."

Elegguá stood tall and said, "To become prosperous, wisdom is what you must seek, and that wisdom will be your wealth."

Unle thought about this silently under Elegguá's watchful eyes. Finally, he asked, "How may I acquire the wisdom of which you speak?"

"To acquire wisdom, you must serve each of your elders for eight years. Through service you will learn wisdom. At the end of that time, with the wisdom you acquire, you will use that wisdom to create wealth and abundance in your own life."

Unle thanked Elegguá for his advice, and he sought out his elders. He served each of them for eight years, and learned not only what they taught openly, but the secrets they hid even from each other. At the end of that time, there was no one on Earth whose wisdom was greater than Unle's, and even though he was now an old man, he used his wisdom to create wealth and live comfortably throughout his old age. Unle gazed at himself in a mirror, and saw the very face that Olódumare had given him in Heaven staring back at him. He knew that it was time to fulfill his destiny on Earth.

These are the stories of how he did this.

Unle Builds a Home

After years of wandering and serving his elders, Unle was no longer a young man. His body was old, his energy was fading, and he knew it was time to build a home of his own, ceasing his travels. Wanting to live someplace serene and quiet, he searched the coast of West Africa until he came to a small village.

It was well populated, but not overly so, and Unle noticed that the people who lived there were the saddest, most miserable humans he had ever seen. "I can help these people with my work," he thought. With his earnings as a diviner, Unle hired the strongest and most skilled of the villagers to build a modest home; and although it was modest, it was still grander than the homes of those who were his neighbors. They were envious.

When his home was done, Unle moved in, and he divined for himself. Eight mouths opened on the mat. Unle said, "Death [Ikú] held me and left me. Sickness [the sisters Aro and Ano] embraced me and fled. I have survived the evil plans of my enemies." He marked ebó for himself; he made ebó, and the orishas told him that he was to offer all manner of food, drink, and kindness to any strangers who came to visit him. Unle vowed to prosper in his chosen home, and he resolved to do all the orishas told him.

Little did Unle know that the land he claimed as his own, while outwardly serene and beautiful, lay in the middle of the sixteen osogbos who chose to settle on Earth as well. It was for this reason that the villagers were sad and miserable—because misfortune plagued them all the time. Ikú, Ano, Aro, Eyo, Inya, Tiya-Tiya, Ona, Ofo, Ogo, Akoba, Fitibo, Égba, Arayé, Oran, Epe, and Ewon (osogbos personifying various types of misfortunes and evils) all owned sixteen plots of land between them, and their lands encircled the village with a vice grip. Each owned an equal expanse of forest around one central plot; this land in the center was the most beautiful and fertile, while the sixteen plots around that were almost equally so, but to avoid fights about who would have the absolute best, they decided to keep that land neutral and in the center of them all. And as humans sought new places to conquer and live, the osogbos were glad to let them settle in their midst; the misery they brought the humans brought joy to their hearts. But they could sense that Unle was different. He had ashé. And while the osogbos weren't yet sure what that gift entailed, they sensed it would loosen their grip on the world.

Unle was a skilled diviner, and people from far lands sought him out. They would travel through the abodes of the osogbos on their way to visit Unle and make ebó, and there, at the mat, Unle would know the osogbo whose land they had traveled through, and he would mark ebó so the osogbo could no longer hurt his client. Quickly they would make ebó, and this would only anger the osogbos more when they would travel back through their lands, and they were powerless to touch them again.

That night, Ikú, Ano, and Aro met in darkness; the night was cold, and they lit a fire against the chill. Some time passed awkwardly as they warmed themselves. Finally, Ano spoke. "Unle is an arrogant man. The world is a huge place, yet he chose to settle in our midst. I will drive him out. I will visit him tonight!"

"And what will you do? Give him a cold?" taunted Aro. "Unle may be elderly, but he's an extremely healthy man. Any illness you give is fleeting, easily cured." She gazed into the fire and smiled. "No, let me go tonight. I will visit him and make his remaining existence miserable."

Ikú frowned. "So you give him a lasting illness, Aro? And make him weak? He's already an old man. He is weak. And while he suffers from your visitation, he will still remain in our midst. He will wither for years, and not only will we have to put up with him, but also his brothers and sisters and godchildren as they make their way to pay their respects and nurse him back to health. And let us not forget that the other odu and diviners are powerful; even if you vex him well, there is still a chance that one of them might have the power to destroy us. No, let me visit him tonight. Death is the only way to be rid of him. Not even the orishas can bring back the dead."

The three osogbos came to an agreement: Ikú would be the one to visit Unle, for death was the only way to remove the old man from their midst. Each supplied Ikú with their power. Ano gave him all the fleeting illnesses of the world to use against Unle, and her sister, Aro, gave Ikú all the lasting, terminal diseases she had at her disposal. Ikú hid all these under her cloak; it swayed and billowed with their evil, as if whipping in an unfelt wind. Blessed with all the gifts of the two sisters, Ikú stole away, invisible to the world, to Unle's palace.

As Ikú scraped at the front door, seeking entrance, Unle felt her presence. He called out to the night, "Who is here?" as he opened his front door in welcome, remembering his own divination from when he came to Earth. "I can't see you, but I can feel you; I know that a powerful spirit has come to visit me tonight. Show yourself, and let us know one another."

Unle knew that it was Death herself who had come to visit him; and he knew that Ikú only came when it was time to die. Yet Unle was a wise odu, and he knew many ways to thwart death for a time. Ikú, surprised at the warm welcome by the naive man, called together a disguise; she presented herself as a middle-aged woman, pleasant to gaze at, but worn from years of toil. As her disguise coalesced and congealed, Unle was surprised. He had expected a fearful specter, but found Ikú to be warm, almost inviting. Still, Unle was not ready to die, and he intended to stretch out his time on the newly created earth.

Before Ikú could strike, Unle offered her a place to sit and rest her weary feet. Quickly, he offered her food and drink, bringing out all the already prepared foods he had from that day. As they spoke, Unle busied himself in the kitchen, and before Ikú could remember why she was at his house, the odu presented her with a wide array of yams, fruits, meats, and desserts. Unle continued to distract the osogbo with warm conversation while she gorged herself on the food before her; she was so full that she was lazy. And while Unle chatted on, Ikú thought to herself, "I can't ever remember a victim who has fed me so well!"

Then, she rose to strike; only she was so gorged that she could barely move. Unle, sensing danger again, brought her a huge share of liquor and encouraged her to drink. So quickly did she drink, and so quickly did she become drunk, that she could no longer hold a coherent thought. She soon forgot why she had come to Unle's house. When Ikú was beyond intoxicated, Unle gasped and said, "Why, it is nearly morning, and we have been up all night eating and drinking. I have a long day ahead of me, and I must have at least a few hours' sleep." He helped Ikú up from her chair, where she was all but passed out. "Before you leave, my friend, let me offer you this, the fattest chicken from my coop. I am sure you have a large family yourself, and will need to feed them, too, when you get home." Ikú was so drunk, so full, so tired, and so confused that she could only thank Unle for his hospitality, and with the night slowly melting as sunrise approached, she left.

It was morning when Ikú stumbled back to the embers that remained of their fire. She was visibly drunk and gorged, and the two sisters were angry when they saw she returned without Unle's soul. Aro hissed, "Why did you not kill him like you promised? He still intrudes on our land!"

"You dared taunt me, Aro, because all I could do was give him a cold? And you, Ikú, I had images in my head of you slicing and dicing him to pieces with your scythe. Instead, it seems you had a merry time with the old man. Kill him indeed! Only way to get rid of him, indeed! You are a disgrace. At least if I'd gone, he'd be drowning in his own secretions by now!"

Ikú, shaken and dizzy, merely offered, "Perhaps we should just leave him alone?" She was still sated on Unle's kindness.

"We will finish what you could not do!" screamed Ano, as she took back all the misfortunes that she and her sister had piled upon Ikú. "You are useless. We will gather the other thirteen osogbos, my sister and I, and tonight we will rage upon Unle's home like a storm from Heaven. We will do what you could not!"

The sisters left Ikú there, by the fire, and soon she fell asleep.

Later that day, after Unle rested, he divined for himself once more. The diloggún told him that he was facing osogbo again, and quickly he made ebó with a goat, a ram, and sixteen roosters. With these he prepared a huge feast, and set his table for sixteen guests. He also laid out sixteen bolts of cloth as his divination demanded. Then, exhausted, he sat down to rest, and waited for his divination to fulfill itself.

It was at sunset that the fifteen remaining osogbos decided to assault Unle and his home; with them, they also brought Eshe, all the general afflictions of the world that they did not control amongst themselves. Because Unle already proved with Ikú that he could see them regardless of how they appeared, they came in their full power and normal forms, assaulting his home from without, seeking entrance.

Unle heard them as they scratched at his walls, and remembering how he was told to entertain all strangers that came to his home, he threw open his door and called out into the night, "Friends, it is cold outside and warm within my walls. Come inside, and let us know each other."

Aro called to the other osogbos, "This is too easy. To be invited is to guarantee one's own destruction. Follow me!"

All the osogbos rushed inside Unle's house, and the modest man was aghast at the nakedness of his guests. Before any of them could raise their hands against him, Unle gathered up the sixteen bolts of cloth and presented each osogbo with one. "Clothe yourselves," he offered, "for it is not seemly to be traveling naked."

Such was Unle's surprise and modesty that each osogbo blushed before him, and quickly they wrapped themselves with the cloth offered. As they dressed, he ushered them to his table where the feast had been prepared. It was then that Aro understood how Ikú was thwarted. "Old man," she hissed, "someone has told you our weaknesses. You know that we cannot harm those who offer us random kindness."

"No one has told me anything," insisted Unle.

"Someone must have!" The other osogbos, comfortable in their new clothing, were feasting, oblivious to Aro's growing frustration.

"I merely divined, and did what divination told me. I made ebó to the orishas, and then laid out this feast and waited for the guests I was told would come."

"You are a diviner? There is a diviner living in the midst of our kingdom?" Suddenly Aro knew why all those they afflicted were saved, and they remained powerless to destroy them after that. "Now we will lose all our powers in our own kingdoms."

"No one knows your secrets. I myself did not know, not until you told me just now. I only did for you what the orishas told me I must do to avoid misfortune: I received strangers with kindness. And now that I seem to know your greatest secret, I will do for you what I do for everyone who confides in me as a diviner. I will keep your confidence. Unfortunately, I must continue to help those that come to me for divination; those, I am afraid, will be saved from your evil if they choose to make ebó. But don't worry—not everyone who comes to me for divination makes ebó. Even if I continue my work, which I assure you, I will, you will still have plenty of victims to prey on."

Aro stood, confused, angry, and hurt; she had not yet put on the cloth, and she was cold. She had not yet touched the food, but hunger overwhelmed her.

"Come, lady; clothe yourself. And eat. The night is still young, and there is much to discuss, is there not?"

Aro smiled as she dressed herself. "It was Ikú herself who came to see you yesterday, and it is your kindness that kept her from killing you the moment she walked through the door. I am Ano, sickness, and it is your kindness now that keeps me from laying waste to you. No human, orisha, or odu has ever granted us such kindness. We will not harm you today. We won't harm you tomorrow. And, definitely, we won't harm you the day after that. But watch yourself, Unle; always remember us. For it is the nature of life to wither and die, and one day, while we won't come to you as an enemy, we will come to you again. It is what we do."

But that night, for once, all the osogbos were Unle's guests; he tended and treated them all well. And when the sun rose the next day, they parted as friends. True to his words, Unle remembered each of them with kindness and never betrayed their secrets; and since not all his clients who came for readings made the prescribed ebós, the osogbos still had their fill of human misfortune.

This is how Unle thwarted all the osogbos of the world with his wisdom and lived to a ripe old age, even in a land surrounded by misfortunes.

Unle Becomes a Farmer

"Lazy men may live by their wisdom, but fools will never know how to manage their affairs." This was the advice that the odu gave Unle when he was trying to determine how to earn his wealth in the world. For quite some time, he had worked as a diviner, and this had provided him an adequate living, but as people made ebó and loosened the chains of osogbo that were upon them, they came to visit Unle less and less. Having lost ultimate power in their lands, the osogbos had packed up and fled, and soon Unle was surrounded by humans who made their living through various means. Most of these were farmers. As the masses of clients seeking his wisdom slowed, Unle found his income dwindling, and soon had to decide what he would do to maintain his wealth on the earth. All his neighbors, too, wondered what Unle would do, for no one could live without a skill or trade. Finally, Unle announced to the world, "I have acres and acres of land for myself. I will be a farmer."

Everyone who knew Unle laughed. He lived alone; he had neither a wife nor children. He was elderly, and had not the strength to clear his own land, plant his own crops, or reap the harvest. Unle divined for himself as to how he was to become prosperous as a farmer, and the odu told him, "Lazy men live by their wisdom and become wealthy, but fools will never know how to manage their affairs." With that proverb in his heart, Unle set out to become a farmer.

He took the money he had saved and hired sixteen men to build three huge storehouses on already cleared land. One he built for corn. One he built for yams. One he built for beans. By his order, each storehouse was huge, large enough to hold more than half the crops produced by the surrounding village. All his neighbors laughed, for between his home and three storehouses, he had little land left that was clear for farming. He also had little wealth left on which he could live. But Unle had a plan.

The next morning, Unle went outside and on his remaining land, he built sixteen mounds of earth. In each mound he scattered seeds, not crops, but medicinal herbs that he knew could be used for curing a variety of illnesses. Lovingly he pushed them into the earth, and then carefully watered them so that the earth was not disturbed. He spent his day doing this, leisurely building mounds and sewing handfuls of seeds.

No one knew what he was planting, but everyone was sure that the harvest he reaped from such a small amount of seeds would barely fill the cupboards in his home. So they laughed, and watched.

"Don't laugh, neighbors," warned Unle. "For I am building up my farm, and in time you will all understand my wisdom."

Everyone forgot about Unle and his mounds; the harvest season came and went, and as was the usual, every farmer's storehouse was stuffed with an abundance of crops. Everyone's except Unle's. They sat empty and unused. But the seeds he planted did grow, and while everyone else was toiling to dig out roots and tubers, or shucking corn and beans, Unle was lazily hanging and drying his herbs by his fireplace. They were dried and ready for use when the first chill winds of winter came.

With those winds came sickness, epidemics, and plagues that threatened the lives of the farmers and their families. Knowing that Unle had knowledge and skills none of them possessed, when illness struck, they came to him for help. Unle provided them each with medicine, but in exchange for the medicines he owned, he charged eight sacks of beans, eight sacks of corn, and eight sacks of yams for each cure. Willingly were goods exchanged, and as each was cured of illness, more sick people came to him. In time, Unle's three huge storehouses were filled; he owned half of the village's wealth and harvests.

Word of his miraculous medicines spread beyond the village, and as they had when the earth was young and new, humans from all around came to be cured of the most heinous diseases. They brought corn, yams, and beans, but Unle's warehouses were full and he had no more room for such things. The price for his medicines changed. From each patient he cured, he exacted a promise of eight workers for eight days; and when the promised workers arrived, he set them to the task of clearing the forest that existed on his land. He had them strip and sand the wood, and he became wealthy off the sale of the lumber.

The colder months came, and with them an icy grip was over the land, and still, the sick came to him to be healed. But he had food. He had clear land with which to farm the next season. And he had wealth obtained from the sale of lumber. He continued to exact promises of workers for eight days in exchange for his medicines, and when the warmer months came, and sickness again left the land, he called upon those who owed him, one at a time, to send in their debts. This he did, one set at a time, throughout the planting and harvesting season. Because he had such an abundance of manual labor, Unle soon had the most productive farm in all the land; and he himself passed his time by leisurely growing medicinal herbs by his house for the next cold season.

This is how Unle became a wealthy farmer.

Obatalá Eats Heads

Olófin wakened.

As he had for centuries, he woke early, and his mortal body was weary. Flesh had many advantages, but weariness was not one of them. Day after day, he worked on the earth directing the orishas in their affairs: He nurtured them as they created; he calmed them when there was chaos; and he judged them when there was conflict.

He held up his withered hands, turning them to look at the back and the front. "They are old. They are tired." He sighed. "I am old. I am tired."

Something changed in Olófin that morning, just before the sun began its daily ascent in the eastern sky. Exhaustion overwhelmed him, and he knew he was done. With a deep breath, and a tear in his eye, he lifted his arms to Heaven, calling Olódumare to bring him home.

All creatures great and small felt Olófin's departure. In the twilight before dawn, the air grew thick, oppressive with its weight, and a great wind swept over the earth. The world shuddered; then, everything was quiet.

Olófin was gone, but no one panicked at first. Travel between Heaven and Earth was an easy thing for an orisha; for them, the wise one was only a footstep away. Unknown to anyone but Olófin, however, Olódumare closed and locked the gates between the realms.

"How will they come to me when they need me?" Olófin complained to God.

"You are retired from earthly work now," Olódumare told him. "You will pick another to lead them on Earth."

"How do I choose?"

"That is up to you. When you have decided, I will reopen the gates so you can make your announcement."

It took many days and many nights for Olófin to decide, and during that time, the earth fell into chaos. Like a slaughtered and dying beast with no head, the orishas worked blindly on the earth, exhausting their collective strength. Without Olófin's guidance, they all fell apart. Only the most aged among them, Obatalá, continued to toil in spite of his exhaustion, and while he worked, the other orishas argued about who should be the new king.

"I should be the new king," Shangó announced. "I am a warrior and have the strength to protect us all!"

"Why can there not be a queen?" asked Oyá. "I wield the machete as well as you, Shangó. I carry the flywhisk that frightens Ikú and all osogbo. I control the first and the last breath, bringing life or death!"

Yemayá put her hands on her hips. "My waters cleanse the world of everything. There is no force on Earth more powerful than my oceans. Because of my strength, I should be the queen."

"But I control everything that makes life worth living!" insisted Oshún. "I should rule this world."

Their arguments became feverish, and Olófin heard them all. Watching the chaos unfolding on the earth below, he made his decision quickly and invited everyone to a formal dinner for his announcement.

Olódumare unlocked the gates so the orishas could cross into Heaven to Olófin's palace. They traveled quickly, and only Obatalá remained on the earth. He continued to labor in everyone's absence. "There is too much work to do," he lamented. "It is better that I stay behind and work."

As the evening began, elaborate place settings awaited each orisha at the banquet table. Shangó found his spot in front of the red and white bowl and plate, feeling special because his seat was at Olófin's right hand. "This is a good sign!" Shangó thought to himself, "to be seated at Olófin's right hand. He has picked me as the head of all the orishas!"

The other men found their places quickly, and stood politely as the women wandered around the table, finding their assigned seats. Yemayá stood in front of the blue and white china; and across from her stood Oyá, her place setting a deep, rich burgundy. She smiled a coy smile at her sister and nodded to her in respect as Oyá bowed her head in acknowledgment.

As Oshún made her way to the table, she breathed in deeply, crossing her hands over her heart and smiling warmly at Olófin. Her plate and her bowl were made from deeply polished brass, so smooth she could see her reflection, and her utensils were pressed from fine gold. "Olófin!" she said, almost a whisper but full of delight, "you honor me with your graciousness."

"Beauty such as yours deserves the best," he said. Shangó rushed to her side, holding her seat and pushing it close to the table as she sat. They exchanged a lustful glance. Oyá shuddered, and Yemayá pretended not to notice. Following Shangó's lead, the men pulled the chairs out from the table, offering the women their seats, and gently pushed them close to the table. When all the women were seated, the men seated themselves. Everyone looked to Olófin, as he was the eldest at the table.

"Where is Obatalá?" he asked. A murmur rose as everyone questioned everyone else as to the orisha's whereabouts, and everyone looked to the vacant seat at the head of the table, across from Olófin. His white plate, bowl, and cup were untouched; his seat remained tucked in at the head of the table. "Has anyone seen Obatalá?"

No one answered. After several moments of confused conversation, Olófin called to his servants. "We eat without him."

Servants removed the empty place setting, and brought huge serving trays of food to the table. One by one, each server served the orishas, offering a wide array of meats, vegetables, and desserts. Hungrily, they piled their plates with food, and when everyone's plates were full, they looked toward Olófin, the eldest at the table.

The elder stood. Looking at the guests individually as he spoke, he addressed them. "You all know that tonight is a special night. I have put a lot of thought into this dinner. Why? I have retired from the earth, and in my absence, one of you must serve as the head of all the orishas. I know you are all anxious to hear my decision, and I am anxious to make it. First, we feast. After dinner, I will tell you all who rules in my absence." Olófin sat; he looked around the room one more time, frowning a bit when he saw Obatalá's seat still empty. With dozens of hungry eyes watching him, he lifted his fork, and took his first bite. With that formality over, everyone began feasting.

Olófin ate very slowly, so they spent hours at the dinner table.

It was late when Obatalá finished his day's work; his hands were soiled and his clothes lightly stained when his stomach made its first hungry rumble. The old man rubbed it lightly, straightening and stretching his stiff back. "I am done with my work, and I am hungry!" Then he remembered, "I could go to Olófin's banquet, but I am very late." He looked down at himself, sighing. "I am a mess." He looked up at the sky, and saw the sun sliding down the western horizon. "I have no time to clean up." His hunger outweighed the embarrassment of his soiled cloths, and he left for Olófin's palace.

Nervous chatter filled the dining room; all the orishas were stuffed and sleepy, but no one could leave the table because Olófin still nibbled from his plate, slowly. Mindlessly he chewed, staring at Obatalá's empty chair. Everyone thought he was sad that Obatalá did not come.

Little did they know that he was simply waiting for him to arrive.

Shangó was the first to grow impatient, "Father?" He touched Olófin's arm gently. "We have been sitting here for many hours. May we get up?"

As if awakening from a deep sleep, Olófin looked at Shangó. He sipped from his water glass and swallowed before speaking. "What did you ask, son?"

Yemayá interrupted. "He asked if we might be excused, Olófin," she said, impatiently but politely. "We have been here a long time."

They were silent, waiting for Olófin to kiss his fingertips and touch the table, excusing everyone. The servants lined up against the wall, each ready to remove the plates, two at a time.

The elder put his fingertips to his lips, about to kiss them, when another servant escorted Obatalá into the room. "I am so sorry. My apologies to you all," the aged orisha said, bowing his head humbly. "Olófin, there is so much work to do in your absence, and I was so caught up in it that I almost forgot tonight was your special night."

Quickly, a servant brought Obatalá's place setting back to the table, and offered him his chair. "There is no need to apologize, Obatalá. But we have been feasting for hours, and I am afraid there is not much left to offer you."

"I am grateful for whatever you give me, Father. You are always a generous host."

The server who seated the orisha brought a tray of meat; everything had been picked through except the delicately roasted heads. "This is all we have left?" asked Olófin.

"Father, it is enough." The men sat back in their seats, arms crossed over their chests as Obatalá ate; the women pushed their chairs back and to the side, crossing their legs impatiently. Olófin kept them all trapped at the table while Obatalá ate, and everyone talked among themselves as Olófin watched them all.

The meat found in the head is a delicate meat, sweet and delicious;

but it is a difficult meat to eat because of all the tiny, razor-sharp bones. In spite of his hunger, Obatalá ate slowly and carefully to avoid cuts and scrapes. When he was sated, he kissed his fingertips and touched his plate.

"May we be excused now?' Shangó asked impatiently. "It is time for you to tell us who will rule during your absence!"

Olófin looked at Shangó as he kissed his fingertips and touched his plate; the servers came quickly, gathering the plates two at a time. Shangó was the first to stand; he was pushing his chair under the table when Olófin grabbed his wrist gently and held his other hand up to silence all the orishas. "Shangó, tell me—what did you eat today? Of all the meats that I served, what did you choose?"

"I ate the beef tongue, Olófin. It was delicious."

"And why, out of all the food I served, did you choose the tongue?"

Shangó smiled; he felt that Olófin was testing his wisdom, and he wanted to be wise. "I ate the tongue because tongue is the best food and the worst food in the world. With the tongue, one can create a kingdom or destroy the world! It is full of ashé!" He smiled and puffed up his chest proudly. Shangó was sure Olófin was about to appoint him head of all the orishas.

Instead, Olófin released his gentle grip on Shangó's wrist and turned his attention to Yemayá. "What did you eat this evening, Yemayá?"

She smiled at Olófin. "I ate the liver. Just as my life-giving waters cleanse the earth of evil, so does one's liver cleanses the body of impurities. It is full of ashé!"

"You are very wise, Yemayá!" said Olófin. Shangó glared at her; Yemayá only smiled at him. "And you, Oshún, what meat did you enjoy today?"

Oshún smiled sweetly, folding her hands over her heart as she looked at the floor humbly. "I ate the heart, because without the heart no one can live. No one can love. Without a heart, life itself . . . is meaningless." A single tear slid down her cheek.

"Of all Olódumare's creations on this earth, you, Oshún, are the most exquisite. You are lovely, and you are loved by all things great and small!"

Olófin turned to look at Oyá. "What did you enjoy from the feast today, Oyá?"

"I ate the tail, because with the tail you can scare things away, and I ate the lungs, for without those we cannot breathe."

Finally, Olófin turned to Obatalá. "What did you enjoy today, Obatalá?"

"When I arrived, all that was left were the heads of the animals. I was late; no one waited for me, so I ate those."

"Without the head, no one can live: Without a head, the orishas cannot function. The head you ate, and the head you will ever be," said Olófin. The orishas were all stunned; this was his decision, his choice for their new king. Everyone prostrated themselves before Obatalá, one by one, and humbly, Obatalá blessed them and bid them to rise.

That is how Obatalá became the king of all the orishas, and that is why we say, "Obatalá eats heads!"

9

Osá

Nine Mouths on the Mat

*When the winds of Osá blow, everything changes: life
becomes death, and death becomes life; the great fall, and
the fallen rise; those who betray are besieged by betrayal,
and the best friend becomes one's worst enemy.*

Opening with nine mouths on the mat, the diloggún sits before the
diviner in an explosive yet mysterious pattern. Osá is open. This odu
represents the destructive side of nature, the forces that cause one quality to mutate into its opposite. Floods, hurricanes, tornadoes, typhoons,
earthquakes, volcanic eruptions, and forest fires all derive their destruc-
tiveness from this sign. While its aggressive nature may seem frightening, in truth it is only a part of the renewal of Olódumare's designs.
Our world is neither stable nor stagnant; everything moves in a continual cycle of change, destruction, and creation to revive and revitalize
the earth. To grow, there must be decay; this feeds new growth. Birth
guarantees death. Osá ensures that this cycle moves continually but
randomly. To understand the odu's power, meditate on its symbols: the
wind, the market, the cemetery gates, and the moment between life and
death. Each of these shows the eternal yet ephemeral transition, something predictable in occurrence but not in time. Osá warns us that all
things will change, and there is nothing we can do to avoid it.

Yet these are Osá's qualities on a macrocosmic level, and in the ritual of diloggún divination, these have little to do with a client's day-to-day life. To apply these universal themes to an individual's life, one must think in terms of both personal evolution and humanity's daily trials—trials endured for no reason other than we are ephemeral, mortal beings. Death, then, becomes a central theme to this odu; and death affects us in ways that have far-reaching consequences.

I chose two of the stories in this chapter for just that reason: "The Death of His Love" and "A Son's Loss." The first story, "The Death of His Love," investigates what happens to those left behind when Ikú takes a life suddenly and without warning. There are many patakís in the corpus of Osá investigating what happens to loved ones when something they care about is swept away suddenly to the next world; however, in my research I stumbled across a story few know about, a patakís that speaks of what happens to people when total strangers are touched by the passage of the deceased. "A Son's Loss" is more poignant; it speaks of not only the unmet needs of earthly survivors, but also the unmet needs of the deceased themselves. Hurt feelings, unmet needs, and human greed have irreversible consequences in this patakí—and in the end, both deceased and survivor suffer eternally.

The remaining stories examine Osá from different angles: "A Beggar's Story" teaches us that through the ashé of Osá, with Elegguá's help, the most destitute can become rich, while "The Brag of the Boastful Boy" brings up another important lesson of Osá—one should not promise, or boast about, things that one cannot deliver. Finally, "Shangó's Imprisonment" is one of my personal favorites from this family of signs. Such were Oyá's obsessive affections for the orisha Shangó that she kidnapped him and hid him in the land of the dead; and after many days and many nights of undisturbed lovemaking, there, in her world, Shangó learned that no woman beyond Oyá had the skills to keep his passions satisfied. When Oshún freed Shangó from that shadowy domain, he returned to Oyá willingly.

Death, change, unrequited love, unrealistic boasts with almost fatal consequences, and random change—these are themes found in the lives for whom the odu Osá falls, and all of the stories presented here represent those themes well.

The Death of His Love

Death took her one day, without warning. She was young and beautiful when she died.

The man sat on his bed, mourning. He was dirty, unwashed, as were his clothes and his sheets. His hair was knotted, his beard uneven, and his eyes reddened. He tried to cry, but the tears wouldn't come; and his orbs felt dry and gritty in their sockets.

"She was the only woman I've ever loved," he whispered. No one answered.

"She was the only woman I've ever loved!" he screamed, pounding his chest with his fists.

There was only silence.

He sat there hugging himself, unmoving, until he admitted, "She never knew how much I loved her." His lips trembled, and his body shook violently. "Now, she'll never know I loved her at all."

That was the truth.

For the man loved this one woman with all his heart, but he never told her how he felt. They were neighbors, having lived in the same neighborhood all their lives. When they were young, they played together; but time soured their childhood ties, and they grew up as strangers. She was his longing, his heart's desire: He was an anonymous face on the street to her.

Still, he always loved her.

That day was her funeral, and the man cleaned himself up as best he could. He shaded his reddened eyes with dark glasses and hung at the back of the crowd during her service. After the ceremony was over, after the pallbearers lowered her casket in the earth, and after everyone peered into the hole for one final "good-bye," he stayed behind, watching the grave diggers shovel the earth back into the hole.

He stayed behind, and kept vigil that day and all night. When the moon slipped below the horizon, leaving only the useless light of stars, he sat by her grave and cried. Nobody heard him.

Ikú, however, heard him.

Ikú came to him.

He froze as she appeared; at first, she was nothing more than a deeper blackness within the darkness, a curious splotch in the night that could have been nothing more than his eyes blurring with tears. But the wind shifted, the leaves rustled, and something took shape in the air. A solid form, not a dream, Ikú towered above him, a nightmarish statue. In one hand was her scythe, and the other reached out to touch him as he knelt, trembling beside his beloved's grave. Her thin hand rested on his shoulder.

He found her touch curiously soothing, like warm soup on a cold, rainy day. He lifted his shoulder and rubbed the side of his head on the back of her hand for comfort. "So this is how it ends?" he asked, not expecting an answer.

"No, this is not how it ends." She cupped his chin with her cool palm, lifting his face to look at her. Where her face should have been, he saw only emptiness in her hood. "I have not come to take you. It is not your time."

He looked at her with narrowed eyes. "Have you come to punish me for intruding on your land?" He shuddered. He knew it was taboo to be in a graveyard after dark.

"No. I have not come to punish you." She rubbed his lower eyelid with her thumb gently, and caught a tear spilling from its edge. She looked at it on her black skin as though it was a brilliant diamond, and gazed at it for quite some time.

After a strained silence, he asked, "Then why have you come?" There was no more fear, only sadness and curiosity.

"Your tears for this woman have moved me. Your sadness is deep, and your love pure. It has been an eternity since I have felt sorrow and pining this intense."

"She never knew I loved her." Finally, the tears came freely.

"Oh, but she does. She hears you as I hear you. The dead are always around us. Even if we can't see them, they are there." Ikú looked up at the stars, and the man followed her gaze with his own eyes. "Such beauty," he thought, "and totally useless," he felt in his despair.

Ikú shook her head in disagreement as if she heard his thoughts. "No. Beauty is never useless. Futile and fleeting, yes, but it is never useless. Did you know there is a star for every soul that has ever lived on the earth?" she asked. "And just as they burn with a cold, lonely light, every soul that has ever lived has felt loneliness at some time. I, however, feel alone every day that I exist."

The stars didn't seem so useless to the man anymore.

"I want you to go home. What happens in a graveyard is not for mortal eyes. But tomorrow night, at midnight, I want you to come back. I will thin the veil just a bit, and let you see your beloved one last time. So you may have closure."

The man fell at Ikú's feet; he meant to kiss them and thank her, but she melted into the night like so much black smoke. She was gone; and as she told him, he went home.

He came back the next night.

Just before midnight, he was there at her graveside; only instead of hiding in darkness he was surrounded by dozens of lit candles. In his arms he held a simple bouquet of roses, and he waited, standing, for his beloved to appear.

"Why are you here?" a voice asked, almost a whisper. A chilly wind blew through the graveyard, and all the candles went out. There was moonlight, and it illuminated the cemetery just enough for the man to see a faint figure standing before him. "I am happy among the dead. Are you not happy among the living?" Her form became stronger—and he saw it was his one true love.

"I love you!" was all he could say, his heart beating wildly in his chest. He held out the roses to her, trembling with fear and desire, and although she lifted her arms to take them, they fell through her ghostly grip and rested on her grave.

She smiled, but faintly. "The flowers are beautiful, and I thank you for them, but . . . I do not love you." His wildly beating heart stopped so quickly that the man thought he, too, was dead. They stood in silence for what seemed an eternity. When he continued to say nothing, the woman spoke again. "I did not love you when I was alive, and now that I am dead with no relatives to remember my name, all I want is rest and peace. But your devotion to me is so pure, and gives me such light in the next world, that I want to thank you for the love you offer."

She paused for just a moment, and still the man said nothing. He looked at the earth, crushed. With narrowed eyes and pursed lips, she told him, "My father was a very wealthy man. He didn't trust banks, or vaults, and he worried that if we stored our wealth in our house, thieves would murder us in our sleep, and steal what they could carry in a night. So he hid everything far away from our home. In the earth he buried many treasures worth more than the richest king's coffers. Before he died, he told me where our family's treasures rested, and from time to time I raided those to provide for my needs. But since my needs were simple, and because I died so young, I never took much. And in death, I have no need of treasure. I give these to you, if you will live your life and leave me to my death."

His heart was broken, but he listened carefully as the spirit told him where all the treasures were hidden. With all her secrets revealed and no more to say, her form dissolved. She was gone.

And what happened to the man?

Time heals all wounds, at least those that don't kill us, and one by one, he unearthed all the treasures the woman's spirit left to him. No one knows if he ever found love, but everyone can assume he lived as a very wealthy man. If he had nothing else, he had that.

A Beggar's Story

"Penny by penny, a beggar can become a rich man," said Elegguá, sitting beside the beggar who lived on the outskirts of town. "Trust me. It is not that hard."

The beggar looked back at Elegguá. "Do you really think so?"

"Fortunes have been built by lesser beings!" the orisha said.

So the beggar went into town, begging alms. Some people offered money; others didn't. Some were gracious, and others weren't. All the while, Elegguá watched what everyone did.

"There are millions of people in this world!" said Elegguá, giving the beggar a friendly slap on the back. If one million people gave you one million pennies, you would have a small fortune on your hands. Don't be afraid to beg, not even for a penny!"

Every day, the beggar went out into the streets, begging alms; and when someone he met said, "I have no money," the beggar begged, "Not even a penny? Surely you have but a single penny you won't miss?"

It worked almost every time; and in just a matter of weeks, the beggar became quite prosperous.

For, truly, penny by penny, a beggar can become a rich man!

A Son's Loss

When his father died, he was sad; and when the son discovered his father died without leaving a will, he was confused. But when the king's men came and confiscated all the family's wealth, he was angry.

"You cannot do this," the son protested. "This all belonged to my father, and I am his only son!"

The guard looked at the man sadly. "Your father died without leaving a will. And when that happens, all a man's wealth goes to the king. It may not seem fair, and it may not seem right, but that is the law, and everyone must follow the law."

Once the house was stripped of all its contents, and once the coins were removed from his father's coffers, the son stood outside in the street and watched as they boarded up the windows and doors. As they were leaving, one of the men said to him, "You may, if you wish, plead your case to the king. But I doubt it will do any good. If your father wanted you to inherit his wealth, he would have left a will. Only with a will would his things have belonged to you. And since a will is such an easy thing to write, the king will only say he didn't want you to inherit what was his. I am sorry."

The young man, who had once lived a comfortable life with his father, was now a destitute beggar in the street.

In Heaven, the old man starved.

"Why am I hungry?" the man asked to no one, and no one answered. "I am dead, in Heaven. Why do I need to eat?"

A messenger spirit came to him. "You are hungry in Heaven because no one feeds you on Earth."

"Feeds me?" asked the man, rubbing his stomach as if to sooth it. "I never fed the dead when I was on Earth."

"Of course you did," said the messenger. "Every time you prayed to or for the dead, you fed them. Every time you gave obi to the dead, you fed them. Every time you laid out a platter of fruits or meats to the dead, you fed them."

"But I did that no more than once or twice a year."

"And every time you made an offering to your ancestors on Earth, it was multiplied thousands of times over in Heaven. Every drop of blood shed from a rooster became a new rooster; every sliver of coconut put to them became a new coconut. For things do not work the same in Heaven as on Earth."

"Please, go to my son," the father begged the messenger. "Ask him to feed me. He is my only relative on Earth, and I will starve if he does not."

The messenger did just that.

On Earth, the messenger found the man wandering in the streets. He came to him as solid as any other living creature. "Your father sends me with a message," he said.

"My father sends me a message? Go back to my father and give him a message for me. How dare he die with no will?"

"Your father is starving in Heaven because you have not made any offerings to him. Give me just two coconuts to take back to him. In Heaven, they will multiply a thousand times over, and your father will have the strength to help you."

The son had a disgusted look on his face when he told the messenger, "Go back to my father and ask him where he left the money I am to use to buy these coconuts. For he left me with nothing, and I have nothing to give him."

In Heaven, the messenger went back to the father, and found him surrounded by all the priests of Heaven. He addressed them as a group. "Your son is very angry. He claims you died without a will. He is poor and destitute in the streets, and has no money with which to serve you."

It was true, and the father looked down at his feet. "I never had time to write a will. But the priests here say they will help my son, and give him wealth, if he will serve me. He must make ebó so I do not starve to death. Go back to my son. Ask him to forgive me. Tell him I think about him constantly, and ask him for a rooster."

Again, on Earth, the messenger found the son. He was eating scraps from a garbage heap. "Your father sent me back to you to ask for a rooster."

He looked up at the heavenly messenger, his face stained and his hands dirty. Trash hung from the corners of his lips; his clothing was ripped and torn. "Where did my father leave my chicken coop, so I can give him a rooster? I don't believe he left me anything. I am starving myself, and have nothing to give."

The messenger returned to Heaven. "You son is a bitter, cruel man," he said. "He will give you nothing."

A priest walked up to the messenger. "This man is deeply sorry for what he did to his son. We see how he lives now, and all the spirits in Heaven grieve for him. Go back to the son; ask him for a ram. Olófin himself will move Heaven and Earth to make him a rich, pampered man."

On Earth, the messenger found the young man standing in the rain, a burlap sack covering his head for shelter. Still, he was soaked. When the messenger relayed the message, he screamed where he stood. "He didn't leave me a coconut for myself. He didn't leave me a rooster for myself. And now, he expects me to give him a ram? I hope he starves to death again!"

Then he had an idea. "Take this to my father," he said, pulling the bag over his body and lying on his side.

"Sir, I cannot."

"Take this bag to my father."

"Sir, I cannot."

"You can!" he screamed from inside the bag. Sadly, the messenger threw it over his shoulder, and set off for the old man in Heaven.

All the spirits in Heaven rejoiced when the messenger returned with the burlap sack, and the old man fell to his knees. "Olófin is great! My son has forgiven me, and has served me." A single tear slid from his eye as the priests came, preparing for the sacrifice. The old man opened the bag.

"Son!" he gasped, horror creeping over his joyous face. "What have you done?"

"I have come to see my loving father," he sneered, standing up. "See what you have done to me, heartless man?" He displayed himself; he stretched his arms out, and turned slowly so his father could see the filth on his body, and the ripped, torn clothes. "For weeks I have eaten from the garbage. For weeks I have walked in the sun and stood in the rain. I can't remember what it is to bathe or sleep in a soft bed, and you send spirits to ask me for things I do not have for myself? You are wicked, old man."

"Enough!" commanded a priest, holding his hand up in the air. "You, as well, are wicked, young man. The coconuts, the rooster—those were for your father, it is true. But all the bright spirits in Heaven saw that you had nothing, and they saw how you lived, and we felt sorry for you. The ram was to make ebó for you, to give us the power to send all in this room down to Earth, to you." He waved his hand, and a door appeared; and he swung open the door, pushing the son inside.

He fell to his knees when he saw the great wealth the room held.

"Father," he said, crawling back to him on his hands and knees. "I had no idea. Forgive me. I thought you didn't care. I thought you hated me. I will go back to Earth and serve you with a coconut and a rooster. I will send the ram. I will do all these things that you asked."

Sadly, the priest shook his head. "It is too late," he said. "Heaven's gates are closed to mortal beings; while still in the flesh, no one can cross. To come here, even with the messenger's help, you had to die. Your body lies still and lifeless on Earth. Only your soul lives. You, young man, can never go back."

And with no one on Earth who remembered their names, father and son languished in Heaven, starving together.

The Brag of the Boastful Boy

Apala was a difficult child, a boastful boy who liked to brag about anything and everything. Fortunately for him, no one paid him any mind, but bored out of his mind one day, he bragged to the wrong men. The king's guards were gathered in town, and wanting to impress them with his boasts, he bragged, "I am a special boy!"

One of the guards looked at him strangely. "What is so special about you?"

"I can do amazing things!" he said, puffing up his chest proudly.

"What can you do?" he asked, wiping sweat from his brow with a black handkerchief.

"Absolutely anything!" he said again, adding, "I can wash the black right out of that cloth! I can make it white!"

Of course the boy could do no such thing, but his mouth ran in front of his mind, and he said things for no other reason than to have things to say.

The king's guards laughed heartily. "No one can turn a black cloth white," said the guard. Then, suddenly, they all went quiet and fell to their knees. The king walked up to them.

"What is so funny, men?" he asked.

The guard who spoke to the boy told him, "This young man says he is a special boy. He boasts that he can wash a black cloth and turn it white!"

"That is a special talent, indeed!" said the king. "White cloth is expensive. By the time a weaver weaves his cloth, it is stained and discolored. Pure white is a rare thing to have. Is this true, boy?"

Apala did not know he was speaking to a king, for when the king went out in public, he chose to dress as a commoner. He was a humble man, and was a man of the people. As such, he did not tolerate lies. "Yes, sir, it is!" boasted the boy again.

"Well, this is our lucky day!" said the king, smiling brightly. "For you see, son, I am the king, and if you can wash even the color black out of a cloth, leaving it white, you will save this kingdom a lot of money. Show me your talents! If you can do as you say, I will reward you handsomely."

Apala stammered and stuttered. He had lied to the king.

"What's wrong, young man?" asked the king. "Surely, you can wash the color out of cloth as you say. I don't tolerate lies. Those who lie to me die for their dishonesty."

Apala was afraid, and being a foolish boy, did not have the sense to back down. "No, sir, I would never lie to a king. I can wash even a black cloth, and turn it white."

"Gather sixteen royal witnesses from the palace," the king ordered his guards. "This evening, I will send this young man to the river, and I will send the witnesses with black cloth. If he can do what he says he can do, I will be a very happy king." He looked sternly at the young man. "And if he cannot do what he says, I will be very angry."

Apala trembled, and ran home to his mother.

"You said what?" she screamed at him. "Apala, you have gone too far. You are a braggart, a boastful boy who has no business ever opening your mouth to anyone. And you lied to the king."

"I'll never do it again, I swear!" he cried, huge tears running down his face.

"You're right; you won't, because when he sees you can't wash a black cloth white, he will kill you." She cried and paced; this was her only son, and he was close to death. Then she said, "I am going to see Elegguá. He will know what to do."

"I must hide!" the boy said. "I can make myself invisible, and no one in the world will ever find me. I can stand right before the king and tickle his nose, and he will think it is only the wind. I can fly away, high up into the sky. I can . . ."

"Apala—shut up!" She screamed. "I've never met a boy as stupid as you. Shut up, and grow up!" There was silence. The mother had never spoken to him like this; and this was exactly what he needed to hear. So afraid was he at that moment that his tears went dry, and he only trembled in his shoes.

"Well, I can try to hide," he said, not wanting to tell tall tales anymore.

"No. The king will look for you until he finds you. You spoke like a man, and now, you have to act like a man and accept your fate. Hopefully, Elegguá will help us." She paused. "Where did the king tell you to go?"

"He told me to go to the river, mother." He cried again. "I don't know how to wash a black cloth until it is white. No one can do such a thing. I am going to die!"

"Not if Elegguá can help us," she said.

With tears in her eyes, the woman told Elegguá her son's plight. The orisha smiled. "So that braggart boy of yours is in trouble? Who would figure?" he asked. Elegguá thought about the boy and his boast for quite some time, and said, "I will get him out of trouble this once. But I need sixteen bolts of red cloth, sixteen bolts of white cloth, and a *jutía* (an African bush rat) for myself. Can you manage that?"

"Yes, I will do anything for my son."

"Then be quick about it. There is no time to waste."

At the river, Apala stood with sixteen royal witnesses. The guards were there; they were ready to take his life if he lied about his skills. Apala's mother stood with him, crying into the river, and Elegguá was there as well, wrapped in his sixteen bolts of red cloth. But no one could see him except Apala and his mother. He was invisible to everyone else. At Apala's feet were sixteen bolts of black cloth sent by the king.

Elegguá whispered into Apala's ear, "Tell them that is a lot of cloth, more than you have ever washed."

"That's a lot of cloth. I've never washed that much cloth before," he said, trembling.

"Tell them that there is a limit to your power, and if you wash that much cloth at one time, it might use up all the power that you have," Elegguá insisted.

"My powers have limits," the boy said. "If I wash that much cloth at one time, I might lose my powers." His voice wavered. Because no one knew Elegguá whispered in his ear, all the witnesses and guards thought his words were sincere, and they believed the trembling of his body and the wavering of his voice came from sorrow over the possible loss of his powers.

A guard spoke up, "This is what the king sent for you to wash. It would cost him a small fortune to have all this bleached white. If you wash it white with a single bar of soap, he will be happy with that, I am sure." He looked at the Apala, shaking pitifully. "And you will live."

"Start washing," ordered Elegguá.

To teach him a lesson, Elegguá made him scrub the cloth all evening and well into the night. He washed and wrung the fabric until his fingers were raw, and his hands blistered. When Elegguá decided he suffered enough, and learned his lesson, he began substituting the white cloth for the black. When the sun rose the next morning, all that remained were wet, white bolts of cloth; and Apala hung these from the branches of the trees to dry.

The witnesses were amazed. Apala looked at his hands. Washing through the night made them bleed.

"We will tell the king of this miracle," said one of the royal witnesses.

"Quickly," said Elegguá in the boy's ear, "before anyone leaves, ask for the guard's black handkerchief."

"Sir?" he asked the guard. "Do you still have that black handkerchief?" Everyone stopped where they stood, and the royal witnesses watched and listened.

He pulled it from inside his shirt. "Yes. Why?"

Elegguá whispered in Apala's ear again, "Tell him you think you used all your powers up on the sixteen bolts of black cloth, and you want to give them one final test."

"I think washing all the black cloth at one time destroyed my powers. I want to test them again."

The guard gave him the black handkerchief. "Wash," he said.

"And keep washing," Elegguá told the boy, "For this is your way out of your lie. I want you to wash that cloth until the sun sets again. Do not stop, not even to wipe the sweat off your brow. If you do, I will replace all the white cloth with the black again, and the king will kill you. Do as I say, for when the king sees that, truly, you have no more powers, he will be happy with what you have done for him, and he will leave you alone."

The boy washed. And he washed. And he washed. Elegguá wrapped the black cloth around himself, and he walked away. Until the sun set, the boy washed that one black handkerchief until his hands throbbed with pain. The witnesses, sorry that the boy appeared to have lost his powers, went back to the king to tell him of the miracle, and of Apala's loss.

They delivered the sixteen bolts of white cloth, and with that, the king was happy. He never asked Apala to wash again.

By day's end, the boastful, bragging boy named Apala learned his lesson; in time his hands healed, but were scarred as a reminder of his youthful folly.

The boastful boy never bragged again.

Shangó's Imprisonment

Oyá's love for Shangó was an obsession. At the mention of his name, her pulse quickened; and when she saw him from a distance, her heart beat wildly. His touch, no matter how fleeting, brought dampness to her secret places. "I love him so much," she told herself; but she knew that his heart belonged to Oshún.

Passion consumed her; it clouded her mind and dimmed her judgment. "I will put him someplace Oshún can never find him, a place from which he will never escape." She paced inside her palace like a caged beast. "I will keep him there as long as it takes; I will keep him locked up until his heart belongs to me, and no one else!" Her eyes glazed with desire, and something resembling madness, as she plotted.

The next day, her army rose up and stole Shangó away to the land of the dead.

She kept him in a small house with both the windows and doors barred; she surrounded it with the souls of the dead, and at the front door, made Ikú stand guard. "No one gets in but me," she said. "And no one leaves without my consent." Ikú and Oyá had pacts, and although Ikú knew it was an orisha she imprisoned in the land of the dead, the spirit of death had no choice but to comply. Of all that existed in both worlds, only Oyá had the strength to fight Ikú and win. Ikú did not like to fight and lose.

Shangó was a prisoner for longer than he cared to remember; but every night, Oyá came to visit him, and they made love until both were exhausted. In time, Shangó learned that Oyá's skills in bed far exceeded those of any other women he loved, including Oshún. Bit by bit, his heart warmed to Oyá.

Oshún was the first to notice Shangó was missing. Every night, it was his custom to come to her; and they would spend the evening hours locked in love's embrace. Often, he slept through the night in her arms. When he didn't show up the first night, Oshún wasn't worried; she knew he had other lovers. A week passed and still, Oshún was not fearful. Shangó had a wife, Oba, who needed his attention occasionally, and Oyá was a sometimes demanding mistress. Weeks passed with no word, and when the kingdom lamented Shangó's disappearance, Oshún knew something was wrong.

"Shangó can't be missing," she told herself. "He can't!"

For days, Oshún searched the kingdom for Shangó; and her searching was futile. Finally, she went to Elegguá, for he was the one orisha who knew everything, and she told him, "Elegguá, I am afraid."

"Why are you afraid, Oshún?" he asked her.

"Shangó is missing. He is nowhere to be found, and already the kingdom mourns him as if he were one of the dead."

"That," said Elegguá, "is closer to the truth than you know. For Oyá has stolen him away to the land of the dead. She made her legions of souls kidnap him, and they took him to their world."

"No!" Oshún's hands fled to her heart. "But Shangó is immortal, as are we. He can't die. The souls of the dead don't have enough power to hold him in their kingdom."

Elegguá agreed. "But Ikú does. Shangó cannot die; nor does he fear the souls of the dead no matter their legions. But Ikú . . . only that spirit frightens him. Death is stronger than anything. And Oyá has a pact with Ikú. Until Shangó gives up his womanizing ways, Oyá has forced Ikú to stand guard at Shangó's prison, and he cannot escape."

Oshún's eyes narrowed. "If you knew all this, why did you not tell anyone?"

Elegguá laughed. "I didn't tell anyone because no one asked me. Now, there is a way to release Shangó . . ." Elegguá paused. "But unless you ask me, I won't tell you."

Oshún stomped her feet, and sighed. "Fine. How can we release Shangó?"

"Not we," said Elegguá. "You." And in quiet whispers, Elegguá told Oshún how to trick Ikú so she could free Shangó.

It was late evening when Oshún gathered all she needed to free Shangó; and with fear in her soul, but love in her heart, she ventured into the land of the dead. Oshún was not afraid of *egun* (ancestral spirits), for she was a vibrant orisha, full of life, who loved worldly things; but in the land of the dead, the pleasures of the living were absent. The place made her shiver with distaste.

None of the dead dared question her presence, for Oshún had the ashé to wither even their own miserable souls. Hope of a new life was all they had, and since that was the only thing that made their existence tolerable, Oshún, as the owner of all that made life worth living, had the power to destroy them. As she passed, they threw themselves to the ground in reverence; and because she lifted no one, they were afraid to lift themselves.

Passing through their land to Shangó's prison was easy.

Only Ikú challenged Oshún as she approached the prison. "I stand guard here on Oyá's orders," Death said. "You cannot be here."

"And who are you guarding?" demanded Oshún.

"You have no power here, lady; nor do you have the right to make demands of me in my own world. Turn back while you still can."

"Go back?" Oshún asked. "Now?" Innocently, she crossed her hands over her heart, and she smiled at the wicked specter. "But I come bearing gifts, Ikú. I brought you something."

Ikú's eyes narrowed suspiciously. "If you have brought me anything, I doubt it is a gift, Oshún. You have no respect for my ways, or the work I do."

"Oh, but I do," she said, seductively. She threw her shoulders back, lifting her ample breasts, and she breathed in deeply, which only made them seem fuller. Oshún reached up to caress Ikú's face, softly, and she tried her best not to let the cold, clammy skin repulse her. "I have always . . . respected . . . you." Ikú shivered with desire.

"Then show me what you bring?" Ikú smiled, but the smile was more of a fetid crack across the bony face; Oshún shivered, but Ikú thought she, too, shivered with desire.

From her basket Oshún pulled out nine racks of roasted pork, nine bottles of honey, and nine bottles of rum. "You must be famished, Ikú, and I thought we could have a little picnic here in your world." She spread a white sheet on the ground, and sat, offering Ikú her hand. Death knelt, and then sat, and feasted on Oshún's gifts greedily. He never noticed Oshún failed to eat.* Alone, Ikú drank all nine bottles of

---

*In the most of the patakís in this book, Ikú is female. But please note that in the patakís, Ikú's gender is problematic. There are stories in which Ikú is specifically male; there are stories in which Ikú is specifically female; and, there are stories where Ikú lacks gender.

rum, and when he was thoroughly sauced, he fell into a deep, drunken sleep.

Satisfied he would not awake, Oshún stole Ikú's keys, and released Shangó. As they passed the souls of the dead, they were still prone on the ground—none dare rise without Oshún's blessing. She blessed not a one.

Back on Earth, far away from Ikú's kingdom, Oshún lay on a riverbank and reached up for Shangó's hands. She spread her legs seductively and whispered, "Make love to me, my King."

But Shangó had spent nine weeks in the land of the dead; and every night Oyá came to him, and their lovemaking was passionate and powerful. After so many weeks away from life and all it had to offer, Shangó found comfort and solace at her breast, and he yearned for Oyá's embrace, not Oshún's. He looked at her, and then turned away. "I can't. I'm in love with Oyá."

Shangó left Oshún laying there by the riverbank, and sought out the arms of Oyá that night. Thunder and lightning rumbled in the skies, mighty winds and terrible tornadoes touched the earth, and rains beat the forest as Oyá and Shangó both screamed in ecstasy. And for many years, even though Oshún tried her best to reclaim Shangó's affections, he belonged to Oyá.

10

Ofún

Ten Mouths on the Mat

There can be neither life without death,
nor death without life.

Ofún is a sign born directly from Heaven and Olódumare; it is elusive and mysterious, a letter bringing more questions to the mat than it does answers. When discussing it with my godfather late one night years ago, he told me, "Ofún is the odu of phenomenon." I remember his voice; it was ethereal, almost a whisper, and I shuddered. His words filled the air with something that felt preternatural; and when he saw me shaking, he smiled. My godfather's knowledge of patakís and Lucumí lore is encyclopedic, and when he discusses an odu, something in him changes. He not only speaks of the odu with his mouth, but also with his heart, and he vibrates with the nature of the sign itself.

Slowly, he ran through the list of stories and ritual lore born of ten mouths. "Life and death are forever bound together through Ofún. Iré and Osogbo fought for prominence. Ofún was born on the earth to mortal parents, blessed by Ikú herself; and when he betrayed her, he lost his own life. His daughter ran away in fear; she was lost; no one found her. Ochanlá received tremendous power in her old age. In jealousy, a powerful babalawo invoked a curse on the cowries of the orishas, and it took the ashé of both Obatalá and Olokun to remove that curse—and the ashé of every santero who washes orishas in the igbodu of ocha. The constellations are born . . . curses are born . . . all the evils in the world were captured, and set free by an innocent's curiosity . . ." One by one, he rattled off the stories found in Ofún's corpus, and I made a mental note of each one.

Later, after he turned in for the night I wrote down every detail I remembered.

It took almost two years to write the rough drafts of that night's oral teachings, and when I was done, more than 50 stories and 500 pages of typed text sat on my desk before me. Choosing from those stories for this chapter was no easy task: I wanted to show the curse that Ofún is, and the blessings that it brings. I wanted to write about Ofún's mortal life on Earth. I wanted to discuss the importance of life and death, and how they are forever bound; and I wanted readers to understand that no matter how deep a diviner's knowledge of this sign is, Ofún speaks of life's tragic, mortal eventuality—it touches all things that are primal, yet digs deeper to a dark place that is simply unimaginable. More importantly, I wanted to show that Ofún, in spite of its inherent tragedy, provides many opportunities for growth and evolution if faith becomes one's source of strength.

When faced with Ofún on the mat, faith might be the only thing that client has left; and it is only by faith that he will evolve.

Life and Death

Life and Death walked together in the place between Heaven and Earth, the thin, veiled chasm that everyone crossed, but only they lived; they were side by side, as they always were, each looking in opposite directions, as they always did. For a long time there was silence, and finally, Death turned to Life and said, "One day, you will die, and I don't care if you die because your death will only make me stronger."

Life turned to look at Death, and smiled. "One day you will live, and I don't care if you live because your life will only make me stronger."

"Life is weak. Everything dies. While I exist, I destroy all the good that you create."

"Death is weak. Life always finds a way to continue. While I exist, I transcend over you and the heartbreak you bring to this world."

Death frowned. "You think you are so smart. But for this world to be a world, our dual existence is necessary. There would be no life if there was no death."

"Nor would there be death without life."

There, as Life and Death stood side by side, and now hand in hand, they agreed: there can be no life without death, and there can be no death without life. The two were inseparable and inevitable.

That's just how the world is.

The Story of Iré and Osogbo

Iré and Osogbo were twin brothers, yet they lived as rivals. Both coveted supremacy over the earth and neither desired parity. In the beginning, they argued as friends; they chose their words carefully, each not wanting to hurt the other's feelings. Time impassioned their words, and they were harsh. The passage of centuries brought battles and wars for power, each epoch bringing more chaos until there was no peace on Earth. Olófin could take no more, and from Heaven he commanded, "Enough!"

The skies rumbled. The world trembled, and every living thing hid in shadows. Never before had Olófin raised his voice. As its sound echoed and waned over Earth, silence ensued. Even the air was still, but thick with anticipation.

Iré and Osogbo were hushed; neither brother dared defy Olófin in his anger.

Taking form in their midst, Olófin demanded, "This war ends now!" He raised a powerful black fist, withered by age, as he gestured at both. "Brother should not raise hand against brother. Today, each of you will make ebó, and when you are done making ebó, you will come see me. I alone will decide which of you is greater on the earth."

Olófin's form wavered in the air before dissolving like a desert mirage. The twins, still stunned, looked at each other with wide eyes. Then they retreated to opposite ends of the earth.

Once alone, smugly, Iré smiled to himself. He looked up at the skies, and spoke into the air, "I do not need to make ebó. No one on Earth desires death; no one desires sickness; no one desires any of life's misfortunes. Every living thing invites me into their homes and their lives with each prayer they offer to Heaven. All of the world's hopes and dreams and desires begin and end with me." Satisfied that Olófin would make him supreme regardless of his disobedience, Iré settled into a comfortable, peaceful sleep.

Osogbo knew his brother and knew his arrogance. To himself he thought, "When goodness is away, I, misfortune, am all that remains. I am everywhere in the world—it is the natural order for things to fail and decay. I will make my ebó; I will make it twice; I will make it three times over. This I will do not because I desire to be greater, because already I am the greatest, but because Olófin himself has ordered it." Osogbo made ebó as Olófin mandated, and while Iré continued to sleep, he did it again and again. Obedience was pleasing to Olófin, and obedient was what Osogbo wanted to be. Satisfied that he had done his best, Osogbo gathered himself up and flew into Heaven, knocking at Olófin's door.

Olófin was surprised when he saw Osogbo so soon; and he was concerned that Iré was not with him. "Where is your brother?" he asked.

Osogbo's face cracked in an evil grin as he said, "My brother, Iré, did not feel he had to make ebó. He was tired, and he went to sleep after you left. He still sleeps down on the earth; he sleeps while humans and orishas alike pray for his blessings. He sleeps while I, tirelessly, do the work that I was born to do."

Olófin's all-seeing eyes scanned the earth for Iré, and he saw that it was true. Iré was sleeping, smugly convinced that goodness, in spite of his refusal to make ebó, would be supreme on the earth. Olófin looked at Osogbo and saw, in spite of all the evils he embodied, that he was the one brother who was obedient and did what he, Olófin, asked.

With a mighty wave of his hand, Olófin conjured Iré to appear before him; he wiped the sleep and confusion from his eyes as Olófin pronounced, "To end the eternal warring between you and your brother, I demanded that you both make ebó. After making your ebós, I demanded that you both come before me for my final decree. Iré, you slept while the world begged your blessings, and your brother, Osogbo, made his ebó not once but three times over."

A horrible expression of fear and confusion crept over Iré's face as Olófin continued, "Osogbo, because you made ebó, you are first in all things. You are not that which is desired, but you are that which fills the world. You are not that which is called, but you are the one who will come. For being obedient you are the greatest, and the most powerful. Humans will get but one chance to ask for a blessing, and if a blessing does not come, you will be all that remains. Humans will get but one chance to hold onto that blessing, and if they are not obedient, it will melt away as if it were never there. You will be all that remains."

Olófin took a deep breath, and looked lovingly at Osogbo, "And for your obedience, my son, know this: That although you think all you bring to the world is evil, with your misfortunes will come much good. For it is human nature to seek out blessings, to grow and evolve into something greater. Because of you, civilizations will grow and flourish as they try to banish you back into the shadows; great books will be written, and art will be created. The weak will be destroyed, and the strong will become stronger. Each generation will grow into something greater and more powerful because tragedy encourages human nature to grow and persevere, while undeserved blessings make the heart grow weak and lazy. You will be both the catalyst and motivation for my creations to achieve great things."

Iré was silent. His disobedience cost him much.

So it has been: since that day, misfortunes follow humanity always, and those who hope to achieve anything great in life must do it with great suffering and sacrifice. Osogbo became the first and the greatest, not because he was sought by those living on Earth, but because of the two brothers, he was the only one who made ebó. This was the beginning of the world's evolution.

Ofún, the Godchild of Ikú

The old man could hear his children outside playing loudly in the afternoon sun; the warm breeze blowing through the open front door brought their voices with it. Normally, their playful sounds made him happy, and while listening to them, he would rock in his chair, laughing at their delightful squeals. Delicious aromas suffused his home; and usually his stomach would rumble with hunger as he wondered what his wife was cooking for lunch. Every afternoon was like this—his nine children outdoors playing, his wife in the kitchen cooking, and he in his favorite chair rocking lazily.

Only today, the smells from the kitchen didn't make his stomach rumble, nor did he rock in his favorite chair. There was a strange tightness in his chest that made breathing a chore, and an exhausting heaviness in his legs that made rocking cumbersome. It was more comfortable to sit still with his legs relaxed; only in stillness was his breathing unlabored. None of this bothered him; the old man figured it was old age sapping his strength, and he sat still, worrying about other things he thought more important.

His wife emerged from the kitchen; she was dozens of years younger than he, but she walked with difficulty. Her stomach was large and protruding; she was eight months pregnant with the old man's child. She called out the front door, "Lunch is almost ready! Come in and get washed up!" Nine little pairs of legs came running through the house, disappearing into the next room; the old man heard splashes and squeals as nine pairs of hands were washed.

She looked at her husband sitting still in his rocking chair; his color seemed ashy, and his shoulders stooped. "Are you all right?" she asked, kneeling beside him and putting a cool hand on his forehead. "You don't look well today."

He shrugged her off. "I'm just worried. That's all."

"About what?" The young woman stood with difficulty, supporting her stomach with one hand.

"About this," he said, nodding toward her unborn child. "We have nine children, and now there is one more on the way." He looked up at her, and saw that she was sad. A single tear hung at the corner of her dark eye.

"But husband," she told him, "children are wealth, and we are wealthy! The orishas have blessed us greatly!"

The old man was touched by his wife's devotion; but he looked at her stomach hanging low and full in her dress, and he sighed. "Yes, children are wealth, and I love them all dearly. But we have more than we can handle." Sadly, his wife rubbed her swollen belly, and he watched her, sorrowful. "And we are about to have another. How will we raise him? I am old, and already you are burdened with nine others. How much longer can I live on this earth? And if something happens to me, what will become of you and the children?"

When the tears came, the old man stood up and hugged her as best he could; the size of her stomach kept him at an arm's length, and he could do little more than place his hands reassuringly on her shoulders. She looked at him with wet eyes. "We will find a way to get by. We always do."

"Yes, we always do." He felt a strange flutter in his chest, and shrugged it off.

It was barely sunset when the old man turned in for the evening. "I'm tired, that's all," he said to his wife. Worry creased her brow. She watched her husband walk, and although he was old, tonight his gait made him seem older.

"Are you okay?"

"I'm fine. It was just a long day, that's all." Gently, he kissed her on the brow. His lips were cold, and as he stood back, she noticed that they seemed bluish.

"I will come to bed soon. I'm doing my prayers first."

He smiled. His wife was always praying. Strangely enough, it seemed her prayers were always answered. "Say a prayer for me, too." She smiled, and as he walked away, her smile turned to a worried frown.

For quite some time, she sat there alone, rubbing her tight belly.

When all she heard were the snores and deep breaths of her husband and children filling the house, she rose and went to her ancestral shrine. Slowly, she lit each candle, and when they were all lit, she prayed, "Please help us. My husband is old; he may not live to see our oldest child grow up. And I am burdened with nine other lives. Please, give us strength."

A chilly breeze blew through an open window. It made the candles flicker and dance before their flames went out. She strained her eyes in the darkness as a shadow rose before her; it was darker than the room, and solid; and she felt an icy hand reach out to fondle her stomach. "Your devotions touch me." The shadow's voice was as cold as the breeze that blew through the room.

She stepped back from the icy caress, covering her womb protectively with both hands. "Who are you?" She shivered where she stood.

"Ikú," said the shadow. "And your devotions have touched me. I will be godmother to your son, and will help you raise the child."

"I have my husband for that," said the young woman, frightened of the specter that stood before her. "He will help me raise my child."

"He won't," said Ikú. "He can't. I came for his soul while you were praying. Your husband died tonight, alone in bed while you were here speaking to your ancestors. I was leaving when I heard your pleas. They touched me. I will help you raise the child. It is your tenth, and you are to name him Ofún."

"Ofún," said the young woman.

"Yes, name him Ofún. It will please me if you do." The chilly breeze came again, melting the shadow that was Ikú, and the woman stood alone. Ikú's words died with the wind.

Slowly, the candles relit themselves as if they had never extinguished. Carefully, she made her way to the bedroom; and when she saw her husband's lifeless body lying stiff beneath the sheets, she had no doubt that the specter had been real, and Ikú herself now stood as godmother to her unborn son. She rubbed her belly mindlessly, whispering, "Ofún," with a mournful sigh.

The child in her belly kicked. It was then that she crumpled to the floor in shock and grief.

༄

As the years passed, Ikú brought many favors to the household, and the young woman found that she had everything she needed and more to raise her family. One by one the children grew up, venturing into the world to find their own fortunes, and when the youngest, Ofún, came of age, his godmother came with the night to visit her only godson. He was afraid when she materialized before him.

"Don't be afraid," she whispered, her dark clothing whipping and folding as if caught by a strong wind. "Do you know who I am?"

Shivering with cold and fear, Ofún whispered, "You are my god-mother, Ikú?"

She cracked a wide grin, and although for her it was a warm smile, to Ofún it seemed an evil grimace. "Yes. I am your godmother. I am Ikú. And now that you are a man, I have come to ask you what more I can do for you. What is it you want . . . out of life?" The word *life* rolled out of her mouth like an evil, vile thing, and it made Ofún's skin crawl.

Defiantly, he told the specter of death, "I want to be a doctor, and save peoples' lives. I want to save them from death!"

Hollow laughter filled the room. "You want to save them from me? That is very noble of you." Gently she caressed his face with one hand; it was cold, like ice, and by instinct Ofún withdrew from it. "Don't worry," she said, "my touch isn't lethal to those I love." With her other hand she took one of his. "Let us go make our pact then."

There was dizziness, and a wind so cold that it seemed Ofún's breath froze in his chest; for a moment, he hung between the realms of life and death, and when he was able to draw in another breath, he was standing outdoors with his godmother. The forest rose around him with trees so ancient he thought they had been alive since the beginning of time, and he sat amid the tangled roots of an ancient Iroko. "This was the first one," Ikú said with a hollow but reverent voice. "When the orishas themselves came down to Earth, they climbed down the branches of this ancient tree. When I first came to be, it was here, with this Iroko as witness, that I first drew form. And it is here that I make my pact with you."

"What pact?" asked Ofún. There was no fear, only curiosity.

"The pact with which I give you power over death itself!" Her voice was strong, full, and it echoed through the forest. Dark birds took flight as her words shook the branches in which they slept. In her hands she held out a branch covered with leaves, and carefully, Ofún took it from her. "This is the one herb that has power over me, and over all death. Remember it well. It grows sparsely throughout the forest, but with your keen eyes you will find it wherever you go. Just look for the oldest Iroko tree you can find, and there, you will find this."

"And what am I to do with this?" asked Ofún, holding the leaves to his nose so he could smell their woodsy scent.

"Whenever you are called to heal the sick, if they respond to no other treatment, they will respond to this. Clean those for whom all hope is lost with this herb and all sickness will flee their bodies."

"And I can save anyone?"

"You can save almost anyone, but not everyone. Before you clean a patient with this herb, look at his feet; if, with your eyes, you see a candle burning there, a candle that no one else but you can see, do not clean him. That person's life belongs to me, and you must allow me to take it."

Ofún smiled. "I accept our pact, godmother."

Thunder rumbled in the distance to witness his words. "Then you will be known among your peers as the greatest doctor who ever lived."

Ofún began his work as a doctor; one by one, the sick came to be healed, and he treated them all. Those who were hopeless, he cleaned with the herb; but when he saw the candle burning at their feet, he said, "There is no hope. You are too sick." For these, he administered herbs that brought pain-free sleep, and he waited patiently at the bedside for death to take them. From his work, he became a wealthy man.

The day came that the king himself lay dying in bed, and Ofún was called to heal him. Before he began his examination, however, he saw a candle burning dangerously low at the king's feet, and he whispered,

"Sir, I am sorry, but your illness is fatal. There is little I can do."

The king took Ofún's face in his hands, and pulled him closer so he could hear him speak. With a weak voice, the king said, almost a whisper, "Ofún, my good doctor, I know you are wise and will do what you can. But you must save me. If I die, this kingdom will fall into chaos. The greater good calls for me to live."

For quite some time, Ofún sat at the king's bedside; he fell into a deep, fevered sleep, and Ofún watched as the candle began to flicker and die. "I have to save him," Ofún thought, "for the greater good." From his bag he pulled out a small branch. "Godmother, forgive me," he whispered as he touched the branch to the king's head, and began cleaning him in long, sweeping movements to his toes.

The candle faded, and in its place stood Ikú. "Ofún!" she cried, her voice thin but sharp. "Did you not see my candle? It is this man's time to die!"

Shaking with fear, defiantly Ofún continued to sweep the branch down the king's sleeping form. He smiled as color returned to his cheeks. "I am sorry, godmother," he said, afraid to look at her. "I do this not for myself, but the greater good of the kingdom. If this man dies, there will be lawlessness and chaos. People will suffer."

Ikú smiled warmly, grasping Ofún's chin with her icy hand; she forced him to look her in the eyes. What was warm for Ikú seemed evil and vile to Ofún, and he shivered with fear. "I love you. You are a noble man, and I understand your reasons for this." She looked at the king, who was starting to move and turn beneath the sweat-soaked sheets. "But this is your final warning. Never again heal a man who has my candle burning at his feet. That life is for me to take, and not for you to save. Do we understand each other?"

Silently, Ofún shook his head several times in acknowledgment.

"And remember this, my godson: Life is about balance, and if it is nothing else, it is but a path to death. To save a life claimed by death, another must die in its place. Remember that." Ikú's form faded away as if she had never been there, and the king awoke.

Slowly, the king sat up in his bed, and with renewed strength in his legs, he stood for the first time in weeks. As the king walked from his chambers, Ofún at his side, there was a scream, and a great cry rose in the palace. A woman ran down the hall, toward the king. "You are alive and well!" she said, forgetting her manners and embracing him brashly. But her surprise at his health melted quickly, and she told him, "Your daughter is ill. She fainted. She is burning up with fever. Bring your physician and come quickly!"

Everyone ran to the sitting room, and Ofún's heart sank when he saw the king's daughter crumpled on the floor, barely breathing, with a sputtering candle at her feet. "Her life is about to be extinguished," said Ofún, remembering his godmother's words.

"Help her!" cried the king. "Help her before she dies."

"You won't take this life before its time, godmother," said Ofún under his breath as he held the herb to her cheek. She felt hot; her fever burned her skin like fire, and Ofún knew that while he cleansed the sickness from the father, it had only jumped to the daughter. "You won't take this one, godmother," Ofún said again as he swept the herb from her head to her feet.

Everyone watched in amazement as the young girl's eyes fluttered open; it was the last thing Ofún saw before he himself went limp.

"I told you that death cannot be defeated," said the dark shadow from the foot of his bed. Ofún opened his eyes. It took great effort to open them. He touched the back of his hand to his forehead. He was burning up.

Slowly, the shadow standing before him came into focus. It was Ikú. Between the two of them burned a candle; it was almost consumed by its own flame. It sputtered and flickered, its light dying slowly.

"You can't defeat death, Ofún. You can only move it from one person to the next. And because you broke our pact not once, but twice, now it has moved to you. I am sorry. I do love you. And because I love you, your own death will be quick and painless."

The candle went out, the room went dark, and Ofún neither saw nor heard another word.

The Loss of Ofún's Daughter

"Father, I can see him. He's riding across the field now!" Ofún's daughter was gazing out the window. For what seemed hours, she had been waiting there, watching for her suitor's approach. The sunlight coming through was bright and unflattering to everything in the room, but on her delicate black skin it brought out her natural sheen and made her complexion glow.

"Oh, to be young again, and in love," Ofún thought as he watched his daughter jump away from the window and smooth her dress. She was eighteen and barely a woman, but she had a grown woman's body, and it was lovely. "I don't know why you wait beside the window so impatiently," he teased her. "He comes the last day of the week and arrives at the same time every day."

"But I worry, father." She pouted, and her full lips seemed fuller. "He comes such a long way from Oshogbo. Do you know how far a journey that is? It is dangerous."

"He is a strong, resourceful young man, daughter. I am sure he can take care of himself."

She giggled as a strong knock came at the front door. Throwing her shoulders back and lifting her head high, she answered it gracefully and curtsied just a bit at the knees and the waist as the young man came in. He took her hands and kissed her briefly on the cheek; and then, he turned his attention to her father.

"Sir, I have something important to ask you. Will you step outside with me?"

Ofún looked to his daughter, and she looked to him quizzically as he stood up. "Of course, if it is that urgent." The two men stepped outside, and Ofún's daughter tried desperately to listen at the door. They spoke in unintelligible whispers.

When Ofún burst back in, his face was spread with a huge, joyous grin; and on his shoulders was the finest silk cloak he'd ever worn. "Look what he gave me, daughter. Your gentleman is most generous!"

The young man knelt at the young woman's feet and took her hands in his. "Your father has given me permission to ask you . . . to marry me."

She almost fainted where she stood.

Ofún wasted no time with preparations. His daughter was his life, and he wanted nothing more than for her to be happy. "A man such as this comes along but once in a lifetime," he told her. "He is young, handsome, and rich; but more importantly, he is a good man. I have no worries that he will care for you well, perhaps better than this old man."

"Daddy," she cried, and her tears were like diamonds on her ebony skin, "No matter how much he loves me, he could never love me more than you." Father and daughter embraced; it was an embrace that seemed to last an eternity.

In the land of Ofún, however, it seemed that happiness was ephemeral, and suffering was eternal. A week before the wedding came the plague.

Coughs and sneezes, fevers and sores, delirium and insanity—these were the things that the plague brought. Ofún was a healer, and one by one the sick came to be healed, but no matter how many potions or salves he administered, everyone who fell ill died—including his daughter. By nightfall, all the villagers were dead and only Ofún was left alive.

Even in death, his daughter was as lovely as she had been in life.

Grief assailed Ofún like a terrible specter, and he wailed as he tore at his hair. In despair, he shredded his robes with his bare hands and lay in bed, praying that he, too, would die. After a night of trembling, shaking, and crying, convinced that Olófin would take his life as well, he fell into a deep sleep himself, so deep he was as one of the dead.

He didn't awaken when morning came.

The young warrior returned that afternoon; and his heart froze when he saw bloated, pox-marked bodies lying in the streets. Death's odor was strong, and even a cloth wound tightly around his mouth and nose didn't block the stench. He rode as fast as he could to his future wife's house. Furiously he knocked at the door, and when there was no answer, he kicked it in. There was only darkness and silence.

"My love?" he called quietly, and then he screamed, "Where are you?" Silence was his only answer.

Fearfully he walked to her chambers and saw her lying in bed, her arms crossed on her chest and her face frozen peacefully; even after a full night, she looked as if she were still alive—her beauty was that deep. The young man wailed; it was soulful and mournful, terrifying to hear.

And Ofún awoke at the sound.

The wailing he heard was deep and otherworldly; it was fatal, like that of a wounded animal. Fearful, his heart frozen, he rose from his bed slowly, mechanically; and terror made the color drain from his face until it was an ashen grey. He prayed to Olófin in the ancient tongue no one used anymore, trying to banish the specters he believed walked the streets, and his house; and his chanting sounded inhuman, even to his own ears.

In the next room, the young man heard Ofún's voice, but he, too, thought it belonged to the dead. Cautiously, he walked to Ofún's room; and when he saw Ofún walking as one of the dead with a pallid complexion, he screamed. Ofún screamed; and in their fear they ran in opposite directions.

Neither man stopped running until they were in separate yet adjacent villages.

Around midnight that same night, Ofún's daughter stirred; at first, it was a gentle flicker of the fingers, almost imperceptible, perhaps a reflex, but she sighed deeply and put her hands to her head. It was pounding. Although the plague had infected her, it had not killed her; it only made her breathing shallow and her heart slow until it seemed life drained from her body. The sores that erupted healed cleanly; not a single scar marked her delicate skin. She walked through the house, confused; and when she didn't find her father in his chambers, she walked back to the front of the house. The door was broken. Fear gripped her heart.

"What has happened here?"

She stumbled into the streets, still weak from the sickness, and screamed when she saw the bodies littering the roads. "Is everyone dead?" she asked the wind. And then she screamed, "Father! Ofún! Where are you?" Only an echo answered her.

Covering her nose and mouth with the collar of her dress, she wandered through town and cried. The devastation was nightmarish. She assumed the worst for her father, and kept walking.

No one ever saw her again.

The next morning, the young man returned with warriors: After a few days of death, the bodies were horribly bloated; they rippled and belched in the morning heat, and flies gathered, feeding off the dead. One by one, the men wrapped the bodies in white cloth and buried them in the forest. When the sun set that evening, no one had found the bodies of Ofún or his daughter; and so weak from mourning was the young man that he had to be lifted onto his horse and slowly guided out of town.

And the next day, Ofún returned with a band of warriors himself; and when they found the town empty of bodies, his heart sank. "The dead have risen," he moaned, "and they have taken the bodies of everyone, even my daughter." With a broken heart, Ofún sank to the earth and wailed; the men searched the town house by house. No sign of the living was found; and the dead were gone. Puzzled, they carried Ofún out of the town; and no one ever returned.

Since that day, Ofún's hometown was known as "the village where the dead steal the dead." No one returned; no one remembered it; and we can assume that the centuries have eaten what remained of the people who lived there.

Tragedy and sorrow—these followed Ofún all the days of his life, and he never recovered from the loss of his only child.

How the Leopard Gained His Strength

Of all the predators in the forest, there was none stronger than the leopard. He ran faster than the gazelle; he had the strength of ten men; he had claws the length of small daggers; and he had teeth that were razor sharp. The sight of him in the forest brought panic and confusion to all the animals who lived there. Everyone agreed—the leopard was the most powerful of them all.

The day came when the leopard wasn't so powerful. His teeth became loose in his mouth, and they wiggled when he chewed his meat; his claws dulled, and his strength waned. He could barely run without gasping. He fell to the earth in an exhausted heap, burning with fever, and he slept.

"What a pathetic creature you are!" said all the animals of the forest. "No one is afraid of you anymore."

Shamed, the leopard found his way to the house of a diviner, and begged the old man to help him. "I would rather be dead than be like this," the leopard told him.

"And if you remain like this, you will surely die," agreed the diviner. Carefully, he marked ebó for the giant cat, and although it took everything leopard owned to make his ebó, he did as he was told. By the next morning, his strength was restored.

Yet he had one more gift that he did not possess previously: His loud, resounding roar. As he opened his mouth to praise the diviner, a great roar erupted from his jaws, and it was so loud that it sent all the birds in the forest flying, and all the animals running. No one taunted the leopard ever again, and every time one hears his roar in the forest, one knows he is praising the diviner who helped him regain his strength.

The Spinning of the Web

Of all creatures that walked the earth, the spider was the smallest. She was fragile and weak, unable to defend herself; but worse, she had no way to catch her prey and feed herself. Desperate for help, she sought out the orisha Obatalá for help.

"Obatalá," said the tiny spider, "I am among the weakest creatures on Earth. And I am always hungry, because I am too tiny to catch my prey."

Obatalá looked at the small spider. "But spider," he said, "Even though you are small, you have sharp fangs; and in your mouth is a poison so deadly that it is strong enough to kill most men."

"But I am too small and too slow to catch prey!" she cried. "Even with my sharp fangs, and even with my poison, the minute someone spies me coming, they run away; or worse, they smash me. I will never prosper on the earth like this."

Obatalá knew what the spider said was true. "I will help you," he said. "But first you must bring me something."

"Anything!" said the spider.

"I need a piece of white silk cloth. Bring that to me, and I will give you ashé that will make you a powerful hunter in your own right."

The spider agreed that she would bring Obatalá what he wanted, and she ran into town as fast as her little legs would carry her. She found a seller of cloths at the market, and in his booth, she found a white silk handkerchief. Carefully, she caught the edge of the cloth in her fangs, and as quickly as she could, she pulled it back to Obatalá's home.

No one noticed the small spider dragging the cloth through town.

"Obatalá!" she cried, finding the orisha sitting on his porch. "I brought you the cloth that you asked for. Now, will you help me?"

Obatalá picked the cloth up from the floor, and saw that it was made of the finest silk. "But of course!" he said, picking up the spider and putting her inside the cloth. Gently, he folded it around her. "Go to sleep, my little friend, and when you wake up in the morning you will have a brand new ashé in the world." Peacefully, she slept.

When Obatalá woke up the next morning, he went outside to his front porch and saw that the awnings were covered in fine strands of silk, and the spider stood in the center of them, feeding off a fly that had landed in the web. "Marvelous!" said Obatalá. "You discovered your ashé."

For the spider had learned to spin a sticky silk web, and with it she was able to trap prey her own size. And once they were trapped, she could kill them with her venom, and feed off their juices.

And that is how the spider spun its first web.

Obatalá Makes Ebó

The years passed, and Ochanlá, who was once young and vibrant, became an aged woman. Age brought weakness and frailty, and even in Heaven, she suffered. No one paid any attention to her.

In desperation, Ochanlá went to the heavenly diviners. She asked them, "Is this all there is for me? All my life I have served Olófin on Earth, and I have followed the will of Olódumare for my life. And now that I am in Heaven, still I age, and I am too old to even walk without stooping or exhaustion. I would rather cease to exist than spend all eternity frail and weak."

The diviner looked at her sadly. "Let us divine and see what the will of Olódumare is for you in your old age." Ofún opened on the mat. "No, Ochanlá, this isn't the end for you, and you don't have to suffer. Ofún tells us that you must make ebó, and once you've made your ebó, all things will become clear again."

Ochanlá had faith; she was an orisha, and had seen miracles worked in the lives of others when they made ebó on Earth. There, in Heaven with Ofún as a witness, she made ebó herself. And then, exhausted, she went to sleep.

Ochanlá awoke the next morning, and she felt different. She looked down at her hands; the skin was still creased and wrinkled, her joints still swollen. She stood up, but felt strength, and went to the mirror. Nothing had changed. Her face was wrinkled, and her eyes creased, but they held a certain youthfulness that betrayed her age. "Curious." She thought.

And then she went outside, and felt ashé coursing through her veins. No more was her body filled with pain; no more did she walk hunched over; no more did standing tire her. She felt powerful, as if she could fly.

And fly she did.

When Ochanlá opened her arms to greet the new day, she felt the sun's rays caressing her, and she was floating, down from Heaven and to Earth. Her white garments, which were once yellow with age, were again blazing and brilliant with the rays of the sun, and as she floated down from the skies, the entire world paid homage to her with the brilliance of a new day.

She was worshipped forever on Earth, thanks to the ashé of Ofún.

11

Owani

Eleven Mouths on the Mat

The road to death is paved with disobedience.

Years ago, I befriended an Ogún priest named Evaristo Perez (now deceased). His Lucumí name was Ogundei. I remember him as a quiet, shy man in secular circles, but when surrounded by priests and aborishas, he became very animated. The orishas were his one true love, and the religion was what brought him meaning and purpose. We met just before Inner Traditions published *The Secrets of Afro-Cuban Divination* in 2000, and when it hit the bookstores, he bought a copy before I could give him one. That same year, when he came to Orlando for the ordination of his godson to the orisha Shangó, I went to see him; he was at his godson's house, and when I walked in the door, he was holding an already worn copy of the volume. He being an elder and I still so young, I was embarrassed when he held out the book and asked me to autograph it.

I loved that man.

As I held that copy of my book by its spine, the volume fell open to the chapter on Owani. Highlights and underlining filled those pages, and there were notes in the margins. I looked at Evaristo questioningly; and as if imparting a great secret (for indeed, he was) he told me, "If a blind man lies very still, no one knows if he is sleeping, or if he is awake!"

I smiled, not sure what to say. "Owani is like the blind man," Evaristo told me. "If you think he's sleeping, and you get too close, he can reach up and grab you by surprise. Worse . . . with a weapon . . . he can kill you. On the other hand, he might give you a hug, or even a kiss. Whether she sleeps or fakes sleep, Owani likes to lay very still while she decides what to do with you, or how to act. She can embrace you with her arms lovingly, or choke you in anger. Remember that."

Through the years, when dealing with Owani and the clients who come to my divination mat with that odu, his is a lesson never steering me wrong. Sometimes it is the client faking sleep, spiritually speaking; and sometimes it is the odu lying still while she decides which blessings or misfortunes to put in the client's path. Always, as a diviner, I keep a cautious distance while I watch both the sacred and mundane dramas unfold.

Evaristo and I spent that evening discussing the odu Owani. He had a deep respect for that family of signs, and although he never privileged me with the knowledge of his itá, I always suspected that he was a child of Owani himself. We shared many patakís that night, one of them being a story included here: "Eshu at the Crossroads." Although I made no recording of his recitation, and although I never committed the story to paper because it stuck in my head so well, as I wrote my version of it, I heard Evaristo's voice in my head, and I cried while putting those words on paper. I miss that man; he taught me so much about the corpus of Owani, and other things. *Ibae bayen tonu, Evaristo Perez, Ogundei, ibae.*

I chose the remaining stories in this chapter to illustrate various themes found in this odu. At first reading, "The Climbing Vine and the Okra" might seem a parable whose moral is "make ebó to prosper over adversity." It has a plot that is simple and concise, repeating a theme found throughout the diloggún: If one has a problem, sacrifice can solve it. Yet a more careful reading of that patakí reveals several issues prominent in this odu; the story itself is deep and difficult, as is the odu Owani. It speaks of personal boundaries. It is cautionary against unintentional friendships. It is a reminder that one cannot be objective with one's self—sometimes it takes an impartial third party to acknowledge and sort out difficulties in relationships. It teaches us that the orishas can and do take sides between their adherents; and often the side chosen is based not only on fairness, but also on obedience. Finally, this short fable is but a small piece of a much larger saga by which the okra received its ashé to thwart death; that saga, however, is beyond the scope of this simple chapter.

The next two patakís I presented are some of my favorites; just as the simple story of the climbing vine and the okra illustrates multiple themes from the odu Owani, these two stories reveal more of the sign's nature. Not many among our ranks know the story titled "The Death of the Egungun Priests." Theirs was a priesthood devoted to the ancestral spirits that we know as egun. As an organized entity, it no longer exists; orisha priests and priestesses freely perform rituals once the sole responsibility of those initiates. This pataki explains why. The next story presented, "Disobedience Becomes the Road to Death," is the basis of a proverb for this odu—the road to death is disobedience. It has a child-like moral to it: Disobedience is what disobedience does—disobedient. After a long, hard day dealing with unruly children, I can only imagine frazzled fathers and overworked mothers tucking their children into bed with this story. Its "I told you so!" quality is powerful.

Realizing that Owani is an evolutionary odu, I wanted to end the chapter with something inspirational. For once Owani destroys the qualities of weakness, frailty, and disobedience in a person's life, it uses what remains to push the client to new heights of prosperity and evolution. Of the dozens of stories I had illustrating this, I chose two: "Oshún's Ebó" and "How Osain Saved the Ill-Prepared Man." In "Oshún's Ebó," we learn that there was a time the richest and most blessed orisha of the Lucumí pantheon fell down on her luck, and she fell hard. If an immortal orisha can lose her luck and wealth, how much easier is it, then, for mortal creatures such as us to suffer for no reason other than the world's fickle nature? Yet Oshún retained one quality so many profess, but so few have—faith. It was her faith that restored her to greatness and wealth. In "How Osain Saved the Ill-Prepared Man," we learn that no matter what, the orishas have pity on the human condition, which more often than not is folly. No matter how many stupid mistakes we make, no matter how ill prepared we are to deal with life's tragedies, there are times that the orishas intervene for no reason other than their love for us. Bad things do happen in this world to people with good hearts, and when they do, the goodness of our hearts motivates the creators of our lives to save us for no other reason than they love us.

Evaristo Perez taught me much about this sign; and although most of what he spoke of was fear, a central theme to Owani often overlooked is this—life is hard, but faith and a good heart, and sometimes ebó, saves us from even ourselves. Owani might be sleeping, but she watches, and no matter what, she knows what we do and do not deserve. This is just one more reason to love ourselves and others with reckless abandon. For as Evaristo said as we ended our discussion on Owani that night many years ago, "We are all watched, and we are all known, and in the end, we suffer or prosper accordingly." If I were to sum up the ashé of Owani in one sentence, that is the one I would use.

Eshu at the Crossroads

It was early morning, and Eshu was gulping rum and running through town between drinks, yelling to all who would listen, "There is danger afoot! Take care as you walk. There is danger afoot! Take care as you walk."

Men, women, and children were afraid, and everyone in town walked slowly and carefully. Many chose to stay home. For Eshu was a wise orisha, and when Eshu gave a warning, there was a reason. So slowly and so carefully did they move that nothing got done that morning, and by late afternoon everyone was angry that they found no danger.

"We've been tricked!" they complained. "There is no danger today! And our day is half-gone! That Eshu is nothing but a trickster!" Everyone went about their business, ignoring Eshu and his random warnings.

"But there IS danger," Eshu thought. "Watch this!" he told himself.

Thoroughly drunk, Eshu ran to the crossroad. From his small animal-skin bag he pulled out huge gallons of red palm oil; and like a child who spreads finger paint on paper for the sheer joy of making a mess, he smeared the oil on all four branches of both streets. He ran; he jumped; he slid through the oil wildly, all the while drinking more and more rum.

When Eshu was thoroughly sauced, a young man came to the intersection, and when he saw Eshu spinning frantically in the middle of both streets, he called out to him. "Eshu!" he yelled. "May I cross safely?"

Eshu stopped mid-spin and looked curiously at the man. In his mind he thought, "Is he crazy? The roads are slicked with oil, inches deep!" Instead, he stood there and said, "It is safe to pass, my friend."

The man took but one step; he fell down and busted his head on the pavement. Covered in oil and blood, he looked at Eshu angrily, and without a word, crawled back the way he came.

"I told you there was danger!" yelled Eshu, skipping and skating wildly in the oil-slicked streets. He stopped as he saw an old woman walking with a cane. "Young man," she called out to him, "I need to cross here, but the road looks dangerous. Will you help an old woman cross the street? Please?"

Eshu smiled warmly at the lady and offered his arm. She held him tightly, and together they crossed the street safely. "Oh, thank you, young man!" she said, holding his hands warmly before walking away.

Eshu stood there and cried. "They told me there was no danger. They were right. I was wrong."

By now, so drunk was Eshu that he saw himself standing in front of himself, and he asked his doppelganger, "Eshu, I heard there was danger in the streets, and the crossroad looks unsafe. May I cross the road safely?"

Eshu said, "I was told that there is no danger today. If there is no danger, it must be safe. Of course you can cross safely!"

Trusting in himself, Eshu took a few careful, faltering steps, but the oil was thick and slick and he fell down hard. His leg snapped in two pieces, twisting at an unnatural angle.

"That trickster . . . he lied to me!" Eshu screamed, in agonizing pain.

But his anger did not last long. On his broken leg, Eshu danced, and he laughed at Eshu's folly and pain. "The next time I tell you there is danger," he told himself, "I bet you will listen!"

The Climbing Vine and the Okra

A field of okra lay untouched when the wind blew a single seed in its midst. "How curious," thought the okra, "that a strange seed would land in the middle of my field." He thought about this seed for a long time and decided that it might be nice to have a friend with whom to pass his days. So the okra gathered his leaves around the seed and pushed it gently into the earth.

With the earth nurturing it and the okra protecting it, the seed sprouted into a healthy, green vine. "Well, hello!" said the okra.

"Hello to you," said the vine.

"My name is Okra."

"And I am the climbing vine!"

The two became fast friends, sharing everything they had. Quickly, however, the climbing vine grew; it sprouted more vines, and these spread across the field until the okra was covered beneath it. "This is not fair!" protested the okra. "I cannot see the sun. You are covering me completely."

"It is not my fault," said the climbing vine, "For climbing and spreading is what I do. I cannot stop."

"But I will die if you do not stop!"

The climbing vine felt badly that it was keeping the okra from having its share of sunlight, and he did not want to kill his friend. The two plants called to Elegguá for help. He smiled at them and asked, "What can I do for you?"

"I cannot stop growing," said the vine.

"And because he cannot stop growing, I cannot see the sun," complained the okra.

"And because he cannot see the sun, I am afraid my friend will die!"

Elegguá rubbed his chin and thought for a moment. "Both of you must make ebó. I want a machete and a rooster from you both. Then I will help you."

Okra made his ebó first and encouraged the climbing vine to do the same quickly. He refused. "I don't mind growing and climbing; truly, I enjoy it. The one with the problem to be solved is you, okra. You are the one who cannot keep up with me. You are the one who cannot see the sun. Since you've made ebó, I trust Elegguá will help you." The climbing vine continued to grow and to climb.

Elegguá was happy when he received the rooster and the machete from the okra, but he was angry that the climbing vine refused to make ebó. He cleaned the chicken, and took both the meat and the machete to a farmer who lived nearby.

"Have dinner with me," Elegguá offered.

"I would love to have dinner with you," the farmer said. He dressed the chicken and put it in his oven to roast. "What vegetable would you like to have with your dinner, Elegguá?"

A mischievous smile crept over his face. "I would like some okra."

The farmer scratched his head. "Okra? What is okra?"

"It is the most delicious vegetable you will ever eat!" he said. "No one in the world has ever eaten any before. A field of it grows not far from here; however, there is a vine covering the okra plants, and I'm afraid if the vine is not cut away, the okra will die off and there will be no more of it in the entire world."

Elegguá showed the farmer where the okra grew, covered by the climbing vines, and he put the machete in his hands. "You can use this to cut back the vines. Beneath the vines are the plants you want to save. That is okra." The man made quick work of the vine, chopping and cutting until the field of okra was free.

As promised by the orisha, it was one of the most delicious vegetables he ever ate.

Since that day, farmers cultivate and grow the okra; and whenever the climbing vine seeks to grow and overwhelm their fields, they cut it back. Because the okra made ebó, it was desired and it prospered; and because the climbing vine refused to make ebó, he is always chopped away.

The Death of the Egungun Priests

Alapiní was one of the eldest priests of egun in Cuba, and Molo, who was crowned Elegguá, was his wife. Theirs was a troubled partnership; for eleven years, the two were married, but each day that came drove a wedge deeper into their marriage. As are most of Elegguá's children, Molo was curious about everything her husband did, from his daily affairs to his religious duties; and Alapiní, ever the henpecked husband, was weary of his wife's constant questions and accusations.

Conversations were never happy and were always strained.

One day, Alapiní was working very hard to ignore his wife, and Molo was working very hard for her husband's attention. He was too busy to care. In eleven days was the huge egun masquerade, and he needed to prepare.

He was making preparations when Molo asked, "Alapiní? What are you doing?"

Alapiní stood at the door to his egun shrine, unlocking it. "I'm going into my sacred room for egun, the one you are not supposed to look inside."

Molo sighed. Whenever her husband went inside his room to address egun, he was in there for hours, and she was bored. "Will you be long?"

It was a simple question, but it distressed Alapiní; his wife was overly concerned about his religious affairs. Being uninitiated to egungun's cult, she had no business in them. For a moment, he was angry, but he took a deep breath and said calmly, "No, I won't be in here for long. In eleven days, we have our feast for egun, and I want to take their clothes outside to air. The room gets stale, and the clothes and scarves need to be fresh for the ceremony." It was too much explanation for his wife, as far as he was concerned, but the words just came out without feeling or emotion. Alapiní felt as if he were explaining things to a child, and it aggravated him.

He opened the door just a bit and backed into the room, glaring at his wife. She averted her eyes; what was inside was not for her to know. She thought to herself, "What is it about that room that is so secret?"

"She's not even an initiate," Molo whispered to his ancestors. "Why does she need to know anything about what we egungun priests do?"

Without another word, Alapiní came out with bolts of cloth draped over his arms. Freeing one hand, he relocked the door with difficulty and went outside to hang the multicolored fabrics on tree branches. She followed him.

Molo noted that there were dark storm clouds in the distance. "It looks like rain."

"It's not going to rain," he answered.

"But the clouds are in the west, and look at your cloth. It is blowing toward the east." Gently, the materials he hung were flapping in the breeze. Alapiní knew that Molo was right about the direction the winds blew, but the clouds were too far away to bring rain here. "The wind will bring the rains," she insisted.

"Not today, Molo." Alapiní's voice was terse. He was aggravated with his wife. In silence, he finished hanging up the clothes and scarves and colored fabrics. The silence was strained. Without looking at his wife, he said, "I have to go into town. I'll be back later."

"But it's going to rain, dear husband," she mocked under her breath. Alapiní did not hear her.

While Alapiní was gone, the winds picked up; they blew frantically, whipping and turning egun's cloths in the air. The dark storm clouds that earlier were miles away billowed and twisted in the sky, and soon, it was dark. Lightning flashed, and thunder rumbled in the distance. As the first drops of rain fell, Molo was outside, gathering her husband's things.

"I told him this would happen." If Alapiní were here, she would have nagged him relentlessly.

Instead, she was alone, and Molo brought everything indoors silently. She draped the fabrics over a chair, and looked toward the door to the egun shrine. Curiously, it was ajar.

Molo looked from the door to the fabrics, and back again to the door. Before she realized what she was doing, she had gathered them up in her arms and walked to the room. "I can close my eyes and take them inside. I won't see anything," she reasoned. She did just that: she closed her eyes and opened the door blindly. "But how will I know where to lay them? What if I lay them on a candle? What if I set them on top of an ebó? That will ruin the fabric." She reasoned that one quick glance would do no harm, just one peek to find a safe place to set her armload of fabrics.

She looked inside the room.

What she saw both surprised and unimpressed her. "Why is all this so secret? It's a stick, a stone in a terra cotta dish, a bundle of sticks, and a bunch of masks hanging on the wall." A funny feeling fluttered in her chest and reddened her cheeks; it was a mixture of embarrassment and shame. Molo would never let anyone meddle in the affairs of the Eshu priests; and because of her curiosity, she had just overstepped her bounds. "There is no reason for my husband to know I've seen his secret things," she said to herself. Not wanting to lie to him, she closed her eyes tight and walked into the room to lay the fabrics on the floor. "If he is angry that I went in the room, I will just tell him that I went in with my eyes shut. That will not be a lie! What he assumes is his problem."

She was just closing the door when her husband burst in; her hand was still on the forbidden doorknob. She opened her eyes in surprise. "What are you doing, Molo? Where are my fabrics and cloths?" Alapiní was wet from the rain, and he stood there dripping on the floor, looking ridiculous all wet like that with anger twisting his face.

"I told you it would rain." She walked past him, holding her hands behind her back and looking at him innocently. "You should change. You're getting the floor wet."

Alapiní grabbed her arm and spun her to face him. Her eyes were wide with fear. "Where are my things?" He emphasized each word. "My egun cloths are gone!"

She wretched her arm free and jumped back. It was a reflex against his sharp voice and menacing stare. "They're in your room. It started to rain so I decided to do you a favor and put them in there for you before they were ruined."

"You went in my egun room?"

"My eyes were closed." She rolled her eyes at him.

"You went in my sacred room?" It was both a question and an accusation.

"Yes, I went in your room." Molo was afraid; in all their years of marriage, this was his only rule for her. She lived by this rule. Now that she had broken this rule, even though she did him a favor, she was afraid of the anger that flushed crimson in Alapiní's face.

"You, woman, are cursed. Death is the punishment for breaking the rules of our cult. In eleven days you will be sacrificed in the bushes for the dead. Egun will drink your blood and eat your flesh. And there's nothing neither I nor anyone else will do to save you."

Alapiní banished his wife that night; he threw her out of the house with only the clothes on her back. She left quickly.

In fear, Molo did what she knew to do; she sought out Eshu, her spiritual father, and asked him for a consultation. Eshu smiled. "Molo, you must make ebó to egun so they don't take your life."

Her eyes were wet with tears and her face pale and streaked where they burned her skin. "What do I give them, Father?" It broke Eshu's heart to see his priestess in such a state.

Eshu thought for a moment. "The day before the festival, at the same bush where your husband and all the egungun priests sacrifice to egun, make ebó to the dead. On a large fishing net with a red ribbon tied to it, give those spirits eleven *jícaras* (the dried gourds into which offerings are poured) of rum, eleven jícaras of beer, and eleven jícaras filled with fried foods. Then leave, and don't look back."

Molo did as Eshu advised, and the day before the great masquerade,

she laid out a feast for egun. She turned and walked away without looking back.

Eshu was hiding in that bush as Molo made ebó; and when she
walked away, he came out of hiding and looked at the foods she prepared. "Excellent," he said. Eshu walked to the ebó and waved his hands
over the offerings. Magically, they multiplied eleven times over, and
there was enough food, rum, and beer for a small army.

Eshu sought out Alapiní, who was busy with his preparations. As Eshu
approached, he whispered, "You are very hungry, Alapiní." When he
was next to him, Eshu heard the man's stomach rumble.

The old man was surprised when he saw the orisha standing before
him, and he went down to the floor in reverence. Eshu lifted him. He
heard the priest's stomach rumble again. "Alapiní, what is this? You are
hungry. You must eat!"

"There is no time to cook, Eshu. At least, I do not have the time
now. My wife is gone. The masquerade is tomorrow, and I must meet
the other priests soon to prepare."

"Strange," said Eshu. "Someone prepared a huge feast already. It is
laid out beside the bush where all the priests meet to feed egun."

"Really?" His stomach rumbled again, more insistently; it was
almost painful.

"Yes, someone did. There must be 121 jícaras of beer, 121 jícaras
of rum, and 121 jícaras of deliciously fried foods set out on a huge net.
Someone went through a lot of trouble."

"Then let me call the other priests, and we will feast as we
prepare!"

Eshu smiled, and went away.

The priests gathered at the bush. Greedily, they ate.

The next day all the priests, including Alapiní, were gathered again at
the bush; the opening ceremonies were about to begin. An evil smile
crept on Alapiní's face when the eldest priest asked, "Where is the sacrifice for egun?"

"The sacrifice is my wife!" Alapiní said.

Everyone murmured among themselves; this was blasphemy. They were in disbelief at Alapiní's words. The eldest priest held his hand up, palm open, and commanded, "Silence!" Everyone was quiet. "Alapiní, this is no time for games. Why would you say we are sacrificing your wife?"

"She broke our rules, and entered my sacred shrine. I cursed her and her life. For her blasphemy, it goes to egun. Those are our laws, and the laws of egun." He paused. No one spoke. "They are ancient laws; it's true they haven't been used in centuries, but a law is still a law and as priests, we must follow it."

Eshu came from nowhere and stood among them. The eldest tried to drop down in reverence, but Eshu held his hand up, forbidding him. Turning his back on the elder, he looked at Alapiní, addressing him as the others listened. "You are sacrificing your wife? You are sacrificing my priestess?"

"Yes. It is our rule."

"So be it," said the eldest priest. "We will sacrifice your wife to the ancestors we serve. It is the law. It is an ancient law, but we all know that our laws have never changed. It is still a law, and we must follow it."

Eshu addressed the assemblage of priests. "Did not his wife make ebó to the dead yesterday? I believe it was a huge ebó: 121 jícaras of rum, 121 jícaras of beer, and 121 jícaras of fried foods. She offered that ebó in penance for the evil thing she did. I am sure egun will pardon her. Surely you all saw that ebó."

"That was a feast for us, not egun," said the eldest priest. "Alapiní invited us all to that feast. And while we appreciate the meal, the dead had no part of that. We cannot pardon her for feeding us."

"No, that ebó was meant for egun, not their priests. Alapiní lied to you all!" Eshu insisted.

"Eshu," Alapiní roared. "You told me that a feast had been laid out!" His face was twisted with anger and pale with fear.

"Yes, a feast had been set out, but you, Alapiní, misinterpreted what I said, and you ate food that was meant for the ancestors you serve."

Alapiní's mouth fell open when he realized what Eshu said was true. "And all of you ate as well."

Everyone was silent. No one dared breathe a word.

"And correct me if I am wrong," continued Eshu, "but I believe that the price for eating food that was meant for the dead . . . is death. Is that not one of your most 'ancient laws'?"

A great roar went through the crowd; and it died as suddenly as it began. For their offense, and their unwillingness to pardon Molo, egun came and claimed as their ebó . . . the lives of all the priests who were there. The spirits all ate; the priests all died; and with no one left to perform the sacrifices, Molo's life was spared. They spared her because she made ebó.

And this, some say, is how the cult of egungun died in Cuba. Once all the priests were dead, there was no one to initiate anyone else into their mysteries.

Disobedience Becomes the Road to Death

It was early evening when Elegguá found Disobedience standing at the gates to the road of Igbade, the Mountain of the Dead. Disobedience was alone, leaning against a thick, polished stick; he stood facing the west, gazing mindlessly at the Mountain. Although it was so distant that its base was lost just below the horizon, it loomed large against the sky, a ragged, cragged monolith with peaks hidden in dark clouds. A dying sun slid behind it, and shadows stretched out over the earth, bringing darkness to the path bit by bit even though the rest of the world was still filled with pale light.

Elegguá was immortal, an orisha, yet the road to Igbade made him shiver like a mortal. He wondered how Disobedience could stand there so calmly, staring at the Mountain. He didn't hear Elegguá's approach.

"Good evening!" the orisha said cheerfully, his voice not betraying his concern. Startled, Disobedience jumped, losing his grip on the stick. When it fell to the ground, Elegguá saw it was a hoe, the razor-sharp blade pointing up at the sky. The man laughed nervously, bending over to retrieve it, but Elegguá was faster and had the hoe in his hands before Disobedience could grab it. "What are you doing in the middle of nowhere with this?" he asked.

His disobedient son smiled a nervous smile. "I am thinking of starting a farm there," he said proudly.

"A farm?" asked Elegguá. "Where are you starting a farm?"

"Over there." Disobedience pointed down the darkening path.

"You want to farm the road to Igbade?"

"Well, not on the road itself. Perhaps on both sides of the road, so the road runs through it easily." He smiled; he was proud of his plan.

"My friend," said Elegguá, handing Disobedience his hoe, "the road to Igbade is not meant for farming. It is a road built by old age, disease, sadness, anger, loss, regret, and tears. Only those who are dead or dying can go there. Nothing can grow there."

"Oh, you are wrong, Elegguá." Disobedience looked at him, and the orisha saw the arrogance and madness of disobedience burning in his eyes. "The land has lain fallow for centuries. It is virgin and rich; and no one has dared claim that land for their own. Anything I plant here will prosper wildly."

"I know you have good intentions, Disobedience, but the road to Igbade is paved with good intentions. You must listen to me. You cannot farm there."

Elegguá's words fell on deaf ears, and Disobedience did what Disobedience does—what he wanted, and nothing more. The man took but a single step past the gates, and he raised the hoe above his head, bringing it down on the earth sharply. A great rumble rose from the earth, like thunder in the sky, and Disobedience shattered into a thousand small pebbles that rolled down the road to Igbade, catching and settling in its cracks.

And that is how disobedience became the road to death.

Oshún's Ebó

Oshún is the owner of all things making life worth living: love, abundance, beauty, and eroticism. So limitless are her blessings that she shares generously with those who worship her; so vast is her wealth that she gives freely to her children.

Things were not always like this.

There came a time when Oshún wandered the earth in poverty and despair. So deep were her sorrows that instead of creating wealth with her touch, she destroyed it; and instead of molding beautiful things with her hands, all she caressed withered and died. Helpless and hopeless, Oshún went to the diviners to learn what she had to do to leave the misfortunes in her life behind.

The diviner told her, "You must make sacrifice, but it will be no simple thing. Not only will it take all your remaining material wealth, but also it will require all your spiritual faith."

"I will do anything to increase my station in life," said Oshún. "In spite of what I do not have, all I have left is my faith. What is required of me?"

"Take every bit of money you have and go to the market. Buy all the red palm oil and honey you can find. If you have even a single penny left in your pocket, then you do not have faith—and this ebó requires faith."

He waited for Oshún to speak. Sadly, she asked, "And after I do that, what do I do?"

"Before sunset, pour all of your oil and honey into the river. Olódumare will bring all that you desire, and more."

Oshún despaired, for she had so little left and was loathe parting with it, yet she had faith in God and the diviner's skills. So she took all her money to the market and bought all the red palm oil and honey she could find. Knowing who she was, and knowing she had fallen on hard times, the merchants gave her extra just because she was Oshún. "I may be penniless, but already my luck is improving," she thought to herself.

Sunset came, and Oshún sat at a river's edge surrounded by her jars of palm oil and honey. She lifted the first jar of honey and took just a taste. "My life has come to this," she sighed to the river. "My last taste of sweetness, and then I have no more. I have nothing. I am lost."

Oshún cried as she poured the honey into the river; she cried as she poured the red palm oil into the river; and as the sweet and greasy swirls settled into the river's sands, she cried some more. Her tears hung on the grasses like delicate morning dew.

Then she cried herself to sleep on the riverbank. Oshún had nowhere else to go.

While Oshún slept, Eshu came to the riverbank. He saw her sleeping form and stopped. "Poor little girl," he said, walking to the edge of the river and swirling his finger under the water, into the sand. He put his finger in his mouth, and tasted the palm oil and the honey. "Good little girl." Eshu smiled, and took a taste of the ebó to Heaven, to Olódumare.

"Look what your daughter has done," said Eshu. "She made ebó with everything she had, and now she sleeps at the riverbank, crying in her sleep. She has faith in you, Olódumare."

Olódumare closed his eyes, and with his inner vision looked down on the earth. He saw it was true. Oshún had nothing left but her faith; and now, she slept with despair.

"She was the last of your creations, Olódumare, and the health of the world depends on her happiness. It cannot go on if she is so sad."

"I know, Eshu," said Olódumare. "You think to tell me about what I created? She will be rewarded for her faith."

"But how will she be rewarded?"

"You will see."

Sunrise came, and with the new day Oshún awoke. She turned on her back and stretched delicately; she ran her fingers through the soft grasses on which she slept and felt something hard and cold against her hands. Stiffly, she sat up.

Oshún blinked. She did not believe her eyes.

Sometime during the night, her tears had turned into tiny jewels, brilliant diamonds that sparkled in the early morning light. She cupped her palms, holding a handful close to her face. "Maferefún Olódumare!" she gasped. "I am blessed."*

She put the handful of jewels in her pocket, and slowly she realized that the riverbank was strewn with brilliant jewels. "This is unbelievable. These were my tears!"

Wanting to wash the sleep from her eyes, Oshún walked to the riverbank, and stopped when she saw the bottom of the waters. No longer was the bank made of sand. It was all brass and gold.

While she contemplated this mystery, Eshu came to her. "You look surprised, Oshún," he said, smiling.

"Do you not see the river? Do you not see the riverbank?"

Eshu pursed his lips as he looked around, and rubbed his chin as if lost in thought. "It looks like gold, brass, and jewels, Oshún."

"I made ebó last night. Into the river, I poured red palm oil and honey."

"And you cried."

"How did you know?" She put her hands on her hips.

"I know because I took your ebó to Heaven," Eshu said proudly, puffing up his chest. "Olódumare turned the red palm oil into brass, the honey into gold, and your tears into jewels. And because the river is yours, everything here is yours as well!"

That is how Oshún became the richest orisha on Earth. She made ebó with all she had, and God himself rewarded her faith.

How Osain Saved the Ill-Prepared Man

An ill-prepared man made preparations for a long journey.

He had no horse, so he decided he would walk. It was only a single day's journey, he reasoned. He had no backpack in which to carry food, so he ate before he left, and believed that to be enough. It was only a

---

Maferefún Olódumare is a phrase meaning, "all praise be to Olódumare."

single day's journey, after all. He had neither a map nor a compass, but the land to which he traveled was in the north, and he reasoned that he would follow the sun to its highest point, and keep walking straight ahead. It was only a single day's journey, after all, and how lost could any man get in a single day?

Ill prepared, the ill-prepared man set out on foot, with no supplies, no compass, and no map. It was a recipe for disaster.

After many hours of walking, he was lost. Worse, he was hungry. Even worse, he was thirsty. The hot midday sun bore down on him like an angry beast; he was tired, dizzy, and burning with fever. He knew he was in trouble.

Nightfall came: the ill-prepared man was nowhere near his destination, and he sank to his knees in despair. As the darkness deepened around him, he saw a dancing light ahead. It was a fire. Exhausted, he walked toward it, sometimes stumbling, sometimes falling, and sometimes crawling.

He thought it was his salvation! A small group of men sat around that fire, and beside them was a pool of water. With the last of his strength, he crawled to that pool and drank greedily. The men laughed. "That's it; drink that water, man!" one of them said. They all laughed heartily.

For the men were a group of bandits, and had neither the morals nor the desire to let the ill-prepared man know that the pool was stagnant and poisoned.

He fell into a deep sleep. The bandits robbed him of all he had; and when the ill-prepared man woke later that night, he was naked and sick. Nausea overwhelmed him; fever burned him; and delirium threatened his sanity.

The ill-prepared man realized just how ill prepared he was and resigned himself to death. "Please, let me die quickly," he prayed.

Instead, he dreamed.

In his dream, a deformed man walked up to him, as he lay prone and helpless on the earth. He limped on one twisted leg. The deformed man stood beside the ill-prepared man, looking down in pity, and then knelt on his good leg, his twisted leg jutting out in front. Carefully, he pushed a withered hand behind his head, and lifted it gently; with his good hand, he put something damp to his lips, and tipped it up. A shockingly sour liquid filled his mouth, but he was so thirsty and hot, and it was so wet and cold, that he swallowed greedily.

The heat in his veins subsided; his stomach settled; and finally, he fell into a comfortable space between sleep and consciousness where he felt no pain. While he rested, the deformed man bathed him with the same liquid, and wiped his feverish skin with the leaves of the forest.

Morning found the deformed man sitting beside the ill-prepared man; he woke, and thought he was still delirious. "Good morning," he said to the waking man as he wiped sleep from his eyes. It was almost a whisper, and the leaves in the trees rustled as he spoke. "You feel well?"

One large eye, one small eye; one good arm, one deformed arm; one good leg, one twisted leg: The man gasped in surprise. It was Osain.

"I feel well," he said, sitting up. "It wasn't a dream. You took care of me?"

"I saved you. I saved you with my herbs." Osain's voice was not coming from his thin lips; it came from the forest itself. "Next time you make a journey, use this." He held out a bag sewn from animal skins. "If you carry nothing else, take this, and carry fresh water. Death was close last night."

A branch fell from a tree; it startled the ill-prepared man, and he looked toward the sound. When he turned his head back, Osain was gone; however, the bag made from animal skins remained. It was filled with sweet water, and he drank greedily.

This is how the canteen was born; and the ill-prepared man was never ill prepared again.

12

Ejila Shebora

Twelve Mouths on the Mat

*There are no arms so strong that they can hold
the sun; there is no mouth so powerful that
it can command the day.*

Ejila Shebora was difficult when choosing patakís; it is a volatile odu, and the themes referenced here are varied. Shangó, Aganyú, Oshún, Dada, Oyá, Oba, Osain, Iroko, Obatalá, Orúnmila, Oké, and others speak so prominently here that I could present dozens of patakís and still not exhaust the essence of what Ejila is. Still, no discussion of Ejila is complete without exhausting two themes: the evolution of Shangó and the evolution of our oracle, the diloggún. When choosing stories to present in this volume, I focused on these.

The name Shangó is more than a name; it is a word from the old Yoruba dialect known as Lucumí. Translated, *shangó* means "problems." While we see this orisha as a phenomenon, a powerhouse who not only unified the Yoruba nations but also unified the Lucumí people in Cuba, at one time his entire existence was one huge problem after another—to both himself and those close to him. It is in the odu Ejila Shebora that Shangó reaches his lowest point. Everyone abandons him, and he gives up. In desperation, he seeks out the diviner Mofá, and, in the context of a simple divination, discovers that life is not about war and conquest.

Simply, it is about living, and living well. That was the turning point in his life, and the point in which Shangó became an orisha not to be feared but loved. He learned that no matter how powerful he became, there were forces more powerful than he was, and Shangó committed himself to evolution, not conflict. Ejila Shebora was the beginning of his greatness.

Of course, within this odu there are other patakís describing how Shangó learned that greatness comes not from war and conflict, but by just rule; however, this patakís is the simplest, and it is my favorite.

The bulk of the stories presented in this chapter detail the spiritual evolution of our oracle, the diloggún. Those wanting to know more of the history involved can reference my previous work, *The Diloggún*. Chapter 13 of that volume provides the bare-bones history behind this evolution. Here, in this volume's chapter about Ejila Shebora, I wanted to provide the spiritual basis of this system's evolution—its beginnings in the hands of Orúnmila, its placement in the hands of Oshún, the origin of the *òpèlè* (divining chain), and Yemayá's quest to know the primal energies of the 256 odu of creation. Finally, I wanted to write about how Yemayá acquired intricate knowledge of the 256 composite odu herself, a quest that ended her own union with Orúnmila. The stories are dramatic—they involve love, marriage, and betrayal. They speak of spiritual yearning and the immortal quest for knowledge. They also explain the limitations of both oriatés and babalawos, and give hints as to why spiritual schisms exist between these two priesthoods.

In spite of these patakís, over the years I have learned that if Ejila Shebora is nothing else, it is an odu bringing fear. It brings fear not only because it is inherently dangerous, but also because each initiate observing the diviner's work brings his or her own preconceived notions to the mat. Even if the diviner manipulating Ejila is an experienced oriaté, less experienced priests will be afraid of him making a mistake affecting everyone who witnesses the ritual divination we know as diloggún. Some will expect him to close Ejila Shebora, and others will expect him to proceed. Of those expecting him to proceed, some will protest if he attempts to read any composite beyond Ejila Meji (12 mouths followed by 12 mouths) on the mat. Yet when one studies the patakís explaining the reasons for the controversy espoused by this odu, one understands that with the proper training, a diviner can not only deliver a competent reading with the patterns in this sign, but also offer ebós to the client that will placate its volatile energies.

"Fear is born of ignorance," a wise oriaté once told me. "People fear what they do not know. And with an odu as intense as Ejila Shebora, whose patakís have been held secretly by both oriatés and babalawos, this fear is hard to dispel." Yet fear serves no useful purpose in the quest for knowledge; and it is knowledge, not ignorance, that frees us from spiritual slavery. Freedom is born of knowledge; and knowledge itself is the beginning of spiritual evolution. Ejila Shebora encompasses all of that, and more.

Shangó's Losses

At first, Shangó thought it was fog that shrouded the battlefield, but his senses sharpened and a sour, acrid odor burned his nose: smoke. Another odor came with it, that of rot and decay. All around him were dead soldiers, their bodies sprawled on the earth in unnatural positions. Further away lay those recently dead, and beyond those were the dying. Distance muffled their miserable moans, yet they washed over Shangó like a wave of despair.

A single shaft of light broke through the gloom; it began in the sky and ended in a patch of bloody, scorched earth at Shangó's feet. "My son," a voice whispered; it seemed to come with the light itself. "These are the wages of war; these are the bodies of your enemies, and your own loyal men . . ."

Shangó awoke, screaming, his body damp with a slick sheen of sweat. A tight band of panic squeezed his chest as he fought back the troubling dream that had tormented him for weeks. His head throbbed; his mind felt numb from the nightmare's gelid grip.

Needing a human touch, Shangó turned on his side, reaching for his favorite wife. She was gone. For the first time in his life, he was alone.

"Even my wife has abandoned me," he said to no one. He did not want to admit it to himself, but he knew: He had hit rock-bottom.

Sitting on the edge of his bed, in darkness, Shangó thought about how his life came to this. In spite of his great ashé and cunning, he was a mess. Once, his subjects cheered him for successful crusades to expand his kingdom. Greed for expansion, however, brought battle after battle. People died for Shangó's causes everyday; but as more wars raged, his own soldiers questioned the worth of each.

His soldiers no longer wanted to die.

Always, Shangó's head was hot and his temper flared. Exhaustion warped his mind. When the kingdom's elders advised caution and rest, his words to them were harsh; and when they tried reasoning with him, he was beyond reason.

His elders no longer wanted to advise him.

Battles lasting only weeks now raged for months; at home, his wives languished from loneliness. He, too, was lonely, and took exotic women in foreign lands to his bed. With so many sensual delights, he was never in a rush to get home.

His wives, however, no longer wanted to wait.

When morning came, it found Shangó still sitting on the edge of his bed in misery. Yet something inside him had changed, and he vowed to set his life straight. He dressed and went to see the one person who had not turned his back on him, Mofá.

"What can I do to put my life back together?" Shangó asked Mofá.

Ejila Shebora fell on the mat. "What is born of war shows the scars of war," said the wise diviner. "Do not fight so much. When you do go to war, do it for honor, and when you win, treat your fallen enemies well. Listen to your elders; seek out their advice. Do not argue. Be a good husband to your wives. But most importantly, live by making ebó, for the orishas never turned their backs on you, and even at your lowest point you were still the favored child of Olófin."

Shangó did all the wise diviner, Mofá, said. It took some time, but his life was renewed, and he never suffered loss again.

The Marriage of Oshún and Orúnmila

The grass mat was covered with a white sheet, and Orúnmila sat there, facing his client—an elderly man seated on a low stool. Orúnmila's wife, Oshún Ibú Ólólodí, sat in the corner on a soft, cushioned chair, waiting for her husband's instructions. As she waited, she listened carefully to everything he said; and she watched, attentively, every manipulation of the sixteen cowrie shells in his hands. Her mind was sharp, her memory almost perfect, and she remembered every word he said in every reading. Years of service to her husband taught her the meanings of the signs, and she herself could have delivered the readings he gave; however, even now, she preferred to sit and listen instead of flaunting her own knowledge. From time-to-time, Orúnmila did approach the odu from new avenues, and these were the nuggets of wisdom she wanted to learn.

When he was done, and it was time to make the ebó of the mat, Oshún was the one to gather the needed items while Orúnmila and his client waited patiently.

"I need seven plates, Oshún," said Orúnmila. "I need a plate with a coconut and a white candle, a plate with the four strips of cloth in Ósun's colors, a plate with corn meal and okra, a plate with toasted corn and black-eyed peas, a plate with a calabaza, a plate with charcoal, and a plate with twelve *otás* [smooth black stones representing the soul's immortality and strength]." Oshún nodded her head and went to the cupboard where Orúnmila stored his items for ebó; however, before he rattled off his list, she already knew what he needed. Ejila Shebora had come for his clients before, and she knew well the ebó the odu entailed.

She helped him perform the ebó; she knew all the songs and all the motions by heart.

For years, this was Oshún's life. Orúnmila divined: Oshún assisted. More importantly, Oshún learned as Orúnmila was her unwitting teacher. Every day went just like this.

Every day, that is, until the messenger from Oyó arrived.

Oshún was cleaning up from the ebó, sealing the ebó's bag and setting it outside the front door when the stranger arrived. He was dressed in the royal robes of Oyó, surrounded by several armed men, all on horses. While they remained mounted, he dismounted, and walked up to Oshún, bowing reverently. "This is Orúnmila's home, is it not?" It was more of a statement than a question and cautiously, Oshún answered, "Yes."

"May I come in?"

Oshún guided the stranger into her home. Everyone in the waiting room eyed him nervously. He was well-dressed, although obviously a servant, and youthful; he walked with an air of lent authority, self-assured, but only because another gave him purpose. She invited him to sit, but he refused. "I am here on the Oba's business. Shangó, the King of Oyó, has sent me. I must see Orúnmila as soon as possible."

From his workroom, still seated, Orúnmila heard the messenger and the insistence in his voice. He got up from his mat, and stood in the doorway. When he saw the man's royal dress, he knew the business was urgent. "Come in," he said to the young man. "We can speak in here."

When the door was closed and Orúnmila, Oshún, and the messenger were assured of privacy, the messenger spoke slowly, but deliberately, "The king of Oyó, Shangó, has great need of your skills as a diviner. He has requested that I escort you back to his compound in the kingdom. There are pressing needs that require your advice and wisdom."

Orúnmila thought about his waiting room. It was filled with dozens of people who had come for help, advice, and ebó. He looked at his wife, Oshún; Oyó was many days' travel, and it would be weeks before he returned. "Who will care for my clients?" asked Orúnmila. "Who will watch over my wife?"

"You cannot go," said Oshún. "We need you here. I need you here."

"Shangó will reward you handsomely," said the messenger. "Many times over what you would make here divining for all these clients." He paused. "And do not forget, sir, the fame and celebrity that come from working at the request of the king."

A thousand and one thoughts ran through Orúnmila's head, but at the front of them all was this: a king was asking for his services, a king who would pay him handsomely for his work. He weighed the dozens of plain people and their mundane problems against the life of a king and his concerns running the wealthy kingdom of Oyó, and managing its tributaries. A hint of greed and opportunity flashed in his eyes as he looked at his wife, but before he could speak, she insisted, "Husband, there is no one else here to do your work. Who will minister and care for all your people? They depend on you. I depend on you. And how safe is this trip, truly?"

Her voice was sharp and nagging, but tempered with concern and worry.

"Shangó is not a patient man," said the messenger, "and he is expecting you. There are other doctors and healers and wise men in Ilé Ifé, and they can carry on your work while you are gone. And if the people do not choose to see others, your wife can reschedule them upon your return."

Orúnmila sighed. The call of duty was strong from both Oyó and his home, Ilé Ifé, but in his mind the promise of riches and prominence from working for a king outweighed the needs of his own people. "I have to go, Oshún. It is my duty. And the messenger is right. There are others who can do some of my work, and you can reschedule those who insist on seeing me." He turned to the messenger, his back to Oshún, "How long will I be gone?"

"It is a week's travel to Oyó. Your business there should only take a couple of days. You will be home in three weeks, if not sooner. Of course, I will accompany you back as well. And as for safety," he addressed Oshún with these words, "we will travel exclusively through the tributaries of Oyó, and we will be accompanied by armed horsemen both ways. There is nothing to worry about."

Orúnmila embraced his wife warmly; she was stiff and unyielding. "It is not that long. Three weeks is nothing." Oshún sighed, and nodded her head in agreement. Still, she was fearful.

Orúnmila finished divining for those who came that day while Oshún packed his travel bags. The next morning, the messenger and his guards accompanied Orúnmila to the palace at Oyó. And, as Oshún feared, people continued to come every day, plagued as they were with osogbo, and Oshún, sadly, had to turn everyone away.

She worried every day that she was without her husband, the way a wife worries when she is lonely and afraid.

Before the third week ended, the unthinkable happened in Ilé Ifé: drought came to the city, and to all the lands surrounding it. It started innocently as a mild, dry heat wave. It was a welcome break from the sweltering stickiness of summer; and for many days of the planting season, outdoor labor was slow and easy, almost tolerable under the clear, blue skies. Slowly, the heat grew, and as the days grew hotter both the farmers and their beasts of burden exhausted themselves as they plowed dusty soil. Soon, the earth was sapped, and the crops lay shriveled and exsiccated in their furrows. Fear menaced Ilé Ifé like a hungry beast; panic ate at their hearts. When even the rivers ran dry, civility among the kingdom gave way to savagery, and everyone fought over the last stores of fresh water.

Farmers came to the diviner's house day after day. "When will Orúnmila return? Our crops are dying. People in the city are crazed with thirst and hunger. We must see him and make ebó!"

Day after day, Oshún told them, "He will return tomorrow, and then your sorrows can be lifted!"

Yet each new day came, and Orúnmila did not return. There were no messengers bringing word, and Oshún was fearful that something terrible had happened. They were well into the fourth week, and the second week of drought, when the oldest and sickest in the kingdom began to die from hunger, thirst, and disease. Afraid for her people, Oshún Ibú Ólólodí decided to put the sixteen cowries on the mat herself, at least to mark an ebó to end the drought. Everyone in town was there that day as fearfully, she let the diloggún roll from her hands onto the mat. She trembled, unsure of herself or her skills. "What if I make a mistake?" she thought to herself. "What if I really don't know what I am doing, and I make things worse?" Carefully, she remembered all her husband did as he marked ebó, and she marked a sacrifice that she hoped would end the drought Ilé Ifé and its surrounding villages were facing. Quickly, each farmer set out to make the offerings she marked.

The next day, the rains came. Soon, her home was filled with people needing help; only this time, they came to see Oshún, and not Orúnmila. At first she tried to turn them away, but as the day continued their numbers increased. Confident with her first success at divination, and moved by the masses who professed faith in her skills, one by one, she divined for them all, and soon word spread through the land that Oshún was a great diviner herself. Some claimed her skills were equal to those of her husband.

Oshún spent the bulk of her days working on the mat with the diloggún; for another week, with no sign of Orúnmila and no word of his fate, she busied herself as a diviner and lost herself in the work. Any fears she had of overstepping her boundaries melted as she became more secure in the art of divination.

After five weeks, Orúnmila returned to Ilé Ifé. His bags were fat with gold and cowries, and he was well rested after so much leisure time in Shangó's court. His fame in Oyó grew quickly; and all the townspeople there, as in Ilé Ifé, regarded him as one of the wisest men on the earth. When he returned to find his house filled with people, he was not surprised. At first, he felt pride. "They are all waiting on my return," he thought to himself. His waiting room was packed; it overflowed to the outdoors, where dozens of people stood, fanning themselves. No one acknowledged Orúnmila's presence; it was as if they had forgotten him. Then, he stood and listened to the quiet whispers around him. Everyone spoke of the miracles Oshún worked in the lives of their loved ones. "My wife a miracle worker?" he mused to himself. "What does she have to work miracles with?"

Then he walked into his divination room. At first his mind did not register what his eyes were seeing, but as the surprise melted, he realized his wife was sitting on his divining mat, and in her hands were a set of his cowrie shells.

Oshún looked up angrily, bothered by the sudden disturbance; and then she realized who it was. "Orúnmila! My husband! You are home!"

Surprise became anger, and Orúnmila leaned against the wall, arms crossed and eyes narrowed. "Don't stop on my account, Oshún," he said. "Finish what you are doing. And then, we will speak."

Anger welled up inside her. "Five weeks he is gone, and he glares at me?" Oshún thought to herself. Then, slowly, she realized his anger was not at her, but at what she was doing, and that is when the fear overcame the anger, and Oshún began to tremble. "I should have never meddled in his work," she realized. Then, she took a deep breath, and continued divining for her client.

Orúnmila waited silently, and watched as his wife, trembling, finished the divination. Her hands shook and her fingers twitched as she touched the diloggún; and her voice trembled and wavered as she delivered the messages of odu. Every word she spoke sent another cold wave of something he thought was anger, but which felt like despair, through Orúnmila's body—every word that came out of her mouth was one that he himself spoke in years past.

The client left worried and confused: the messages of odu were clear, but the tension in the room struck something primal in his chest. Oshún barely managed a smile as she showed him out of the divination room, and closed the door on the remaining clients.

His face a mural of confusion and anger, his features twisted into a bizarre cacophony of expressions, Orúnmila asked, "How could you?" It was meant to be a question, but sounded like a threat.

Silence: Oshún knew he was angry, and returned his own vacant stare with one that was pleading. "Do you love me?" she asked. It was all she could think of.

"What?"

"Do you love me?" Her voice broke like a prepubescent girl's. "Because I love you."

"Yes, I love you. But I'm disappointed in you. You know that I am the only man on Earth allowed to divine with the diloggún. You are my wife! You are my helper. You're not meant to be the diviner in this house. And that's not my mandate, Oshún. That is Olófin's mandate. You've broken an ancient pact that he and I have, and those who break pacts with God suffer horrible fates. If anything, I fear for you."

"You fear for me?" she asked, her face twisted in amazement. "You. You fear. For me?" It became an accusation. "You should fear for your people. They were dying! You should fear for yourself! You had responsibilities here, and you left them to seek fame and fortune with the king!" She narrowed her eyes and opened her palms to emphasize her words. "With your knowledge and skills come sacred responsibilities. Olófin didn't give you the gift of divination to cater to kings and queens! He gave you that gift to take care of his people on Earth. You betrayed your pact when you went running to a faraway land after fame and fortune. Shangó has his own diviners. We had no one!"

"You, my own wife, dare reprimand me and tell me what my responsibilities are? Who are you to accuse me? Shangó is a man, just like any other man to whom I minister."

"But you went to HIM, and not him to YOU. You catered to one man because you thought him more important than all the people you were leaving behind! That is not part of your pact, is it, husband? I was left alone with thousands of dying people, and I had to do something. THAT was your pact."

Waves of shock sent shivers down his spine. "You arrogant woman! You dare accuse me of breaking pacts? I am Orúnmila, witness to creation! Who are you?"

"I am your wife, and no one on this earth knows you or your responsibilities greater than I. You left me here alone; your people were dying; and I had no choice but to do what you were not here to do!"

It was the wrong thing to say; something inside Orúnmila snapped, and his ears shut down to Oshún's futile words. His body tense, his face devoid of any expression, Orúnmila walked to her, slowly; and she found herself backing away from him, defensively. Every hair on her body was rising with cold shivers. It was the same metallic fear you feel when seeing a snake just inches away from your feet in the grass or when you realize a stranger with a weapon is hiding in shadows just a few yards away. Her back against the wall, unable to flee, Oshún resigned herself to whatever fate awaited at her husband's hands as he grabbed her wrist.

He spoke a single, unintelligible word. The room melted. Everything went dark, and Oshún woke on the floor of Olófin's palace.

She lay still on the floor, looking around through glazed eyes. Olófin sat in his throne, a huge, silver chair adorned with soft, white cushions, and Orúnmila sat on the floor to his right, speaking softly and looking at him with pain showing on his face. No one noticed when Oshún first awoke, and she listened to what she could.

"Father . . . it is treason . . . I did not mean . . . a woman cannot divine . . . yes, I love her but . . . no, Father . . . you promised me the diloggún was mine alone . . ."

Olófin noticed that Oshún was no longer asleep, and he smiled at her. "Oshún, come to me," he ordered; but when he said it, it sounded more like a pleasant request. Afraid, Oshún lifted herself, gathering her yellow skirts tightly to her body as she approached Olófin, and lay down on the floor before him in reverence.

Olófin's aged but strong hands touched her shoulders lightly, blessing her. She rose, and the two embraced. The old orisha sat again, bidding Orúnmila to rise and Oshún to remain standing.

"We have a serious problem here," he said.

Before he could finish, Oshún burst into tears, and she fell on the floor, pleading, "I know, Father, and I am sorry. I only divined because Orúnmila was gone, and everyone was dying. I felt helpless and powerless. I knew I could mark an ebó, but I had no idea how powerful it would feel to be on the mat, reading the odu. If I'd stopped there, maybe my actions would have been excusable. But it felt good. It felt right. And I couldn't stop. Too many people in this world need help!"

She looked at her husband with blurry eyes, and wiped the tears on her face with her hands. "I said horrible things to my husband when I was the one who deserved to be reprimanded. Whatever punishment you give me, Olófin, I will accept without complaint, and I will bear its burden honorably."

"What punishment, Oshún?" He looked at her with a warm smile; she returned his with confusion. "There is no punishment to be had. The universe is a marvelous place filled with infinite possibilities. This isn't about right and wrong, or punishment. This is about evolution."

"I have made up my mind, Orúnmila," Olófin said, looking only at him. "The diloggún no longer belongs to you. You are never again to touch the shells with your hands. I am giving it to Oshún."

Orúnmila's jaws dropped, and he took in a sharp breath. "Olófin, what have I done to deserve this?"

"Nothing: you've done nothing wrong, Orúnmila. I'm giving you a gift."

The air in the room seemed to thicken and shimmer as Olófin held his right hand up, fingers curled and palm facing upward. There was a flicker of light; ashé moved and flared across his palm. When the air again thinned and the lights were gone, the old man held a curious chain with eight golden disks.

"This is yours now, Orúnmila. It is called an òpèlè, a divining chain. As with the cowrie shells, you can access the 256 odu of creation and improve the lives of those who come to you for help; however, it has one benefit that the diloggún does not have."

Reverently, the diviner took the chain that was offered to him; a thin current, almost electrical, tingled his fingertips. The chain had power, and for just a moment, Orúnmila thought he heard the sweet voice of Olódumare singing in its gold. "What benefit is that?" he asked, completely focused on the talisman he held.

"The diloggún has a flaw that you have never encountered. It can refuse to speak in a shadow that is but is not an odu: Opira. All mouths can touch the mat when you cast the diloggún, and only the blank sides face Heaven. When that happens, the diloggún refuses to speak. In your hands, Orúnmila, it never refused to speak."

"But in my hands?" asked Oshún.

"There are times it will refuse to speak. The òpèlè does not have that flaw. Opira is not a possibility with its castings."

"Then, what do I do when Opira comes," asked Oshún.

"When you divine, if Opira comes, you take your client to Orúnmila. Just as husband and wife need each other, so the diloggún and òpèlè will depend on each other."

Orúnmila looked at his wife, Oshún; in his hands was the òpèlè, and he was still bewitched by the incredible, but subtle ashé that flowed from it into his hands.

"There is one more thing," said Olófin.

"What is that, Father?" asked Orúnmila, his eyes still on the òpèlè.

"As long as you are married to Oshún, you are responsible for teaching her what she does not already know about the diloggún and its mysteries. You have higher mysteries at your disposal, and it's your duty to make sure what you left behind is not forgotten."

Oshún and Orúnmila remained married for many years after this; however, while he forgave her of what he believed to be betrayal, his heart never forgot the pain this brought him. In time, the lessons he gave Oshún in the casting of the diloggún became less and less, and one day he told her, "I can no longer teach you. It pains me too much."

"But Olófin said . . . the day you no longer taught me was the day he would annul our marriage."

"I realize that," said Orúnmila. "I still love you, but it hurts too much to be with you."

There was no more to be said. Their marriage was over that day. Sadly, the two orishas went their separate ways.

Yemayá's Quest

With no husband and no home, Oshún Ibú Olólodí did the only thing she knew to do: She fled Ilé Ifé, and traveled to Abeokuta to live with her sister, Yemayá.

In her home, the years passed slowly. Oshún busied herself with the work of the diloggún, divining for those who came to her from all over Abeokuta for help, and Yemayá, curious about the work her sister did, assisted her, and learned all she could about the divining shells. Eventually, Oshún began teaching Yemayá one-on-one, and before too many years passed, Yemayá was almost as proficient a diviner as she.

One day, Yemayá Ibú Achabá asked her sister, Oshún Ibú Olólodí,

"You always speak of these signs, and how the mouths that face upwards mark the 'odu.'"

"Yes, you caught on very quickly to the odu and their names. There are sixteen of them."

"Yes, but we are always 'marking' the odu with the shells. We tell our people the proverbs and meanings of the odu that fall. We use the odu to mark the ebós and sacrifices that improve their lives, and cleanse them of osogbo. But, what are the odu, Oshún?"

"What do you mean, 'What are the odu'?"

"I mean just that. What are they? We mark them. We talk about them. We say they influence people's lives, and they get caught up in their spiritual currents. But what are they exactly? And where do we find them?"

Oshún was silent as she thought. "I don't know," she admitted finally. "My husband never taught me all there was to know about the diloggún. Olófin told him as long as we remained married, he was to be my teacher, and we were to work hand-in-hand with the two oracles. But he grew weary of teaching me, or perhaps he grew afraid that a woman would know as much as he. We always talked about the odu and what they meant, but we never talked about what they were, or where to find them."

Yemayá laughed a sarcastic laugh. "Maybe he himself did not know? I want to know what these odu are. I want to know where they live. I want to know them. I will find them!"

"But, how?"

"Sister, I am Yemayá! I can do anything. Watch me."

Yemayá Ibú Achabá left Abeokuta that day; she left in search of the sixteen sacred odu. For what seemed an eternity, she traveled the earth, looking in its most secret places, and speaking to the wisest men and women she could find in each place about these things called "odu." Finally, when she realized the earth did not contain the secrets of the odu, she went to Heaven, and scoured its most secret, holy places for the sixteen odu. She wandered and searched there for many years; still, she did not find them.

Olófin, however, heard of her quest. And when Yemayá was exhausted and about to give up, he called her to his palace in Heaven.

Yemayá answered Olófin's call, and she found him in his palace, seated on his throne as was his habit whenever he received guests. In spite of his advanced age, Olófin was an orisha whose presence emanated ashé; his lightly wrinkled black skin was supple, almost evanescent in appearance, and his white, wooly hair glowed with a preternatural sheen. His robes were beyond regal; they shimmered and scintillated with a white light that seemed to originate in the fabric itself. Olófin was the perfect embodiment of wisdom and ashé in Heaven.

Before such a powerful display, Yemayá threw herself to the floor from side to side, a horizontal, stylized curtsey in homage to the mighty Olófin. Strong hands brushed her shoulders, and bid her to rise. They embraced.

Yemayá looked at Olófin lovingly; to her, he was always the perfect father. "Why have you summoned me, Olófin?"

The wise orisha smiled; and Yemayá marveled that his teeth seemed the perfect ivory, a beautiful contrast against his dark lips. "I heard about your quest, Yemayá, to find the sixteen primal odu of creation. All of Heaven and Earth knows that you are looking for the ultimate power and wisdom." Yemayá bit her lower lips, unsure if she was about to be congratulated or castigated for her searching. "Have you found them yet?"

"No, Olófin, I haven't. I have searched everywhere, and I'm starting to wonder if such a thing really exists."

"They exist, Yemayá. They are hiding, in secret, waiting for the time when they will be unveiled to the proper orisha. Such is their power that they could never fall into the wrong hands, no matter how much someone looks."

His voice was kind and caring, yet Yemayá knew she had just been chastised. Even when angry, it was not Olófin's nature to raise his voice, or make idle threats. "I am sorry, Father. I didn't mean to overstep my boundaries. I only wanted to know . . . what they were."

"And know them you shall!" Olófin smiled a huge, loving smile, and again he embraced Yemayá. "But it is not your ashé to know them directly. Another orisha must reveal them to you, slowly." Olófin turned his back to Yemayá, and he reached beneath his throne. He pulled a simple, plain calabash from beneath it. The massive lights that surrounded his throne seemed to dim, but just slightly.

"Take this to Orúnmila for me, Yemayá, and take it quickly. Don't stop to look inside, because what I hold is meant for Orúnmila's eyes only. If he chooses, it is up to him to share what is in this box with you."

"But what of the knowledge of the sixteen holy odu? How will I find them?"

"Yemayá, there are more than sixteen odu. There are 256 odu. And you will know them all in time."

Yemayá took the calabash from Olófin's hands; ashé stronger than any she had ever known flowed into her body, and for those few fleeting moments she knew . . . everything. Everything, that is, except for the fact that she held the most sacred, 256 odu in her own hands. But she did know that the secrets in that container did not belong to her. They were meant for Orúnmila. So with that box, and with Olófin's consent, she took that box down to Earth and put it in the diviner's hands.

"Olófin told me to give this to you," Yemayá said, touching the floor with her fingertips and then kissing them in respect for the wise diviner.

"Another gift from Olófin?" he asked, taking the box from her. When he felt its ashé, he thought he would faint. He didn't, and instead stood there gazing at Yemayá while the most sacred, secret knowledge of the universe flowed into his body and his mind. Love for all things in creation welled up in his heart as he knew . . . everything . . . and when he looked at Yemayá Ibú Achabá, he thought that his heart was filled with love for her.

"Marry me?" he asked, still under the spell of the ashé that coursed through his body.

"What?" asked Yemayá, stunned. She looked at Orúnmila; he was the wisest man in all the land, and since abandoning Oshún, was one of the most eligible orishas in all of Heaven or on Earth. And he wasn't a bad-looking orisha, either.

Again, Orúnmila asked, this time on his knees, and holding the box up toward Yemayá. She put her hands on it, and felt the immense ashé traveling through them both. "Marry me," Orúnmila insisted.

They were wed that night.

Yemayá Learns to Cast Òpèlè

Yemayá never knew that the calabash contained all the odu of creation; and Orúnmila spent hours every day with that container, studying its contents, and this only increased his proficiency as a diviner. What Yemayá did know was this: Orúnmila's skills with the òpèlè grew by leaps and bounds, and there was a waiting list of people who wanted to take advantage of his wisdom.

Although Orúnmila was loathe to let another help him in his work, soon things were overwhelming, and he had no choice but to allow Yemayá to work in the divining room with him. He cast òpèlè, he read for his clients, and Yemayá ran to fetch the items needed to make ebó.

At every session, she compared what she learned from Oshún to what Orúnmila did; with the òpèlè, he did something Yemayá had not learned from her sister, and something she doubted Oshún herself knew. There were composite odu. Instead of one cast of cowries resulting in a single number, Orúnmila cast the òpèlè with a flick of his wrist, and the resulting pattern was what he called a "composite odu." So Yemayá sat through each session, silently, listening to the proverbs, advice, and patakís that Orúnmila told for each composite. Much as Oshún did when she herself was married to the diviner, she memorized every word.

Years passed. Soon, Yemayá knew as much about the òpèlè and its letters as Orúnmila himself. Little did she realize that this was the knowledge Olófin himself promised she would obtain.

Strangely enough, the wise diviner Orúnmila did not see the treason that was coming, nor did he learn from his own history. In time a new messenger arrived from ancient Oyó, sent by the king, Shangó. Much as the last messenger had done, this one presented his case willfully: Shangó had pressing problems in managing his kingdom, and needed Orúnmila's wisdom in his affairs. Once again, the call of fame and fortune was too much for the wise orisha to resist, and without giving it any thought, he kissed his wife on the cheek and bid her farewell.

He traveled with the messenger and his armed men to Oyó that night.

The next morning, as clients lined up outside Orúnmila's home, Yemayá realized that she had an opportunity to test out the òpèlè and its powers. She was well practiced with the diloggún, and seeing that the mechanics of the two systems were similar, she felt secure that she could wield it as effortlessly and skillfully as her husband. She seated her first client on the mat and began divining.

The odu Òtùrùpónméjì opened before her.

Quickly, she gathered the items she needed to make ebó of the mat, and once the white plates were lined up, she began the songs and prayers that would cleanse her client of osogbo. She had not a clue that Orúnmila was just outside their front door.

To this day, no one knows why Orúnmila stopped traveling the night before. No one knows why he set up camp on his own that night, and returned home the next day. Perhaps he realized that this was the past repeating itself, and he had learned from his mistakes; or perhaps he returned to retrieve a necessary but forgotten item.

What we do know is this: Orúnmila was unfazed by the gathering of clients in his waiting room, and without so much as a knock, he swung open the door to his divination room, almost in anger. When he saw Yemayá sitting on the mat with a client and his òpèlè, his face turned ashen.

It was betrayal all over again.

She sat there with her skirts drawn about her like pants, the òpèlè resting between her legs. Before he could count its pattern, he knew the odu Òtùrùpónméjì was open on the mat; he knew this from the plates and their contents, which sat to the side in preparation for *ebó de estera*.

Yemayá looked up, angry that someone had interrupted her prayers, and when she saw Orúnmila poised calmly by the door, his face ashen from anger, she was afraid.

"You look surprised to see me, Yemayá," Orúnmila noted calmly. "Don't stop on my account. Continue. You have a client waiting for your help."

In spite of his calm appearance, Yemayá knew her husband was angry, and she could not move. He, however, moved closer.

"You think you know everything, Yemayá. You think you can divine as well as I divine? Even your sister, Oshún, waited until I was gone for many weeks before she cast the diloggún, and in hindsight, she had good reason to betray me. It was to save her people. But you—I was barely over the horizon, gone for not even an entire day, and here you sit pretending to be a diviner. You pretend to know the secrets of my sacred tool, the òpèlè."

"I am sorry, husband," said Yemayá. She realized her own treason, but there was no sorrow in her voice when she said, "But I can divine as well as you. I know how the diloggún works. I know how the òpèlè works. And I know all the composite odu and the things they take for ebó. From working with you, I have learned well."

Shock coursed his spine like an electric current. "That may be true, but no matter what, the òpèlè is mine and mine alone. Take your knowledge of odu and leave my sight. I no longer want to be married to you, Yemayá. But before you go, know this: For your treason, I curse you and your knowledge. I curse you through the very odu open on the mat, Òtùrùpónméjì. Equal though it may be to Ejila Shebora in your own system of the divination, the diloggún, in Ifá that letter belongs to me. This shall be your curse: You and all like you empowered to divine with the diloggún are powerless to make any ebó beyond Ejila Shebora on the mat. Work with your diloggún if you must; take the knowledge you have learned here and share it with the world if such is the depth of your treason. But know that when any letter beyond Ejila Shebora falls in your own diloggún, you have lost the power to help that client with ebó de estera. The power to make ebó with those signs rests with me!"

Orúnmila watched as Yemayá sealed her fate by closing the odu with ebó de estera that day; and he watched with both sadness and anger as his wife packed her things and fled back to Abeokuta. As he had before, Orúnmila went to see Olófin in Heaven; and with Olófin's consent, decided that if he ever married again, it was taboo for a woman to divine, even with the cowrie shells, under his own roof.

And this is how ebó de estera for all odu beyond Ejila Shebora became closed to the orisha priests; and this is how it became taboo for the wives of Orúnmila, or the wives of his babalawos, to divine in their homes.

Glossary

Lucumí, and the original Yoruba from which it evolved, is a tonal language, like Chinese. Because the Afro-Cubans had neither the time nor the opportunity for formal education during slavery, many of these words have no consistent spelling. While I have tried to keep my own spellings consistent throughout my work, my spellings will differ from those of other authors in the field. However, the pronunciation of the words will be the same. For any Lucumí or Spanish term that does not have an accent mark, the proper emphasis goes on the second-to-last syllable in the word. To facilitate proper pronunciation, I have included the appropriate accent for all words that vary from this pattern. Vowel sounds for all non-English words will approximate those of the Spanish language.

Keep in mind the following points when pronouncing words:

- The *ch* sound is used in Lucumí and Spanish words; these languages have no *sh* sound.
- The *ñ* character (enye sound) is used in Spanish words only, and not Lucumí words.
- The *y* sound in Spanish has a slight edge to it, so that it sounds more like the English and Yoruba *j*. I have used *j* here whenever possible.

Also, note that in each glossary entry one or more words may be italicized. The italicization of a word indicates that it can be found in the glossary as well.

247

Abeokuta: The word translates into "under the rocks." It is the name given to a city in Ogún State of Nigeria sitting on the Ogún River. It is part of the *Yoruba* territories. The original inhabitants of Abeokuta were *Egba;* later, Yoruba settlers came to the area. It is through this interaction of Egba and Yoruba that many of the Egba mysteries were assimilated into native Yoruba *orisha* worship in both Nigeria and Cuba.

aborisha: One who worships the *orishas* of the religion *Santería;* an aborisha has taken at least the initiation of the *elekes* and *warriors.*

adimú: Any type of offering that does not include the sacrifice of an animal. Adimú is usually prescribed during a session with the *diloggún.*

Aganyú: The *orisha* of volcanoes, born from *Oroiña,* the molten center of the earth. He is also known as the father of *Shangó,* and is the ferryman who carries people across the river.

Akoba: A type of *osogbo* in which one's life in general is not good.

aleyo: One who follows *Santería* but is not initiated as a priest or priestess; a noninitiate or outsider.

Ano: One of the *osogbos;* it is a *Lucumí* word that means "illness" or "disease." It denotes any illness which is fleeting and curable (colds, flu, strep throat, etc.) as opposed to *Aro,* which denotes any illness that is durative and terminal (AIDS, diabetes, cancer, heart disease, etc.).

apadí: One of the eight *ibó* used in the divination system called *diloggún;* it is a piece of broken pottery, and it symbolizes loss, defeat, and marriage.

Arará: An area in Dahomey, Africa, now known as Benin; it is the origin of *Naná Burukú* and her son, *Babaluaiye.*

Arayé: One of the *osogbos;* it is a *Lucumí* word denoting "envy," "ill will," "arguments," "evil tongues," and "witchcraft."

Aro: One of the *osogbos;* it is a *Lucumí* word meaning "durative illness" as opposed to *ano,* which is "fleeting illness."

ashé (also spelled aché): A very dynamic universal force; the spiritual power of the universe. It has many meanings, among which are grace, life, fate, power, talent, and wisdom; the meaning intended depends on its usage in speech. Most *santeros* will agree that life is ashé, and ashé is life.

avatar: Many *orishas,* including *Obatalá, Yemayá, Oshún,* and *Elegguá,* have different avatars, also known as paths or roads, which could be thought of as different incarnations of the same spirit. Each avatar is related to one of an orisha's many incarnations on the earth (many orishas have spent mortal lives among humans). Only those incarnations of significant religious, historical, or political importance are remembered specifically and become avatars or paths of that orisha.

ayé: One of the eight *ibó* used in the *diloggún*. It denotes any type of elongated saltwater seashell.

babalawo: An initiate of *Orúnmila*. A babalawo is always male because only men may enter Orúnmila's mysteries. Also known as "father of the secrets."

Babaluaiye: This *orisha* originates in the land of *Arará*, which is present-day Benin. He is the father of smallpox, disease, and afflictions of the skin.

calabaza: Gourds, pumpkins, or squashes. All are sacred to *Shangó* and *Oshún*.

composite odu: A pairing of *odu* that combines a *parent odu* with a second *odu*. Each of the sixteen parent odu in the *diloggún* has sixteen composite odu; there are 256 composite odu in total.

cowrie: The type of shell that is used to create the *diloggún* of an *orisha*.

diloggún: The system of *cowrie* divination by which a priest or priestess of *Santería* learns the will of the *orishas;* also, the eighteen or twenty-one cowrie shells that contain the soul of an *orisha;* also, the set of sixteen shells a diviner casts to perform divination. The exact meaning of the word depends on the context in which it is used.

divination: The act of uncovering the will of the *orishas*, the desires of *egun*, and the trends of the future. The *Lucumí* faith employs three systems of divination: *obí, diloggún,* and *Ifá*.

diviner: One skilled in the art of divination who knows the secrets of *obí* and *diloggún*.

ebó: An offering made to an *orisha*.

ebó de estera: Literally, this translates into "ebó of the mat." It is a function of the oriaté, and it is a special set of rituals done on the diviner's mat. It cleans the client of the odu's osogbo using the same elements that the odu once used to remove osogbo from their own lives. The ingredients vary depending on the composite odu opening before the diviner.

efun: An *ibó* that is a loosely packed, powdered chalk made from crushed eggshells.

Egba: The Egba are a subgroup of the *Yoruba* people living in Western Nigeria, primarily in the region of *Abeokuta*. Once they were a part of the ancient *Oyó* Empire, but the Egba asserted their independence and ethnic identity following the collapse of ancient Oyó in the early nineteenth century. There are many divisions of the Egba, and each division has their own king: Ake, Owu, Oke Ona, Gbagura and Ibara. Because of the interaction and mingling of the Yoruba and Egba in Abeokuta, many of the Egba mysteries have been absorbed into native *orisha* worship in Yoruba land and the *Lucumí* faith in Cuba and the New World.

Égba: A *Lucumí* term that means "paralysis." It is one of the *osogbos* found in the *diloggún*.

egun: The many ancestral spirits related to one through one's blood relatives or one's spiritual relatives.

egungun: One who is possessed by *egun*. In Cuba, it often refers to the now-dead cult of egun—priests and priestesses who dealt only with the ancestral spirits, and not the *orishas*.

Ejila Meji: One of the sixteen *composite odu* found in the family of *Ejila Shebora*. It opens when a casting of twelve mouths (Ejila Shebora) is followed by another casting of twelve mouths (Ejila Shebora).

Ejila Shebora: One of the sixteen *parent odu* in the *diloggún;* it consists of twelve mouths open on the mat. It is the twelfth and final odu that a *santero* who has not the skill of an *oriaté* may read in the diloggún.

Eji Ogbe: One of the sixteen *parent odu* in the *diloggún;* it consists of eight open mouths on the mat.

Eji Oko: One of the sixteen *parent odu* in the *diloggún;* it consists of two open mouths on the mat.

Ejioko: In both *Yoruba* and *Lucumí* belief, Ejioko is the mortal incarnation of the *odu Eji Oko.* It is upon his life that many of the stories found in that odu are based.

elegede, Elegede: A *Lucumí* word translating into "pumpkin" or *"cala-baza."* It is also the name of the woman whose death is said to give birth to all pumpkins, squash, and gourds.

Elegguá: He is often portrayed as Fate, a young child, and an old man; Elegguá is the messenger of all the *orishas,* and the first and last to be honored in every ceremony performed. Without his goodwill, nothing in the religion *Santería* may be done. In *Ifá,* it is said that there are 256 paths of Elegguá, one for each *odu.* Each of these paths is known as an *Eshu* and has its own specific name, such as *Eshu Ayé, Eshu Bi,* and *Eshu Laroye.* In *ocha,* there are 101 paths of Elegguá (each also known as Eshu). In many *ilé ocha,* when an initiate receives the *warriors,* he is told the name of Eshu that his Elegguá enshrines.

eleke/elekes: These are the beaded necklaces given to both *aleyos* and *santeros.* The bead colors denote not only the *orisha* to whom they are consecrated, but also the path of that orisha. In the initiation of the elekes, an aleyo will generally receive four elekes unless the *diloggún* specifies otherwise: the elekes of *Obatalá, Yemayá, Oshún,* and *Shangó.* Sometimes, the eleke of *Elegguá* is given.

Epe: One of the *osogbos;* it denotes a curse.

érìndínlógún: An alternative spelling for *diloggún.*

Eshe: One of the spiritual principles known as *osogbo;* it denotes general afflictions.

Eshu: An alternate name for the *orisha* known as *Elegguá.* While *Ifá* lists one Eshu for each of the 256 *odu, ocha* has only 101 paths of Eshu. Some examples of Eshu that are shared by both Ifá and ocha are *Eshu Ayé, Eshu Laroye,* and *Eshu Bi.*

Eshu Ayé: This *avatar* of *Eleggua* is said to walk on the shoreline where waves lap at the sand. This *Eshu* works closely with the *orisha Olokun.*

Eshu Bi: This *avatar* of *Eleggua* is both a young child and an old man; he is forceful and stern. It is said that this *Eshu* walks with the first two *Ibeyi,* the twins, who were born of *Shangó* and *Oyá* (some lineages believe they were born of Shangó and *Oshún*). He is the protector of twins and also of small children.

Eshu Laroye: This *avatar* of *Eleggua* works closely with *Oshún* and is her constant companion; he is often referred to as the "little, talkative one." He is one of Eleggua's most important and popular paths, being the one addressed and refreshed before any invocation or prayer to the *orishas.*

estera: The Spanish word for "mat." In the *Lucumí* faith, the straw mat is sacred, and many rituals, such as divination, are performed on its surface.

Ewon: One of the spiritual principles known collectively as *osogbo;* it denotes imprisonment.

Eyo: One of the spiritual principles known collectively as *osogbo;* it denotes tragedies that come through legal complications, gossip, and accidents.

Fitibo: One of the spiritual principles known collectively as *osogbo;* it denotes an impending, sudden, and tragic death.

gungun: One of eight *ibó* used in *divination;* it consists of a bone from the left hind leg of a goat used to feed *Eleggua.*

Ibeyi: In some branches of the *Lucumí* faith, these are known as the divine twin children of *Shangó* and *Oyá;* in other branches, they are known as the divine twin children of Shangó and *Oshún*. They are the patrons of both twins and the mother of twins.

ibó: When reading the *diloggún,* these are the tools the *diviner* uses to determine orientation and *larishe.* There are a total of eight ibó: *otá, efun, ayé, owó, apadí, gungun, osán/sesán,* and *orí ere.*

Ifá: A system of divination used by *babalawos* exclusively. It consists of 256 *odu.* Only the priests of *Orúnmila,* the babalawos, may use Ifá.

igbodu: The sacred room where *orishas* are born and initiates are crowned.

ikú, Ikú: When set lowercase, ikú means physical death; Ikú is the *Lucumí* personification of death.

Ilé Ifé: An ancient Yoruba city found in southwestern Nigeria. Modern archaeology has discovered evidence that the city's present site was settled as early as 500 BCE by the Yoruba, and oral history retained in both the *diloggún* and *Ifá* tells us that the city standing today is not the original settlement; over the span of centuries, the original settlement moved as many as five times before today's final city was founded. According to our patakís, the original settlement of Ilé Ifé (whose location has been lost in time) is the original location where Odúduwa and Obatalá created the world.

ilé ocha: The spiritual house of *ocha* or of the *orishas,* headed by either a priest or a priestess who has many years of experience in the *Lucumí* faith.

Inya: One of the spiritual principles known as *osogbo;* it denotes war.

iré: Any type of blessing or good fortune that can befall the client as he sits for a session with the *diloggún.*

Iroko: In Nigeria, Iroko refers to a specific tree that is sacred to the *orishas* and *Olódumare.* Iroko is also a powerful orisha who assisted the descent of *Obatalá* from Heaven to Earth. Iroko spans the sky and the earth; he is the sacred tree before which the orishas gather. In the New World, the orisha Iroko claimed the silk cotton tree as his native shrine.

Irosun: One of the sixteen *parent odu* of the *diloggún;* it is opened when four mouths fall face up on the mat.

jícara: A dried gourd that is cut open to resemble a bowl. It is used to give offerings and to pour libations to the *orishas.*

jutía: An African bush rat, a large rodent; it is a staple offering for many of the *warrior orishas* such as *Elegguá, Ogún,* and *Ochosi.*

larishe: One of the hundreds of remedies that any one *odu* can prescribe to overcome *osogbo* and bring *iré* to the client sitting for a session with the *diloggún.*

Lucumí: A contraction of various *Yoruba* words that translates into "my friend." The Lucumí are the physical, and now spiritual, descendants of the black Yoruba slaves in Cuba. This word also refers to the corruption of the native Yoruba tongue that is now used in *Santería*.

Maferefún: In *Lucumí*, "Praise be to. . ." or "All power be to. . ."

Marunlá: One of the sixteen *parent odu* in the *diloggún;* it is said to be opened when fifteen mouths fall onto the diviner's mat.

meji: Twin, double.

Merindilogún: One of the sixteen *parent odu* in the *diloggún;* it opens when sixteen mouths fall on the mat.

Merinlá: One of the sixteen *parent odu* in the *diloggún;* it opens when fourteen mouths fall on the mat.

Metanlá: One of the sixteen *parent odu* in the *diloggún;* it opens when thirteen mouths fall on the mat.

Mofá: The name of a diviner who appears in *patakís* throughout the *odu* of the *diloggún*. His name is a *Lucumí* contraction of *"Moforibale Ifá,* "I salute Ifá," or *"Mojuba Ifá,* "I pay homage to Ifá." To create the contraction, the "mo" from Moforibale/Mojuba was added to the "fá" from Ifá. This name was used in patakís adapted from the oral corpus of Ifá for use in the diloggún during the time of syncretization and reformation of Yoruba *orisha* worship in Cuba.

Moforibale: In *Lucumí*, "I salute."

Mojuba: In *Lucumí*, "I pay homage."

Naná Burukú: In some *patakís*, this *orisha* was born from *Yembo* when she ascended by her own *ashé* to the palace of *Olódumare;* historically, she comes from the land of *Arará* in Africa and is not *Yoruba*. She was later absorbed into the *Lucumí* pantheon during the time of the *cabildos* in Cuba. She is the mother of *Nanumé* and *Babaluaiye*.

Nanumé: A very old female *avatar* of *Babaluaiye;* so dissociated from him is she that many consider her to be not only an aspect of this *orisha*, but his sister and a separate entity as well (similar to the relationship between *Yemayá* and *Yembo*). She is the daughter of *Naná Burukú,* and she is said by elder *santeros* to be the moon in the night sky.

niche osain: An amulet made of herbal, mineral, and animal substances; it is beaded in the colors of the *orisha* to whom it is consecrated. Every niche osain is made for a specific purpose. Protection, blessings, prosperity, health, and longevity are among the most basic uses. *See also Osain.*

Oba: A *Lucumí* word that denotes a king.

Obara: One of the sixteen *parent odu* of the *diloggún*. It opens when six mouths fall face up on the diviner's mat.

Obatalá: An *orisha* considered to be the king of all the orishas of Heaven; the creator of the human form. Obatalá has both male and female *avatars*.

obí: The system of divination based on the coconut, and also the coconut itself.

Obí: The man who became an *orisha* and then fell from grace because of his own pride, becoming the coconut used in divination. Despite this, Obí is still an orisha and treated with respect in the *Lucumí* religion.

ocha: A shortened form of the word *orisha*. It also denotes the *Lucumí* faith.

Ochanlá: The eldest female *avatar* of the *orisha* Obatalá.

Oché: One of the sixteen *parent odu* of the *diloggún*. It opens when five mouths fall face up on the diviner's mat.

ochinchin: A favored *adimú* of the *orisha* Oshún. It is made with eggs, shrimp, *sazón* (seasoning), and watercress (although for some *avatars* of Oshún, watercress is taboo and spinach is substituted).

Ochosi: An *orisha;* one of the *warriors* and said to be the patron of both the hunt and justice.

Odí: One of the sixteen *parent odu* of the *diloggún;* it opens when seven mouths fall on the diviner's mat.

odu: The many patterns that can fall when using the divination system known as the *diloggún*. There are a total of sixteen *parent odu* and 256 *composite odu*. Each of these has its own proverbs, *patakís*, meanings, and *ebós*. The word *odu* is both singular and plural in *Lucumí* and *Yoruba* usage.

Odúduwa: The founder of the *Yoruba* Empire. He is also an *orisha*.

Ofo: One of the spiritual principles known as *osogbos;* loss.

Ofún: One of the sixteen *parent odu* of the *diloggún;* it opens when a cast of ten mouths falls on the mat.

Ofún Meji: One of the sixteen *composite odu* that exist in the family of *Ofún*. It forms when the initial cast of ten mouths (Ofún) repeats itself on the mat.

Ogo: One of the spiritual principles known as *osogbos;* it means witch, witchcraft, or sorcerer.

Ogún: One of the warrior *orishas;* the patron of ironworkers, civilization, and technology.

Ogundá: One of the sixteen *parent odu* in the *diloggún;* it opens when three mouths fall on the mat.

Okana: One of the sixteen *parent odu* of the *diloggún;* it opens when one mouth falls on the mat. Also, it is the name of the woman upon whose life many *patakís* of the *odu* are based.

Olobatalá: Literally, "the owner of *Obatalá*." The word denotes a priest or priestess crowned with the *orisha* Obatalá.

Olódumare: A *Yoruba* contraction that translates into "owner of the womb." This is the supreme deity of the Yoruba and *Lucumí*.

Olófin: It is said among the *Lucumí* that Olófin is "god on Earth;" he is the eldest *avatar* of *Obatalá* and can be received only by the priesthood of *Orúnmila*, the *babalawos*.

Olokun: The androgynous *orisha* who rules and owns the ocean. In most *Lucumí* houses, Olokun's primary manifestation is male.

Olorún: A Lucumí contraction of two words: olo, "owner," and orún, "the sun." It means "owner of the sun." It is a name for God, his symbol being the sun in the daytime sky.

omá, Omá: This term refers both to the quality of wisdom and its personification.

omo odu: Literally, it means "the children of odu." It refers to the 256 *composite odu* born of the 16 *parent odu* in the *diloggún*.

Ona: One of the spiritual principles known as *osogbos;* it means "afflictions."

òpèlè: A divining chain used by *babalawos;* it has eight concave disks made of varying materials (gold, silver, lead, iron, coconut shells, etc.), connected together on a single chain.

Opira: Although many call Opira an *odu,* it is not an odu in the *dilog-gún.* It is a shadow that falls on the mat when the *orishas* do not wish to speak about the client's concerns. One says that Opira has come to the house when the shells fall so that no mouths are open; they are all face down on the diviner's mat. The *ebó* is automatic: The diviner must send the client to *Ifá.* If Opira falls during a reading but is not the opening odu, there are rituals that can be done to pacify this sign so that the diviner can continue with his reading.

Oran: One of the spiritual principles known as *osogbos* in the *diloggún;* it refers to moral and legal crimes.

oriaté: An expert not only in the reading of the *diloggún,* but also in all ceremonies of the *Lucumí* faith.

orí ere: This is one of the eight *ibó* used in *divination;* it consists of a tiny doll's head. Most *diviners* use the head of a tiny jester's doll.

orisha: A *Yoruba* contraction that means "select head"; it denotes any of the myriad spirits in the pantheon of *Santería* that are an extension of *Olódumare's ashé.*

Orishaokó: The *orisha* who controls the fecundity of the earth. He has two forms: During the day he is envisioned as a handsome black male; at night he becomes a terrifying presence in the darkness. Traditionally, this orisha lives in the *santero's* home for the six months that the fields lie fallow, and then he goes outdoors with the beginning of the planting season.

Oroiña: The *orisha* who lives at the center of the earth. She is its molten core. She gave birth to the orisha *Aganyú.*

Orúnmila: The *orisha* of *Ifá* and its priests, the *babalawos.* Only men are called to his priesthood. He does not speak directly through the *diloggún;* however, certain *composite odu* indicate that he would like the one at the mat sent to his priests so he may speak directly.

Osá: One of the sixteen *parent odu* of the *diloggún* opened when nine mouths fall on the mat.

Osain: One of the most mysterious *orishas*. Osain was created after creation; he sprang forth from the earth the moment the first green thing began to grow. He is the lord of *ashé* on the Earth, knowing all the secrets to the herbs. Without Osain, none of the orishas can work its magic, nor can its children be initiated, or can the orishas be born on Earth. He will live until the last green thing on this planet perishes. See also *niche osain*.

osán/sesán: One of the eight ibó used in diloggún divination; it is the seed of the guacalote tree. It conceptualizes both offspring, and, curiously, illness. One's children and progeny are symbolized here because the seed holds the potential to become a tree and create thousands of new seeds; illness is found here because the fruit hiding the seed must rot before a new tree can grow.

Oshún: The *orisha* bringing love, sweetness, money, prosperity, fertility, conception, and all the things that make life worth living. She is the sister of *Yemayá* and one of *Shangó's* wives. In some lineages, she is referred to as the mother of twins.

Oshún Ibú Olólodí: One of *Oshún's* many *avatars;* she was the wife of *Orúnmila,* and learned the secrets of *diloggún* divination from him.

osogbo: The spiritual principle of misfortune; it is a living, spiritual entity in the *Lucumí* faith. Negative influence; any of the evils that may be predicted for a client through the oracle known as *diloggún*.

Ósun: Ósun is an *orisha;* he guards the head of an *aborisha* from danger.

Otá: Otá is a smooth black pebble representing the strength and immortality of the soul.

Òtùrùpónméjì: One of the 256 *odu* in *Ifá*. It corresponds to the odu in the diloggún known as Ejila Meji, 12 mouths followed by 12 mouths on the mat.

Owani: One of the sixteen *parent odu* of the *diloggún;* it opens when eleven mouths fall on the mat.

owó: Money; cowrie. When referring to the ibó, owó may take one of two forms: a single uncut cowrie shell or two cut cowries that are attached so their mouths face outward.

owó mérìndínlógún: An alternate term for the *diloggún*.

Oyá: This female *orisha* is the patron of forked lightning. She is the gatekeeper to the cemetery, *Shangó's* partner in battle, and the lady of the marketplace. She is also the orisha of fast change and tumultuous cycles. Some also see her in the action of the tornado. This is Shangó's third wife, his favorite even over *Oshún*.

parent odu: The sign giving birth to all sixteen *composite odu* in a single family. For instance, *Okana* is a parent *odu;* it gives birth to the signs Okana Ogundá, Okana Oché, and Okana Obara.

patakís: The many sacred stories and legends found in the *diloggún;* some of these are about the *orishas,* while others are about the actions of historical/mythological humans who lived and died in both Africa and Cuba. All patakís teach spiritual truths found in *odu,* and many are considered historical texts, although oral.

Santería: The name of *orisha* worship as it developed in Cuba; the English translation from the Spanish is "worship of the saints." The name derives from the syncretizing of the Catholic saints and the orishas of the *Yoruba*.

santero/santera: A priest or priestess of Santería.

Shangó: The fourth king of ancient *Oyó,* and the *orisha* of storm, thunder, and lightning.

Tiya-tiya: One of the spiritual principles known as *osogbos;* it denotes arguments, slander, and gossip.

Unle: One of the *parent odu* of the *diloggún;* it is also the name of the mortal upon whose life many of the *patakís* of this odu are based.

Unle Odí: One of the *composite odu* found in the family of *Unle;* it opens when a cast of eight mouths on the mat is followed by a secondary cast of seven mouths on the mat.

warriors: The four *orishas* that are received together in one initiation: *Elegguá, Ogún, Ochosi,* and *Ósun.*

Yemayá: Born when *Olokun* was chained to the bottom of the ocean by *Obatalá,* Yemayá arose to become mother to the world and the *orishas.* She is the patron of motherhood and the fresh waters of the world.

Yemayá Ibú Achabá: One of the many *avatars* of the *orisha Yemayá;* at one time, she was married to *Orúnmila.* She brought him the secrets of the 256 odu of *Ifá,* and learned how to cast the *òpèlè* by watching him work.

Yoruba: The native Africans who originally settled in the southwestern parts of the area known today as Nigeria; their deities, the *orishas,* form the basis of the *Lucumí* faith. The word *Yoruba* also denotes the language shared by these peoples, the native tongue that mixed with Cuban Spanish to become Lucumí.

Index

BOOKS OF RELATED INTEREST

Diloggún Tales of the Natural World
How the Moon Fooled the Sun and Other Santería Stories
by Ócha'ni Lele

The Diloggún
The Orishas, Proverbs, Sacrifices,
and Prohibitions of Cuban Santería
by Ócha'ni Lele

Osogbo
Speaking to the Spirits of Misfortune
by Ócha'ni Lele

Sacrificial Ceremonies of Santería
A Complete Guide to the Rituals and Practices
by Ócha'ni Lele

Obí
Oracle of Cuban Santería
by Ócha'ni Lele

The Secrets of Afro-Cuban Divination
How to Cast the Diloggún, the Oracle of the Orishas
by Ócha'ni Lele

Cuban Santeria
Walking with the Night
by Raul J. Canizares

Drawing Down the Spirits
The Traditions and Techniques of Spirit Possession
by Kenaz Filan and Raven Kaldera

Inner Traditions • Bear & Company
P.O. Box 388
Rochester, VT 05767
1-800-246-8648
www.InnerTraditions.com

Or contact your local bookseller